WITHDRAWN

FAULKNER'S WOMEN:

characterization and meaning

XXIV

XXix

FAULKNER'S WOMEN:

characterization and meaning

Sally R. Page

EVERETT/EDWARDS, inc.

133 SOUTH PECAN AVENUE
DELAND, FLORIDA 32720

Library of Congress Catalog Card Number 78-172792
Everett/Edwards, Inc., DeLand, Florida 32720
© 1972 by Sally R. Page
All Rights Reserved
Published 1972
Printed in the United States of America

To my daughters:
Ellen and Kelly

Contents

Introduction   xi
Characterization and Meaning: Preliminary Issues   xxi

PART I/ Woman: The Image of Romantic Ideality

Chapter 1   The Lure of Sex and Modern
               Alienation   1
Chapter 2   The Failure of the Romantic Ideal   27

PART II/ Woman: The Image of Moral Order

Chapter 3   The Ideal of Motherhood: *The Sound
               and the Fury*   45
Chapter 4   The Ideal of Motherhood: *Sanctuary*   71

PART III/ Woman: The Image of Death

Chapter 5   Sexual Perversity and Sterility   93
Chapter 6   The Female Idealist: *As I Lay
               Dying* and *Wild Palms*   111

PART IV/ Woman: The Image of Life

Chapter 7   The Feminine Ideal of *Light
               in August*   139
Chapter 8   The Male and the Female Principles:
               the Snopes Trilogy   153

CONCLUSION: Minor Figures and Major Motifs   175

Bibliography   189
Index   227

Acknowledgements

The successful completion of this volume is largely the result of the wise guidance of the director of my graduate research at Duke University, Dr. Arlin Turner, who helped me ask significant questions and set reasonable goals. I am especially indebted also to Dr. Baird Shuman whose kind recommendation of this manuscript led to its publication. I am grateful to Dr. Allan S. Hurlburt for his support and encouragement and for the financial assistance made available to me through the Duke University M.A.T. Program which he so ably directed. The Department of English of Duke University provided teaching opportunities and other financial assistance without which my graduate study would have been impossible. Three of my former students deserve recognition for their contribution to my understanding of the values of literary study — Steve Tilman, Elizabeth Heard Guy, and Heather Tosteson Reich.

I am much indebted to Dr. Edwin Wilson, Provost of Wake Forest University, who, despite the demanding responsibilities of his position, gave freely of his time to read and criticize this manuscript. I am grateful also to Mrs. Patricia Willis for her editorial assistance.

I wish to acknowledge my deep appreciation for the inspiration afforded me by the dedication, the discipline, and the integrity of three of my college professors — Mr. Rufus Norris, Dr. John Broderick, and Dr. Edwin Wilson.

The privilege of graduate study and of the leisure to write were the gifts of my parents and of my husband who have supported me through innumerable acts of practical assistance and have shared with me the tasks of child-rearing which are usually a mother's alone.

Throughout my research into the mass of secondary sources on Faulkner's fiction, I was continually impressed by the sensitivity and the integrity of the commentary of Professor Cleanth Brooks. It is the highest of honors that Professor Brooks consented to write the introduction to this volume, not simply because he is a man of eminence in American literary scholarship but because his work represents to me the best analysis of Faulkner's fiction in existence.

Introduction

William Faulkner came out of an old-fashioned society and his fictional world is an old-fashioned world in which the roles of the sexes are clearly defined. Between the sexes there is a definite polarity — though this need not and generally does not entail antagonism. Yet just because Faulkner's conception of woman is traditional, it has been frequently misunderstood by contemporary readers. These misunderstandings and misstatements are particularly rife in the work of early commentators on Faulkner. Egregious examples can be found in the writings of Leslie Fielder and Maxwell Geismar. Faulkner is said to have hated and feared women; he could portray with sympathy only girls below the age of puberty or else white-haired matriarchs.

Some of the characters in Faulkner's fiction do hate and fear women; still others are incapable of understanding them. But such attitudes are not to be attributed to Faulkner's male characters generally, nor to Faulkner himself. A further point is worth making: Faulkner did not have to wait for middle age to mellow sufficiently to approve of women between the ages of fifteen and forty-five. In his first novel he depicts a decent and generous (though nubile) woman in Margaret Powers, who shows kindness, understanding, and a genuine graciousness to the men around her.

At the University of Virginia, when Faulkner was asked whether he found it easier to write about men or women, he replied that it was much more "fun" to try to write about women, and he gave a reason: "because I think women are marvelous, they're wonderful . . . ." But that he found women wonderful does not rest merely upon his own say-so. His fiction provides the overwhelming evidence of his interest in women, his sympathy for them, his acknowledgment of their force and power, and his belief in their crucial importance to the human community. (Why not? They produce human progeny and dominate the formative years of every child's life.)

Yet we need a book on the subject of Faulkner's conception of women, for some of the old misunderstandings persist. Moreover, our present decade is likely to produce new obstacles to a just comprehension. Now that the relation of the sexes has become a matter for much polemical rhetoric as well as reasoned debate, contemporary readers may encounter fresh difficulties in coming to understand the position of woman in Faulkner's world. At any rate, we do need a good book on the subject, one that will view the whole matter in range and depth. Sally Page has undertaken to survey the whole tremendously complicated scene presented in Faulkner's stories and novels and to make an intelligent assessment of it. One does not have to agree with every nuance of interpretation in her study — and very frankly I do not — in order to say emphatically that she has given us an admirable study.

She is thoroughly aware of the danger of sweeping generalizations. She knows that Faulkner's purpose was to provide us with fictional characters who in their concreteness and particularity would carry conviction and suggest something of that mysterious uniqueness of flesh-and-blood men and women, and that he was not in the least interested in merely stating and illustrating certain abstract principles. Yet her task is very properly to generalize and to make classifications, for a measure of this is required if we are to make any sense of Faulkner's world.

In that world, women are closer to nature than men, more practical than men, and more realistic. They remain closer to their primary role of bearing children, nurturing them, sustaining the family, and keeping the human community in being. Such a role is not confined to women like the simple and almost bovine Lena Grove. Miss Jenny Du Pre, witty, civilized, patrician, displays in her own way just these virtues. Literally Miss Jenny has no children, but for her motherless nephew Bayard Sartoris she fulfills this essential maternal role.

Faulkner's men, on the other hand, are the idealists and the romantics. Since they are less closely tied to nature, they devise codes of conduct, and succeed or fail in their efforts to live up to them. These codes are often regarded by the women as impractical and even quixotic. Yet the more understanding of the women comprehend the men's plight: whereas a woman can find her role simply through being a woman, the man has to achieve status — pass certain tests — do something to prove his right to manhood. All of this is familiar enough: we have all read enough anthropology to know that primitive tribes exemplify such patterns in their mythologies and in their practical behavior. To come closer home, such has been the basic pattern of earlier European and American culture. But I have already noted that Faulkner's is an old-fashioned society, and what makes it seem strange and different is not its innovations but the tenacity with which it has held to these traditional patterns.

Because men have to find themselves through conscious exploration and test themselves in action, whereas women do not, Faulkner's male characters often attribute to women some kind of secret wisdom. Women "know" without ratiocination — they intuit — whereas men must struggle to discover reality and themselves.

Some further consequences of this view of the difference between men and women may be worth mentioning. Men are "innocent" in a way that women are not. An extreme instance would be Horace Benbow (of *Sanctuary* and *Sartoris*). Benbow is a naive idealist and learns only the hard way, through bruising personal experience. He discovers that mankind is not good, that even his charming stepdaughter, Little Belle, is not really "innocent," but is capable of using her charm to manipulate men, including her own stepfather, and that nature itself is not innocent. In a passage cited by Mrs. Page, Benbow exclaims: "That's why we know nature is a she; because of that conspiracy between female flesh and female season." And then he goes on to say, a paragraph later: "There was a mirror behind [Little Belle] and another behind me, and she was watching herself in the one behind me, forgetting the other one in which I could see her face, see her watching the back of my head with pure dissimulation. That's why nature is 'she' and Progress is 'he'; nature made the grape arbor, but Progress invented the mirror."

Still later, Mrs. Page quotes Horace's remark: "My Lord, sometimes I believe that we are all children, except children themselves." Though the last clause may seem puzzling, it makes perfect sense in Faulkner's total world view. For his children, like his women, are close to nature and, as he has one of his characters observe, if there is one thing that is not "innocent," it is a child.

The danger run by all of Faulkner's men is that they may mistake their ideals and their abstract codes for reality. Such codes range from the naive but high-minded configurations that a Horace Benbow tries to force upon reality to the grandiose but inhuman "design" of a Thomas Sutpen. Men tend to get into trouble with their idealism and their other abstractions, and it is clear that nearly all of Faulkner's "villains" are men who try to distort nature or who reject it altogether. Usually, their rejection involves a concomitant rejection of women and of the female principle itself. A tragic example is that of Joe Christmas, one of the several of Faulkner's characters who is more sinned against than sinning. Joe attempts the desperate action of cutting himself loose from nature. The feat is of course impossible and the attempt ends in Joe's death.

In Faulkner's world, woman is the goal and the end of action. Typically she is not herself a romantic, but in the eyes of the male she often wears a romantic aura. Her ability to stimulate his romantic imagination is part of her power, which she may use responsibly or cruelly and selfishly. Thus in Faulkner, as in so much of the traditional literature of Western civilization, woman, especially the young woman in her springtime beauty, is nature; or she may be the temptress, exploiting her attraction for selfish ends; or she may be the life-giving being who comforts, sustains, and completes man. It is interesting to note — as of course Mrs. Page does — that in Faulkner's very first novel, *Soldier's Pay*, we have the three roles clearly defined: Emmy, the naive girl of simple and spontaneous emotions, who gives herself to her lover with no questions asked or promises exacted; Cecily, the brittle, artificial and thoroughly selfish young siren; and Margaret Powers, who, though still young and sexually attractive, shows the selfless love, the "agape," that one more often associates with some of Faulkner's older women.

In *The Sound and the Fury*, Mr. Compson cynically observes that women "only use other people's codes of honour . . . ." We don't have to take Mr. Compson's remarks literally, particularly since we realize the reason for his bitterness. His wife is a cold-hearted and neurotic woman who has poisoned the whole family relationship. Yet even this bitter assessment does have a relation to Faulkner's general outlook. Women do not live by codes of honor. Their clear-eyed apprehension of what can be done and ought to be done usually compels them to regard as hopelessly abstract the ethical patterns that men impose upon themselves. For illustration: Mink Snopes, smarting under what he regards as a humiliation publicly inflicted on him by Jack Houston, shoots his enemy from ambush. Since he does not confront Houston, man to man, we may regard his concept of honor as a rather shabby one. Yet Mink, though destitute, scorns to rifle the dead man's pockets.

On the other hand, Mink's wife, in her utter devotion to her man, will do anything to get the money that will allow him to get away. Brushing aside any scruples as to how the money is to be got, she prostitutes herself and then presses the money on Mink. But Mink's honor interposes: though his need is desperate, he will not accept tainted money.

Or, to move up to people of better breeding and more exalted codes: Bayard Sartoris feels a compulsion to confront his father's assassin. We find later that he has from the beginning resolved not to try to kill him, as the community expects him to do; yet he must show that he is not afraid to face him. Bayard's Aunt Jenny tries to dissuade him, saying: "I know that you are not afraid." Later, when Bayard tells her that he must go, saying "You see, I want to be thought well of," Aunt Jenny replies: "I do. Even if you spend the day hidden in the stable loft, I still do." Bayard, as his aunt senses, means to go to the confrontation unarmed, even though he knows his opponent is armed. When he returns unscathed from this quixotic exposure of his life, his Aunt Jenny finally breaks down with the exclamation: "Oh, damn you Sartorises! Damn you! Damn you!" But she is obviously terribly proud of her nephew even if she is exasperated almost beyond endurance by his having taken such a risk.

Mr. Compson is in one sense correct: women — at least Faulkner's women — do not live by codes of honor, but this does not mean that they do not have their own standards of courage and justice. Theirs, however, are not quite those of their men, and Faulkner does not expect them to be. In fact, as one explores Faulkner's fiction, it becomes plain that he believes it a mistake for either sex to try to adopt the special values of the other. (Obviously they share basic human values.) The sexes must maintain their roles. Each must learn to love and respect the other, although since both men and women are human, that is not always easy to do.

Faulkner has from time to time been reproached for giving us few happy marriages. Happy marriages do occur in his world, though he does not tend to write much about them. After all, as Tolstoy remarked, happy marriages are all alike. The most interesting are those that are not happy. Nor are most of Faulkner's most interesting men and women happy. Faulkner's masterpieces of character portrayal usually involve instances of frustration, tragic waste, or self-destruction. He gives us the story of a woman deflected from her proper role, or turned inward in bitter frustration, or that of a cold-hearted man incapable of seeing his wife as a fellow human being or so blasted by abstraction that he hates womankind and nature itself. Thus, Faulkner is sufficiently the realist to give us instance after instance of a wife at the mercy of a shiftless or cruel or even mad husband (just as he also depicts more than one husband at the mercy of a selfish or trivial or neurotic wife). But his accounts of the failures of men and women to achieve a proper union point clearly enough to what the ideal union ought to be. In it, woman is not condemned to be a drudge or slave, nor does she have to be "submissive." Faulkner's most strong-minded characters — I except from this category male characters like Joe Christmas and Thomas Sutpen, since they are not so much strong-minded as fatally obsessed — are almost invariably women.

Some of the most interesting of Faulkner's women are those that have been pushed out of their proper orbit — "masculinized" women like Drusilla Sartoris or Joanna Burden. But Faulkner treats even these women with dramatic sympathy and views their plight with pity and understanding. Drusilla is a destructive force, the "priestess of a succinct and formal violence," as she stands in her yellow ballroom dress beside the coffin that holds her murdered husband's body and presents the pistols to her young stepson. He is only a few years younger than she and clearly she is more than half in love with him, and this fact explains why it is "in a voice fainting and passionate with promise" that she urges him to avenge his father. Yet though Faulkner sees Drusilla as corrupted in her obsession with masculine honor, he has shown his reader how she became so. Moreover, he allows her incandescent emotion without making her ridiculous. Finally, he presents her as a woman who has not lost all sense of the good and noble. At the end Drusilla makes the gesture that shows that she too recognizes the heroic significance of Bayard's resolution not to kill.

Even Miss Emily Grierson, who poisoned her lover to keep him from jilting her and who kept the body through some forty years in an upstairs bedroom, is viewed as more than simply a witch or merely a clinical case. The nameless narrator of her story by implication accords her a certain respect as a woman who has proudly maintained her independence through genteel poverty and who has refused to knuckle under to the new ways of the town. In killing her lover, she has pushed the aristocratic virtues to their final desperate extreme. The price she pays for her victory is terrible, and yet, to the discerning eye of the narrator, it constitutes a kind of victory after all.

Faulkner's treatment of woman throughout his fiction indicates that he did indeed find them marvelous and wonderful — in their capacity for horrifying depravity as well as in their capacity for sheer goodness. Human beings in general were for him wonderful creatures — in both these respects — all of which is to say that Faulkner saw women essentially as human beings: their special sex role did not make them inhuman in the eyes of this male novelist. In fact, because of her special role, woman occupied a place at the very center of the human condition.

Mrs. Page's discussion of the various ways in which Faulkner saw woman and the female principle is admirable, both in its scope and in its depth. In some of her comments on the male principle I think that she has occasionally been less discerning; but this observation may simply represent the workings of my own male prejudice. In any event, she regards the male principle as the necessary complement of the female principle. For if the human community devoted itself solely to nurturing children, became simply life-regarding and life-sustaining, and insisted on being eminently practical, putting hearth-and-home things always first, the world would become a parochial community, unimaginative, unspeculative, and almost totally submerged in nature. Faulkner's women obviously do not want that kind of world, nor, as the full sweep of Mrs. Page's book testifies, does she. Faulkner's indictment of male abstractions that get out of hand — "designs," codes of complicated laws, quixotic concepts of honor — is powerful. Nevertheless mankind needs these too. What is called for is a proper tension between the male and female principles.

In her concern to be thorough and to show that she has taken into account what others have had to say about Faulkner (in her bibliography of secondary sources I have counted over 375 items), Mrs. Page sometimes needlessly puts herself in leading strings to others, acknowledging their views and occasionally allowing herself to be too much impressed by them. But her intelligence, her common sense, and her intimate and detailed knowledge of the Faulkner canon keep her from ever going very far astray.

Her book is particularly strong in its power to remind us of the great variety of human types to be found in Faulkner's work. It is strong, too, in the author's skill in making out character patterns and discovering analogous traits that may connect a very obscure character with one of Faulkner's major figures. In reading her book I have learned a great deal. I predict that it will have a salutary effect on Faulkner scholarship — and not on Faulkner scholarship alone. It is a book that will be valuable to the general reader, for it not only illuminates Faulkner's attitude toward women, but it also necessarily deals with his conception of mankind at large and the nature of the human effort. In her account of *As I Lay Dying*, Mrs. Page provides an excellent brief summary of the basic situation so often portrayed by Faulkner. As she puts it: "*As I Lay Dying* is another dramatization of Faulkner's vision of the polarities of choice available to man — man's choice to survive, which requires a compromise of personal visions of transcendence, and man's desire for the achievement of transcendence and ideality which, as his earlier fiction demonstrates, results in isolation and death. Faulkner's variation of the theme in *As I Lay Dying* [i.e., his giving the husband here something of the female role and the wife, something of the male role] indicates both his comprehension of the complexity of human life and the range of mood with which he is able to portray his theme . . . . *As I Lay Dying* demonstrates that it is impossible for man or woman to force out of life a reality that matches the idealism of an inner vision. To persist in devotion to ideality rather than to reality results in personal isolation, individual decay, and death. Submission to life, expecting no good luck in it and accepting fully the limitations of the human situation, enables man to survive."

This is not the last word on the subject, but it constitutes an important word, and it states effectively one of Faulkner's great themes. The hero — more rarely the heroine — attempts to live his vision or to impose it on reality — and generally fails. But out of the failure, if the dream is a high one and pursued heroically, he wins a victory in defeat, or at least suffers defeat only on his own terms. If the ideal is too limited — too cruelly at odds with nature, as with some of Faulkner's "Puritans" and his woman-haters — his effort ends in alienation and final disaster.

CLEANTH BROOKS

Characterization and Meaning:
Preliminary Issues

William Faulkner is one of the most successful novelists of this century because of the sheer imaginative wealth of the fictional world he has created. No other American writer has brought to life such an abundance and variety of human character — both protagonists who have depth, intensity, and roundness and a supporting cast that is vivid and unforgettable. Faulkner, of course, is not equally successful in all his works, but his best novels are masterful presentations of a vividly detailed human world that is unobtrusively, yet coherently ordered by the meaning the fiction has been created to convey.

Faulkner's women are an especially interesting focus for the study of his fiction because they clearly illustrate how Faulkner has designed character to make the fiction reveal the meaning which is the inspiring, motivating force behind the creation of the story. Indeed, an adequate comprehension of the bulk of Faulkner's fiction requires an understanding of his portrayal of women. Conversely, it is impossible to judge adequately the effectiveness of Faulkner's women characters apart from the thematic import of the works in which they appear. Faulkner's female figures have been, of course, the object of a great deal of very negative criticism, a criticism which is the product of a misunderstanding of the fictional purpose behind his characterization of women. In a real sense, to attack the way Faulkner has portrayed women in his novels is to attack the very nature of the fiction he has created, both in terms of its meaning and its method.

Such an attack is explicit in the criticism of both Maxwell Geismar and Leslie Fiedler, who have been more outspoken than any other readers in their disapproval of Faulkner's women characters. In "William Faulkner: the Negro and the Female" (*Writers in Crisis*, p. 147) Geismar suggests that Faulkner's first novel, *Soldier's Pay*, exhibits ". . . a suspicion of women when it is not contempt and contempt when it is not hatred." Basing his argument on his readings of *Sanctuary* and *Light in August*, Geismar proposes that the "twin furies" of Faulkner's fiction are the Negro and the female and that upon them Faulkner has vented all his hatred of the modern South whose fall is symbolized by the fall of the Southern woman. "How shall the artist more aptly convey his total protest than to portray the Female source of life as itself inherently vicious?" (*Writers in Crisis*, p. 180). Geismar's remarks do not even seem especially extreme in comparison to Leslie Fiedler's comments on Faulkner's women. "In no other writer in the world do pejorative stereotypes of women appear with greater frequency and on more levels, from the most trivial to the most profound; had Faulkner dared treat in such terms any racial minority, his books would have been banned in every enlightened school in the country" (*Love and Death in the American Novel*, p. 309). Irving Howe (*William Faulkner: A Critical Study*, pp. 97-100) suggests that Faulkner's emphasis on the destructiveness of woman is so extreme that it represents a psychological imbalance on his part.[1] Are the female characters in Faulkner's

---

[1]This is certainly the implication of Geismar's and Fiedler's criticism also, and Irving Malin (*William Faulkner: An Interpretation*, p. 96) regards Faulkner's "brutal treatment of sex" as "latently homosexual or, if this is too extreme, Oedipal." The destructive nature of Faulkner's women is also the subject of Thomas Lorch's "Thomas Sutpen and the Female Principle" and Samuel Yorks' "Faulkner's Women: The Peril of Mankind."

fiction so narrowly conceived, so evil and destructive that it is only possible to conclude that they are the product of a neurotic hatred of women?

Something of that question was put to Faulkner during the conferences at Nagano, Japan. He responded,

> "The opinion that women cause the trouble is not my own .... They have held families together and it's because of families that the race is continued, and I would be sorry to think that my work had given anyone the impression that I held women in morally a lower position than men, which I do not." (*Faulkner at Nagano*, p. 69)

Rather than regarding woman as the cause of all the "evil and trouble" Faulkner apparently considered her a creative and sustaining force in human life. Indeed, it has been successfully demonstrated that the negative attitude toward women present in some Faulkner novels represents not the view of the author but the view of characters in the story.[1] And a number of critics have noted the positive qualities of many of Faulkner's women characters.[2] It is not a legitimate argument that Faulkner has presented woman merely as a force of evil and destruction. The novelist who created Temple Drake, Belle Mitchell, and Joanna Burden, also created Ruby Goodwin, Dilsey, and Lena Grove. Numerous examples prove that Faulkner's view of woman as he described it at the Nagano conference is borne out by his fiction; indeed, this veiw of woman is a central theme in many of his novels.

It is true, however, that Faulkner's female figures do ultimately fall into one of these two extremes of character

---

[1]See Naomi Jackson's "Faulkner's Woman: 'Demon-Nun and Angel-Witch'," pp. 16-17.

[2]See, for example, Karl E. Zink, "Faulkner's Garden: Woman and the Immemorial Earth" and Cleanth Brooks's comments about Faulkner's women in *William Faulkner: The Yoknapatawpha Country*.

types; either they are creative, or they are destructive. It may seem, then, that Faulkner's women must be merely stereotyped versions of virtue or evil with little variety in personality traits. This is certainly the view of most of the criticism which has concerned itself with Faulkner's women characters. Fiedler's opinion is that Faulkner had respect only for women beyond menopause and that all the other women in his fiction are of one of two destructive types — either they are the fertile and alluring "mindless daughters of peasants" or the "fleshless but sexually insatiable daughters of the aristocracy" both of whom, according to Fiedler, fade into the stereotype of the "Good Bad Girl" in Faulkner's later fiction (*Love and Death in the American Novel*, p. 312). Fiedler's rather sensational categorizing of the women characters is not an isolated example in Faulkner criticism. Virtually every analysis of Faulkner's women *per se* has been basically some scheme for organizing all the major figures into two or three groups of character types who have some dominating trait in common. However, such discussions have been at best an over-simplification of the role of women in Faulkner's fiction; at worst they have resulted in faulty and misleading descriptions of individual characters.

For example, because Howe (*William Faulkner*, p. 98) divides all of Faulkner's women into two groups — the old ladies who are "beyond the age of sexual distraction" and the "young American bitch" — Patricia in *Mosquitoes*, Temple Drake, Charlotte Rittenmeyer, Eula Varner, and Lena Grove are grouped together as "young bitches" without any acknowledgement of the vast differences in their characters. Similarly, in order to place the women into his two categories of "ghosts" and "earthmothers" David Miller (*"Faulkner's Women,"* pp. 3-11) is led to group together indiscriminately such diverse characters as Jenny DuPre, Judith Sutpen, Addie Bundren, Margaret Powers, and Joanna Burden without indicating the tremendous differences in the nature and meaning of their roles in the separate works. To emphasize some vague — or even precise — similarity among certain characters without noting their differences results in the false implication that Faulkner's women are merely unvaried repetitions of two or three character types. Such a criticism denies the very complex nature of Faulkner's fiction and the important place which women characters have in it.

Most of Faulkner's women are too original to be regarded as replicas of other characters or of some stereotyped view of woman. None of those whom Miller and Howe group together as common types are really very much alike either in terms of their individual personalities or in terms of the roles they play in the structure and meaning of the novels in which they appear. Though it is possible to group the characters into the two broad categories of creative and destructive types, this kind of analysis is quite unrewarding apart from the exploration of the relationship between characterization and narrative purpose. When Faulkner's women are examined in the context of the form and meaning of the works in which they appear, their uniqueness and their effectiveness as fictional characters are readily apparent.

It is obvious that many of Faulkner's women do embody the extremes of human nature; Joanna Burden's crazed nymphomania, Temple Drake's mad lust, and the overpoweringly abundant sexual fertility of Eula Varner are not, after all, typical traits of most women. But then, neither is Faulkner's fiction as a whole characterized by a mimetic treatment of human reality. Faulkner did not elect to limit himself to the empirical view or to the observer attitude as a novelist, nor did he limit his subject matter to the routine, outward surface of human life. Instead, throughout Faulkner's major novels reality has been heightened to the level of the symbolic and the mythic. This observation is, of course, a commonplace in Faulkner criticism; yet, too many of Faulkner's critics have been reluctant to admit that this kind of fiction requires an adaptation of realistic methods of characterization. Indeed, such a heightening of reality is the product not only of the language the artist chooses, but also it is the product of the kind of characters the novelist has created. Many of Faulkner's characters loom "larger than life," for the strictest realistic requirements of characterization are not adhered to by Faulkner because his purpose is, if not larger, at least different.

Several recent studies of the technique of the novel have reasserted the importance of character in fiction and have stressed the necessity of considering characterization in terms of the nature and meaning of the novel as a whole.[1] The question that has been raised is, how can the reality and effectiveness of a given character be satisfactorily judged. The reality of individual characters is the product of the total reality of the fictional world they inhabit, and the nature of the reality of a certain character is determined by the nature of the fiction itself. If characters do not function meaningfully in accordance with the total atmosphere and action of the narrative, their "convincingness" as individual beings is irrelevant. A so-called flat character or even a stereotyped character may be quite appropriate and effective because that kind of characterization suits the purpose of the author and contributes to the creation of a fully realized fictional world.[2] Similarly, a character who embodies the extremes of human nature may contribute substantially to the novel's meaning, particularly if the fictional method is symbolic.

For example, a great deal of the appeal of Faulkner's fiction is the result of his creation of an abundant variety of eccentric individuals – people like Miss Jenny DuPre, Lena Grove, Anse Bundren, and Eula Varner. These characters are to a degree flat, for they do have some dominant quality that is immediately apparent whenever they reappear – Miss Jenny's ire, Lena's serenity, Anse's laziness, Eula's sexuality. Yet such characters please the reader because this kind of characterization by the

---

[1]See, for example, the sections on character in Philip Stevick's *The Theory of the Novel* and in Robert Scholes' and Robert Kellogg's *The Nature of Narrative* and Charles C. Walcutt's *Man's Changing Mask: Modes and Methods of Characterization in Fiction* and especially W. J. Harvey's *Character in the Novel.*

[2]See Harvey's chapter, "The Human Context."

very nature of its repetition is vivid and memorable. But more significant is the fact that the very changelessness of the flat character contributes to a basic theme of Faulkner's fiction: his belief in mankind's changelessness, the capacity to survive despite the knocks and bumps of life. If many of Faulkner's women may be regarded as flat or static characters, it is not without purpose. It would be contrary to Faulkner's meaning if Eula Varner were shown in the fullness and balance with which Henry James portrayed Isabel Archer.

At the same time Faulkner's static characters persist in surprising the reader with the revelation of some new and unexpected dimension. Consider, for example, Lena Grove's comic judgments on herself, Miss Jenny's sudden death when she is struck to the heart by Narcissa's hypocrisy, and Eula Snopes's perceptiveness and nobility when she commits suicide to save her daughter. Further, the flat or static characters frequently play such a major role in the structure and meaning of the works that they assume the depth and complexity of the fictional worlds they inhabit. The contrast between the flatness of the character of Caroline Compson when she is considered in isolation and the depth of her character in the context of a work as monumental as *The Sound and the Fury* is obvious.

In accordance with the tendency of his fiction towards the symbolic, Faulkner relies quite heavily on imagery, both as a device for characterization and as a means of linking individual characters to the overall symbolic content of the novel. It is Faulkner's imagery which is the key to understanding the close relationship between his characterization of women and his major themes. If most of Faulkner's women may be broadly categorized as either creative or destructive types, it is because they are intricately related to the central meaning of his fiction. At the heart of each of Faulkner's novels is the dynamic tension between the forces of life and the forces of anti-life,[1] a tension

---

[1]See for comparison Kenneth E. Richardson's *Force and Faith in the Novels of William Faulkner*, especially the section on woman, pp. 65-108.

xxvii

which is made constantly real and intense through the imagery, the characters, and the action of the novels.

Faulkner has not bored us with his women characters. Who can be anything but amused and amazed at them? Taken as a whole Faulkner's women do not jar our view of woman in real life nor of mankind in terms of the extremes of virtue and evil of which individual human beings are capable. Most significantly, Faulkner has carefully designed his women characters to do their part in revealing a larger pattern of meaning which is not only ordered and coherent, but is also a valid presentation of the tensions of human existence as mankind experiences "the conflicts of the human heart." This volume is an examination of Faulkner's women characters in the context of the mesh of character relationships, the imagery and symbolism, the action, and the meaning of the separate works.

Abbreviations

A,A!:	*Absalom, Absalom!*
AILD:	*As I Lay Dying*
CS:	*Collected Stories of William Faulkner*
H:	*The Hamlet*
ID:	*Intruder in the Dust*
LA:	*Light in August*
M:	*Mosquitoes*
MF:	*The Marble Faun*
R:	*The Reivers: A Reminiscence*
S:	*Sanctuary*
SF:	*The Sound and the Fury*
SP:	*Soldier's Pay*
T:	*The Town*
TT:	*These Thirteen*
WP:	*The Wild Palms*
ZG:	*Miss Zilphia Gant*

CHAPTER I

The Lure of Sex and Modern Alienation

One of Faulkner's early poems entitled "Study" portrays a student trying vainly to prepare for an examination though enthralled by lush images of spring and womanly beauty.

> Somewhere a slender voiceless breeze will go
> Unlinking the shivering poplars' arms, and brakes
> With sleeves simple crossed where waters flow; . . .

> Somewhere a candle's guttering gold
> Weaves a tapestry upon a cottage wall
> And her gold hair, simple fold on fold,
> While I can think of nothing else at all
> Except the sunset in her eyes' still pool.
> (Work, work, you fool!—) (*Early Prose and Poetry*, p. 62)

The poem concludes, ". . . I wish I were a bust/ all head.) Of the nineteen poems which Carvel Collins has collected in *William Faulkner: Early Prose and Poetry* sixteen are explicitly about the powerful attractiveness of woman or the romantic love relationship.

1

"L'Apres-Midi d'un Faun," perhaps the most well known of these very early poems, begins with an extensive description of a woman who personifies the beautiful dynamic life of nature itself.

> I follow through the singing trees
> Her streaming clouded hair and face
> And lascivious dreaming knees
> Like gleaming water from some place
> Of sleeping streams, or autumn leaves
> Slow shed through still, love-wearied air.
> She pauses: and as one who grieves
> Shakes down her blown and vagrant hair
> To veil her face, but not her eyes —
> A hot quick spark, each sudden glance,
> Or like the wild brown bee that flies
> Sweet winged, a sharp extravagance
> Of kisses on my limbs and neck.
>   (*Early Prose and Poetry*, p. 39)

The woman lures the faun to a visionary world which represents the ancient pastoral age of perpetual spring. It is her image which is painfully sought and yet unfound in the closely related poem, "Faun." Two other poems, "Sapphics" and "Naiad's Song," also depict the nymphs and goddesses of the ancient world who possess the mysterious power to lure others into bondage and peaceful forgetfulness.

When Faulkner describes a woman of the present age in "To a Co-ed," he makes her attractiveness clear by comparing her to the goddesses of the ancient world.

> I could have turned unmoved from Helen's brow,
> Who found no beauty in their Beatrice:
> Their Thais seemed less lovely then as now,
> Though some had bartered Athens for a kiss.
> For down Time's arras, faint and fair and far,
> Your face still beckons like a lonely star.
>   (*Early Prose and Poetry*, p. 70)

In this poem, as in "Study," the lure of the girl's beauty is a powerful force which, as the star image suggests, is alive, burning, inescapable, and eternal.

This inescapable power of woman is also the subject of "After Fifty Years." Even though the woman in this poem has grown old and has lost the men who once worshipped her youthful beauty, she is still able to bind to her the young man who is the poem's personae until "he feels her presence like shed scent,/ Holding him body and life within its snare" (*Early Prose and Poetry*, p. 53). This poem makes explicit a feeling which is suggested by the mood and imagery of several of the poems in this collection — that woman's allure can bring pain as well as release and pleasure.

In the eight poems which depict a romantic love relationship ("Une Ballade des Femmes Perdues," "Nocturne," "Portrait," "Co-education at Ole Miss," "Fantoches," "Clair de Lune," "Streets," and "A Clymène" — the last four from Paul Verlaine) the emphasis again is on the power of the force of love. The moods vary from the comic to cynical disappointment to the firm fidelity of "A Clymène," but whether love is a live flame, as the lovers themselves are imagined in "Nocturne," or whether the lover merely dreams of the "little ghosts of loves" past, as in "Une Ballade des Femmes Perdues," the force of woman's love is always presented as overpowering, inescapable, and unforgettable.

The golden-haired girl of "Study" and the images of nature, particularly of spring, which so frequently accompany her presentation are the dominant motifs of Faulkner's earliest poetry. These poems portray woman as the possessor of a mysterious beauty which endows her with a powerful and inescapable allure. She can be a source of comfort, and, even more, she can be a source of the deepest and most complete emotional fulfillment. At the same time her power can represent painfulness, as is suggested by the bee-sting kisses of the woman in "L'Apres-Midi d'un Faun" and the "snare" of the woman in "After Fifty Years."

It is not surprising that these themes dominate Faulkner's first attempts at poetry, for they are also the central motifs of his earliest novels. At the core of Faulkner's early fiction is a major tension that is the product of the powerfully alluring image of woman who is often elusive and unattainable and is at times binding and destructive but who, nevertheless, represents an idealized beauty, freedom, and fulfillment which are above and beyond the world of routine realities. The sensation of tension and frustration that envelops the youth of "Study" who is torn between the necessity to complete a drab task and the urgings of imagination and physical desire is the motivating and pervading emotion of Faulkner's first two novels, *Soldier's Pay* and *Mosquitoes.*

The action of Faulkner's two apprentice novels is grounded entirely in the male's obsessive desire for the female as a mate. The combinations of pursuer and pursued are seemingly endless. In *Soldier's Pay* Julian Lowe and Joe Gilligan pursue Margaret Powers, Donald Mahon has courted both Emmy and Cecily Saunders, and George Farr lustfully dreams of Cecily throughout the novel. In *Mosquitoes* Mrs. Maurier pursues Mr. Talliaferro; Miss Jameson, Pete and Mark Frost; Gordon and David pursue Pat Robyn; Mr. Talliaferro pursues Jenny, and at the end of the novel Dawson Fairchild, the Semitic man, and Gordon seek out their respective prostitutes. Janarius Jones in *Soldier's Pay* and Mr. Talliaferro in *Mosquitoes* are in a sense parodies of the more "normal" characters; the lustful satyr Jones quite literally attempts to kiss if not rape every attractive' female he encounters, and the weaker Mr. Talliaferro does the same in his imagination. In both novels the sole motivation of the characters which advances the plot through encounter, conflict, and resolution is the mating urge. The plot structure of *Soldier's Pay* can be outlined in terms of the mating relationships: Donald Mahon, Julian Lowe and Joe Gilligan encounter Margaret Powers; Margaret rejects Julian and accepts Donald and Joe; Cecily wavers between Donald and George Farr, finally choosing the latter; as a result of Cecily's decision Margaret marries Donald; Donald dies; the rejected Emmy succumbs to Janarius Jones; Margaret rejects Joe and the novel is completed.

In a real sense nothing happens in *Mosquitoes* because the characters' motivations to mate end with encounter. They are thrust together, most of them intensely desirous of sexual love, but they neither accept nor reject one another. The plot, like Mrs. Maurier's yacht, is suspended in a lake of no movement. The only exception is the escapade of David and Pat; their departure from the yacht constitutes a change in setting and suggests a forward movement of plot. It is the only event which breaks up the pattern of sameness, but it, too, proves to be futile action. *Mosquitoes* is a successful novel at least in the sense that it creates within the reader the same frustration of expectation without resolution and the boredom of futile encounter that is its subject. From the dream visions of Gordon to the vain yearnings of Mr. Talliaferro, virtually the only human emotion portrayed in the novel is sexual desire which remains perpetually unfulfilled. The characters who are not driven by sexual desire are seemingly inhuman; Dawson Fairchild, the Semitic, and Mark Frost are only talking machines, until the final pages of the novel when the first two visit the prostitutes and Frost visits Miss Jameson. The futility of the *Nausikaa's* cruise is re-emphasized by the revelation of the sterility of Mrs. Maurier's life and by the final comic-pathetic defeat of Mr. Talliaferro's effort to "talk up" a seduction of Jenny.

Obviously, the mating urge is no merely superficial basis for plot action in these two novels, but is, instead, at the core of the thematic concern of both works. Faulkner explores the complexities of the mating relationship by creating a large number of characters who illustrate a wide variety of human responses to love and sexual desire. He devotes considerable effort to portraying pictorially woman's physical beauty in order to suggest the power and mystery of her attractiveness. Not only does Faulkner suggest that women possess an unworldly beauty, but also through certain women characters and the comments of males Faulkner endows woman with an understanding of human needs that men do not possess and suggests that all women have by their very nature capacities for life and creativity denied to the male. Characterization, imagery, and thematic commentary in *Soldier's Pay* and *Mosquitoes* reveal that the frustration and futility of the sexual relationship are indicative of the essential impotence of man in the face of the final and ultimate oblivion of death. Man's desire for woman is an expression of his quest for freedom from the bonds of mortality and human limitation.

The thematic centrality of the motif of the failure of romantic love in *Soldier's Pay* is apparent both in minor episodes and in the whole framework of the novel's plot. *Soldier's Pay* opens as a typical post-war novel with a portrayal of soldiers returning home, half-drunk and riotously enjoying their last taste of freedom from normal civilities as they boastfully complain of the bitter experiences of war. However, with the appearance of Margaret Powers the direction of the novel changes abruptly, and *Soldier's Pay* becomes not so much a novel about post-war despair as a novel about the frustrations of sexual love. The new pattern is initiated by Julian Lowe's adolescent infatuation with Margaret. Lowe is a romantic youth, bitter because his late arrival on the battlefield denied him the heroism of a wound, of death, or even of combat. His childish vision of death at war — "He saw a tomb, open, and himself in boots and belt, and pilot's wings, on his breast, a wound stripe" — parallels his ridiculously sentimental concept of love.

> Lowe told her [Margaret] youngly: "I thought of it [making love to her] on the train when I first saw you. When I saw you I knew you were the woman for me. Tell me, you don't like him [Donald Mahon] better than me because he has wings and a scar, do you?" (*SP*, p. 52)

Julian's confusion of the lusts of the flesh and knightly love and his stupid yearnings for heroic wounds are rendered without any touch of complexity. The portrayal is almost maliciously without restraint, and the whole episode of Margaret's mockery of him becomes distasteful. However, the caricature is neither structurally nor thematically irrelevant. Faulkner does not allow the reader to forget Lowe; throughout the novel major events are punctuated with the periodic flow of his faithful letters to Margaret — sentimental, confused, ungrammatical, misspelled notes to a woman who cannot even remember his name. The "love" which Julian feels for Margaret is totally meaningless, forgotten soon after they are physically separated. Julian's infatuation is typical of youth and his presentation is stereotyped, but Faulkner's attention to him is appropriate, for the episode initiates the motif of ineffectual love which is the central thematic concern of this novel as well as of *Mosquitoes*.

The central complication of the plot of *Soldier's Pay* is that Cecily Saunders, Donald Mahon's fiancée, cannot bear to marry the disfigured war hero. Her current lover, George Farr, is kept in spasms of despair and desire at her indecision. When he finally wins her, it is obvious that even by the time the honeymoon is over, Cecily's deflated ego has already produced a miserably deflated mate. Faulkner suggests that the love the modest and unattractive cook Emmy holds for Donald is genuine, but Donald is in reality nearly dead, and, even at that, circumstance prevents their marriage. Margaret Powers marries Donald to justify herself to her dead husband, whom she feels she married and made love to hypocritically. However, their marriage involves no real union and seems to hasten Donald's death rather than retard it.

Faulkner shows the greatest respect for the love which Joe Gilligan feels for Margaret, but she, because of her past, cannot return his love, and Joe is prevented, again by circumstance, from pursuing her on her own terms. Even his faithful devotion fades as soon as he is separated from her, and he seemingly accepts the rector's judgment that "The saddest thing about love, Joe, is that not only the love cannot last forever, but even the heartbreak is soon forgotten" (*SP*, p. 318). Julian Lowe's "love" experience is not the exception in Faulkner's first novel, but the rule. Even the most admirable and mature characters are prevented from achieving a satisfying love relation either because of circumstance or because of the complexities of their own personalities.

The love experiences in *Mosquitoes* are of a far more futile nature even than those of *Soldier's Pay*. Love becomes entirely irrelevant and the mating urge is reduced to its bare essential of lust. Yet even this proves an inadequate drive for most of the characters who seem unable to force their encounters toward any sort of conclusion, much less to establish meaningful sexual relationships. A more admirable example is David, the yacht's steward, who is utterly possessed by his yearning for Pat Robyn. He shares with her an entrancing nocturnal swim, and they escape the yacht together in a mock elopement which is morbidly ended with the attack of the mosquitoes. Throughout their experience David's sexual need totally immobilizes him; he is incapable of overcoming his modesty and fears in the face of Pat's total lack of sexual desire. Though the feeling he has for her is "like he had just waked up and a wind with music in it was coming across green hills brave in a clean dawn," David can never express himself in any way except to stare constantly at Pat "with an utter longing, like that of a dog." David is a sufficiently strong character to leave the yacht after his humiliation and thus seems to escape the total condemnation to sterility that engulfs the other characters.

The two female characters, Miss Jameson and Mrs. Maurier, represent the epitome of sterility. Although Miss Jameson concerns herself constantly with thoughts of love and attempts at mating, she is totally unsuccessful. Her past bohemian life, complete with an artist lover, left her still a virgin. Every successive affair has been "like those brief thunderstorms of August that threaten and dissolve for no apparent reason without producing any rain" (*M*, p. 103). The total despair of her existence is made plain at the end of the novel when she receives a habitual visit from Mark Frost, her only remaining male friend. Frost phones with the request to have a button sewn on; Dorothy eagerly encourages his visit, reiterating that her parents are away for the weekend. Frost arrives, collapses on the divan, and smokes interminable cigarettes. Miss Jameson delicately departs to her boudoir, flashes on and off the lamps, locks, then slightly opens the door, while she searches for "an embroidered night dress, neatly folded and unworn and scented faintly."

Then, standing where the door, should it be opened, would conceal her for a moment, she slipped the gown over her head and from beneath it she removed the undergarment. Then she took her reckless troubled heart and the fragile and humorless calmness in which it beat, back to the dressing table; and sitting before the mirror she assumed a studied pose, combing and combing out her long uninteresting hair. (*M*, p. 333)

Dorothy Jameson's intentions are brutally mocked, for Mark Frost merely continues to place one cigarette after another into his "pale prehensile mouth" as though it "were a separate organism," dozes, hardly notes his hostess's absence, and finally races away at midnight frantic for fear he will miss the last streetcar home.

The story of Mrs. Maurier's life is the same pathetic tragedy of sexual frustration but with more heroics. Forced into a marriage for money at the sacrifice of a poor but worthy lover, she became a widowed and childless but rich old woman. Fairchild, learning of her past, explains her thwarted character as the result of her loveless marriage.

"Fooling with sex, kind of dabbing at it, like a kitten at a ball of string. She missed something: her body told her so, insisted, forced her to try to remedy it and fill the vacuum. But now her body is old; it no longer remembers that it missed anything, and all she has left is a habit, the ghost of a need to rectify something the lack of which her body has long since forgotten about." (*M*, p. 326)

The host of pathetically sterile characters which Mrs. Maurier assembles for her *Nausikaa* cruise suggests that the novel focuses wholly on tragic despair. Actually a tone of bitter mockery pervades the novel. Faulkner's attitude is more satiric than sympathetic, and though the characters are hopelessly doomed to tragically futile sex drives, the novelist frequently laughs at them. Mr. Talliaferro, the most hopelessly ineffective lover of all, is a comic figure. The novel opens with his declaration, "The sex instinct is quite strong in me." He discusses at length with his friends the exact methods he should pursue in order to seduce the delectable Jenny. When at last Jenny decides to "envelop him" with "the sweet cloudy fire of her thighs," Mr. Talliaferro trembles at the "exquisite, unbearable lightness" that moves "down his arms to his hands, and down his legs" (*M*, p. 189). Then the determined seducer Talliaferro turns and flees, totally incapable of any other response when the invitation is issued. [The scene makes Talliaferro seem more like a Smollett character than Eliot's Prufrock or Joyce's Bloom to whom he has been compared.[1]] The novel closes with a final humorously pathetic deflation of his pretensions. After a cruel rebuff he calls Fairchild for reassurance about a new plan of attack, his decision to be "cruel and hard, until she begs for my love." Fairchild hangs up on him, and a female voice comments sarcastically, "You tell 'em big boy; treat 'em rough." With Mr. Talliaferro the act of love is reduced to an imagined lust enacted only through useless and empty words.

The idyllic mating experience of the youthful Emmy and the pre-war Donald in *Soldier's Pay* is a startling contrast to the predominant pattern of ineffectual love which Faulkner has created in his first two novels. The lovers meet at night in a forest, their nakedness bathed by a pool of pure water and the light of the moon. The scene is entirely still and quiet except for the pastoral cows munching grass. Emmy enters freely and without self-doubt into the experience Donald offers her; she is wholly innocent and completely self-giving. After Donald has made love to her she sleeps peacefully, and he awakens her at dawn with freshly picked blackberries for her breakfast. When she returns home and her father calls her a whore, she dares him to touch the flesh which still feels the sacredness of her experience. When he leaves for war, Donald instructs his father to care for Emmy, and though he carries the photograph and letters of Cecily, the implication of the novel is that it is the experience shared with Emmy that Donald needs to recapture to find peace. Emmy's strength to endure her present existence is

---

[1]See Frederick L. Gwynn, "Faulkner's Prufrock — and Other Observations," pp. 63-70, and Joyce W. Warren, "Faulkner's 'Portrait of the Artist,' " p. 129.

based on the sense of fulfillment and tranquility she experienced with Donald during her youth.

Frequently in the course of the novel the photograph of the pre-war Donald with his "delicate pointed chin and wild, soft eyes" and his thin face "with the serenity of a wild thing" suggests to various characters that he is like a mythological faun. What is known of Donald's behavior as a youth supports the comparison: his hair is unruly, he refuses to conform to proper dress, he wanders through the woods alone oblivious of time, and he woos young women. His seduction of Emmy, his possessions returned from the battlefront – "a woman's chemise, a cheap paper-covered 'Shropshire Lad,' a mummied hyacinth bulb" – and Cecily's quick assumption that he has made love to Margaret are perfectly in character. The comparison of Donald to a faun suggests a possible relationship between the novel, Faulkner's second published work, and his first, *The Marble Faun*, a collection of nineteen related poems.[1] These poems indicate that Faulkner did intend that the pre-war Donald of *Soldier's Pay* would represent an innocent creature of a past world and that the pastoral experience which Emmy shares with him would be like the pure love of the original Golden Age. *The Marble Faun* provides a valuable clue to the themes which govern Faulkner's characterization of woman in both *Soldier's Pay* and *Mosquitoes*. The patterns of imagery based on the beauty of spring and the passing of the seasons which are of major importance to Faulkner's portrayal of woman in much of his fiction were initially expressed in this early poetic work. A knowledge of the structure and meaning of *The Marble Faun* provides a basis for the interpretation of this imagery throughout Faulkner's fiction.

The subject of *The Marble Faun* is the polarity of the female and the male conditions; the former is symbolic of the natural, free, and creative life of a golden age, and the latter is symbolic of the mortal, limited existence of modern man. Throughout the poem the marble faun, a statue in a formal garden, is a

---

[1]*The Marble Faun* was written about 1919 though it was not published until 1924. (It is interesting to note that the poems were composed the year after Estelle Oldham's first marriage.)

striking contrast to the natural world which is personified as woman. The many faces of the feminine world which Faulkner creates in *The Marble Faun* form the basis for his pictorial presentation of a number of the major female characters in his subsequent fiction.

The last lines of the earlier poem, "L'Apres-Midi d'un Faun," indicate the situation which is the subject of *The Marble Faun*.

A sound like some great deep bell stroke
Falls, and they dance, unclad and cold –
It was the earth's great heart that broke
For springs before the world grew old.
(*Early Prose and Poetry*, p. 40)

Like Donald Mahon, the marble faun is a creature of the ancient pastoral Age of Gold grown sad, cold, immobile, and impotent with the aging of the earth. In the prologue poem the reawakening of spring with its warm sunlight creates a painful discontent in the marble faun. "The whole world breathes and calls to me/ Who marble bound must ever be" (*MF*, p. 12). However, in the first six poems of the series the faun either recalls the past or miraculously returns to it, for, lured by the pipes of Pan, he becomes alive again, free to range the woods, mountains, and streams and to participate in the glorious beauty of spring. His love of the beauty of nature is like that which Faulkner suggests the youthful Donald Mahon enjoyed.

The structure of the poem is based on the parallel between the progress of the day and the progress of the seasons. The birth of spring is depicted as a rich and fresh morning experience; the fall of the fruit-tree blossoms ushers in the climactic high noon of late spring and early summer, a still point when the earth sleeps "full and stillily ripe." As sunset nears, the faun is drawn into a peaceful sleep. These first six poems portray the process of life in those first "springs before the world grew old." The only pain is the refreshing pang of birth, and though death might come, it is a death of peace, for the entombed faun would possess forever ". . . about my eyes close-furled/ All the beauty in the world" (*MF*, p. 19). The perpetual spring of the Golden Age never fades, but forever re-creates new life, lush beauty, and inner tranquility.

In the seventh poem the faun is returned to his garden, again statue-bound. The pattern of the spring is repeated; but in the modern age the fading of the fruit blossoms foreshadows the inevitable death of spring, the passing away of the season of life and the movement into the season of cold and snow. In the modern age spring is not a perpetual reality.

> Whisper of an orchard's trees
> That shaken by the aimless breeze,
> Let their blossoms fade and slip . . . .

* * *

> . . . and the swallows' cry
> Calls down from the stirring sky,
> Thin and cold and hot as flame
> Where spring is nothing but a name. (MF, pp. 30-31)

In his marble state the faun can closely identify with this death of the season of life, and he mourns its passing.

> And my eyes too are cool with tears
> For the stately marching years,
> For old earth dumb and strong and sad
> With life so willy-nilly clad,
> And mute and impotent like me
> Who marble bound must ever be . . . .(MF, p. 36)

The movement of the seasons into autumn brings the marble faun closer and closer into the sense of death. The climactic high noon stillness of the former world is transformed into the stillness of night and the season of snow. The garden pool freezes, and the snow drifts; the cold of winter brings peace to the faun, who is also cold and white and dead.

How soft the snow upon my face!
And delicate and cold! I can find grace
In its endless quiescence
For my enthralled impotence: . . . (*MF*, p. 45)

However, the season of snow does not last. In the stillness of the cold night the marble faun is brutally relieved of his momentary peace by the sounds of the re-awakening of spring — the blare of loud brass horns, the "dancers in a blatant crowd," the "unclean heated thing" debauching "the unarmed spring" (*MF*, p. 48). The rebirth of the seasons is an endless pattern in which all of nature blindly, but joyfully participates, never questioning,

Why about the pole star turn
Stars that flare and freeze and burn;
Nor why the seasons, springward wheeling,
Set the bells of living pealing.
They sorrow not that they are dumb:
For they would not a god become. (*MF*, p. 48)

In the face of the reality of death's snow, it is shocking that the seasons are reborn and that Spring conceives anew. Each passing season must now increase the faun's discontent. Though he can imagine peace in the sleep of death, he does not die; he remains a hard and cold statue, the symbol of his eternal impotence. The annual re-birth of spring and the beauty of nature become a cruel mockery of his permanent marble.

Ah, how all this calls to me
Who marble-bound must ever be
While turn unchangingly the years . . .
I would be sad with changing year,
Instead, a sad, bound prisoner,
For though about me seasons go
My heart knows only winter snow. (*MF*, pp. 50-51)

The marble faun is a creature in antithesis with his environment, a natural world which is presented throughout the poem as intensely feminine. It is the call of spring which initiates the faun's desires for freedom, and spring is depicted as a woman full with child, a creature of dignity, serenity, and beautiful sadness as she awaits "the joy and pain of birth." The natural scene is personified as young maidens:

> The poplar trees sway to and fro
> That through this gray old garden go
> Like slender girls with nodding heads . . . .(*MF*, p. 11)

The poplars are "poised dancers," "gracefully slim" with "glistered hair" who lure the faun with their "curving shivering hands." "Old earth dumb and strong and sad" is the eternal mother, mourning the passing years and comforting the stricken faun.

> For my crooked limbs have pressed
> Her all-wise pain-stricken breast
> Until my hungry heart is full
> Of aching bliss unbearable. (*MF*, p. 36)

The moon is a cold old woman whose light peers and pries over earth revealing its signs of death. Having watched the seasons come and go and the earth age, she has grown mad over the "withering of the fair." Traditionally the sign of woman's fertility, the old moon in the formal garden is the symbol of sterility. The pool in the garden, which is like a mirror reflecting the skies of spring and holding the image within its depths even though it is "sealed by ice and snow," is also a feminine symbol.

Spring, trees, the earth, the moon, water and mirrors are extremely important symbols in Faulkner's fiction and they are, as is true in *The Marble Faun*, invariably connected with woman. The faun of the Golden Age, free of his marble bonds, could participate in the natural feminine life and experience the fulfillment of the reproductive beauty of spring. But, the modern faun — a marble statue in a formal garden — experiences a death-in-life existence, for though he is drawn to the beautiful pattern of nature, he is immobilized and impotent.

The Marble Faun makes it clear that man's need of woman as it is portrayed in Faulkner's early fiction springs from emotions far more complex than mere physical desire.

Like the marble faun, the men in Faulkner's novels are compellingly drawn to that "spring before the world grew old." Just as a feminine nature lures the marble faun, the mysterious beauty of woman becomes a sign of the past ideal of fulfillment, the link between the impotence of modern man and the natural life of a golden age. In Faulkner's fiction woman's intense physical attractiveness, her wisdom, and her tranquility indicate that she is a creature of another order not burdened by the limitations of a total humanity. Because woman can participate directly in the natural process, she has an identity and creative role which tie her inextricably to the natural world in which she lives. When she is true to her nature, she can experience the serenity of that past ideal.

Man, on the other hand, is constantly burdened by his alienation from the natural process, the sign of his ultimate death. Like the marble faun, modern man possesses only one April, and when it is past, autumn and winter lead him to a permanent death. Man's life, like that of the "dying gladiator" in another of Faulkner's early poems, is lived in the age of bronze where "Man's life is but an April without a morrow/ Between a snow and a season of snow" (*Early Prose and Poetry*, p. 113). When his one spring is lost or past, man's future holds only impotence and death.

The implication of *The Marble Faun*, that it is the frustrated "why's" of the faun that have created his painful death in life, is verified by the action of *Soldier's Pay* and *Mosquitoes*. Man's very humanity, his capacity for rationality, for introspection, for evil, his desire to "become a god" frustrate the natural process of life. The experience which Donald and Emmy shared cannot be sustained in the present age. The innocent faun is horribly disfigured by war, and the pure woman appears in unattractive, bulging domestic garb occupying herself with ironing, cooking, and serving food. Most of the characters, both men and women, in *Soldier's Pay* and *Mosquitoes* have only a fleeting notion of the beauty of the original world or of the possibility for a fulfilling "April" in the bronze age. They are frustrated and immobilized by confusion and lust, and the inevitable fading of every spring is a subconscious reminder of their primeval loss.

Provided woman is not perverted by her human limitations, she can offer man at least a momentary escape from his sense of futility. However, if the inner nature of woman contradicts her outward appearance of purity, she becomes, like the fading spring, a mocking sign of the ultimate decay of man's existence. On the other hand, when her true beauty is cloaked by outward unattractiveness, man is likely to be blind to her inner serenity, and the salvation she can offer is lost.

Faulkner has carefully designed the characterization of the major female figures in *Soldier's Pay* and *Mosquitoes* to convey his sense of mankind's alienation from the natural creative processes of life and his vision of the tranquility which sexual love should bring to man and woman. The powerfully compelling natures of Cecily Saunders and Margaret Powers in *Soldier's Pay* and of Pat Robyn in *Mosquitoes* are the result of Faulkner's identification of their qualities of femininity with an ideal beauty capable of freeing man from the marble bonds of his limited humanity. However, the discrepancy between the real natures of the women and the powers they seem to represent dooms the heroes to a frustrated and vain search for a beautiful and immortal ideal in a mockingly ugly and mortal existence.

The imagery which depicts the physical appearance of Cecily Saunders makes her the most enticing female figure in the two novels. However, the disparity between her outward beauty and her inner shallowness makes her also one of Faulkner's cruelest satires on man's hope for fulfillment in woman's love. Cecily is the character upon whom the hopes of all the other characters rest; but, ironically, she is the character least able to fulfill any of their expectations. The characters misinterpret the capacities of Cecily because her outward beauty, her freshness and seeming innocence, her youth and femininity stimulate their belief in her ability to renew life. Though Joe and Margaret recognize the depravity of her moral nature, they blindly rely on the chance that she will become the ideal her appearance suggests she embodies. Her behavior, however, is a constant contradiction of this expectation.

The greatest flaw of Cecily's character is the result of the difference between her physical purity and her moral impurity. She is not what she appears, yet she persists in attempting to perpetuate the false image; she totally lacks either personal sincerity or self-honesty. She is motivated entirely by the childishly self-centered desire to be the center of attention and admiration whatever the situation. She is willing to use her sexuality to control her own father, and Margaret notes with surprise that the display of her physical beauty is so habitual that the performance is enacted even for another woman. As Joe Gilligan discerns from her photograph, she is still enraptured with "all the bunk about knights of the air and the romance of battle . . ." (*SP*, p. 41), and she wishes to maintain a position as heroine at any cost. Thus she is constantly putting on another act, pretending the seemingly appropriate sexual roles of innocent fiancée for the rector, the innocent child for her father, the innocent lover for George, or the coy maiden for other men; yet each "act" is juxtaposed with the obvious reality of her shallow selfishness. Despite the shock of Donald's appearance and her rejection of him, she cannot bear to give him up completely for fear that Margaret will win the heroine's role. She plays with George's rather violent emotions for the sake of her own amusement with the role circumstances have given her, and she heartlessly flees to Donald and then withdraws without any regard for his feelings. Cecily's histrionics frequently make her appear both vicious and foolish, though her naïve admirers generally remain blind to her failures.

Despite Faulkner's total lack of sympathy for the character of Cecily, he devotes considerable attention to presenting the magnetic powers of her physical beauty. The central metaphor for Cecily's physical appearance is that of a graceful and slender poplar whose leaves glisten with silver lights, an image taken directly from *The Marble Faun*. (The poplar as a young girl is also the central metaphor of one of Faulkner's early poems, "A Poplar," *Early Prose and Poetry*, p. 60.) The omniscient narrator makes use of the imagery only in a limited way,

describing Cecily merely as a "stricken poplar" when she first
sees Donald's scar, or as a "swept tree" when she feels the
precariousness of her hold on male attention at the dance.
However, in the minds of her admirers the imagery is intense
and profuse suggesting the extent of the fascinating lure of her
physical beauty. The silver highlights of the poplar are stressed
in the descriptions of Cecily in her dance frock. To Mr. Rivers,
who eagerly awaits a dance with her, she is as "fragile as spun
glass" with her "green feather fan" and "silver frock." George
Farr thinks constantly of his intercourse with Cecily, an
experience which has re-defined his life and tied him inextricably to her though she seems barely affected by it. George
repeatedly recalls her "taut body prone and naked as a narrow
pool sweetly dividing: two silver streams from a single source."

This metaphorical description of Cecily is most richly
developed in the mind of Janarius Jones, a man of words and
thus in possession of a vocabulary sufficient to describe what
Cecily's physical attraction is like.

> She was like a flower stalk or a young tree relaxed against
> the table: there was something so fragile, so impermanent
> since robustness and strength were unnecessary, yet strong
> withal as a poplar is strong through very absence of
> strength, about her; you knew that she lived, that her clear
> delicate being was nourished by sunlight and honey until
> even digestion was a beautiful function . . . .(SP, p. 80)

Though Jones cannot resist Cecily's beauty, he quickly discerns
her viciousness. In their first meeting Jones thinks of her first as
a tiger, then as an "Hamadryad, a slim jeweled one" (SP, p. 77).
The meaningless gestures of her hands, undulating like "slim
waves," symbolize for Jones the uselessness of her beauty and
the icy, remote shallowness of her character.

Nevertheless, Jones, as the relentless satyr, continues to
pursue Cecily, and their relationship comes to a climax when
she attempts to use her sexuality to learn how much Jones
knows about her relationship with George Farr. Though Jones
would willingly succumb to Cecily's seduction, he discovers that

she is too stupid to discern his weakness. The scene represents
the height of ineffectual and meaningless love in the novel and
is an "opposite" of the scene of Emmy's and Donald's mating.
Jones is a decadent, interested only in the gestures of love, but
even he is repulsed by Cecily's cold and selfish determination.

Cecily's physical beauty is revealed to be a sham, a glass
beauty without meaning.

> . . . it was as if her whole body became her hand. The
> symbol of a delicate, bodyless lust . . . . A poplar, vain and
> pliant, trying attitude after attitude, gesture after gesture
> — "a girl trying gown after gown, perplexed but in
> pleasure." Her unseen face nimbused with light and her
> body, which was no body, crumpling a dress that had been
> dreamed. Not for maternity, not even for love: a thing for
> the eye and the mind. (SP, p. 224)

Faulkner demonstrates that when selfishness and abstraction
replace love, the gestures of love lead to absolute futility. His
judgment on Jones and Cecily is severe:

> . . . Jones a fat Mirandola in a chaste Platonic nympho-
> lepsy, a religio-sentimental orgy in gray tweed, shaping an
> insincere, fleeting articulation of damp clay to an old
> imperishable desire, building himself a papier mâché
> Virgin: and Cecily Saunders wondering what, how much,
> he had heard, frightened and determined. (SP, p. 225)

Cecily's lure is a false one; her physical beauty suggests that
she is the call of nature to a satisfying physical life, but her
character is totally corrupted. That nature should still endow
her with such beauty and power is but another mockery of
man's hopelessness in his search for innocent love. Jones acutely
senses man's debasement; at the end of the scene he remarks to
Cecily,

> "Do you know how falcons make love? They embrace at
> an enormous height and fall locked, beak to beak,

plunging: an unbearable ecstasy. While we have got to assume all sorts of ludicrous postures, knowing our own sweat. The falcon breaks his clasp and swoops away swift and proud and lonely, while a man must rise and take his hat and walk out." (*SP*, p. 227)

Most of the male characters in *Soldier's Pay* assume that women possess a certain practical wisdom and sensitivity to human needs that are denied to themselves. Early in the novel Joe Gilligan remarks, "I know about some things; but after all women can guess and be nearer right than whatever I could decide on." Margaret Powers is the woman in the novel who most consistently inspires this kind of comment. Despite the assumption of most of Charlestown that her motivation for accompanying Donald home is that she has slept with him, she is immediately accepted by the men as a trustworthy guide. Her maturity and her stability of character are sensed intuitively by such diverse characters as Mr. Saunders and the doctor from Atlanta, who comments to the rector, "You let her take charge of this thing. Women are always more capable than we are, you know."

In contrast to Cecily Saunders, who represents the flighty selfishness of girlhood, Margaret Powers is a mature woman who has suffered. She is physically beautiful, but her beauty has been darkened by her experience of life. Julian Lowe notes "her pallid distinction, her black hair, the red scar of her mouth, her slim dark dress." She is compared to a woman in an Aubrey Beardsley portrait, a figure "dressed in peacock hues, white and slim and depraved among meretricious trees and impossible marble fountains." Margaret's dark past lends a quality of mystery and superiority to her character, and she shows that she has moved beyond the silver tinkle of self-centeredness and hypocrisy that characterize Cecily. She devotes herself to the wounded Donald without regard for the narrow opinions of others — "Men are the ones who worry about our good names, because they gave them to us. But we have other things to bother about ourselves." Whereas Cecily is fascinated and lured by the lustful Jones's sex games, Margaret sharply rebukes his empty play with words. "Let me give you some advice . . . the next time you try to seduce anyone, don't do it with talk, with words. Women know more about words than men ever will, and they know how little they can ever possibly mean" (*SP*, p. 250).

Seemingly, Margaret Powers is the woman in the novel who should be most capable of a meaningful love experience. Joe Gilligan immediately senses her depth of character and remains devoted to her throughout the novel. Although she is willing to take Joe as a lover to satisfy his physical needs, she is unwilling to marry him, to promise him a sustained spiritual love. Her complete inability to respond to Joe reflects her loss of faith in love as a human possibility. Despite her awareness of the shallowness of Cecily's character, Margaret persists in her efforts to gain justice for Donald by insuring that Cecily marry him. It is very late in the novel before she recognizes that Emmy is the proper mate for Donald, and then she fails to perceive the inevitability of Emmy's willingness and capacity to love him. Margaret cannot give Donald, through her marriage to him, the spiritual vitality he needs.

Margaret's failure in love is the fault of her high degree of introspection and moral sensitivity. Her maturity and capacity for unselfishness are the result of her efforts to justify herself to her dead husband, Dick Powers. The fulfillment of their three-day marriage, the result of an intense physical attraction, fades as soon as they are physically separated. Margaret concludes that their romance was only a part of a passing war hysteria, and she writes to free him of any loyalty to her. When Dick is killed in battle before her letter reaches him, Margaret feels betrayed into an eternal dishonesty with him. At the same time the news of his death revives the vitality of her memory of their shared physical love. She doubts the genuineness of that love, yet she harbors the memory of it as something valuable and concrete in a dark and chaotic world. Her confusion, her self-consciousness, her loss of faith in the possibility of love's being either real or lasting make her incapable of responding warmly to anyone. Even the heated physical love she shared with Dick can never again exist for her. Like the marble faun, she knows too much; she has lived too long and has lost faith in the possibilities of life. The coming of spring signifies for her "a world of joy and sorrow and lust for living," a time of "maternity," but Margaret Powers recognizes that her own life is sterile.

The movement of the plot of *Soldier's Pay* is paralleled by extensive descriptions of the natural scene during the rebirth of spring. The novel opens with a hint of spring mixed with the cold dreariness of a Northern early April. When the setting changes to Georgia, the spring is effulgent and rich. The rector's flower garden becomes the embodiment of the beauty of nature. As the action progresses, the season develops — "a pear tree, like a branching candelabra, closely bloomed, white, white . . . ." The sense of conflict is conveyed through the descriptions of the imminence of rain and the sultry heat that follows. Cecily's loss of virginity and her maturity into physical womanhood are paralleled by the maturing of the natural world in spring. Margaret marries Donald and the exotic beauty of the season begins to fade — "fruit blossoms were gone . . . . Leaves grew larger and greener until all rumor of azure and silver and pink had gone from them; birds sang and made love and married and built houses in them . . ." (*SP*, p. 281). The novel closes on a sultry warm night in early summer.

The luxurious renewal of nature in spring is, of course, a mockery of man's pretensions to renewal and life. As in *The Marble Faun*, spring is but a reminder of the discrepancy between the eternally reproductive powers of nature and man's inability to achieve even a single meaningful "April" experience in the face of his own depravity and mortality. Man's sexual drives lure him toward a possible human spring, but the fading of the fruit blossoms warn him that this sign of intense life will inevitably fade in the midst of its beauty. For Margaret, for Joe, for Donald and for Emmy, love fails as completely as it does for a George Farr married to natural beauty corrupted. Man assumes that sex symbolizes life, that spring is the season of joyous mating, rebirth, and new life; but, in truth, sex is the mate of death in its mockery of man's pretensions to life.

Sex and death: the front door and the back door of the world. How indissolubly are they associated in us! In youth they lift us out of the flesh, in old age they reduce us again to the flesh; one to fatten us, the other to flay us, for the worm. (*SP*, p. 295)

In *Soldier's Pay* and in much of Faulkner's fiction man's sexual desire for woman is the hint of a past immortality, but in the present age where man is mortal, sex is a decayed lust without love, a gesture without meaning. It is the sign of death that the ugly satyr Janarius Jones with his bulging tweeds, his yellow goat's eyes, and his empty words captures Emmy, the Atalanta whose capacity for idyllic love is hidden by her ignorance, her ugly garments, her poverty, and her servant's role, while she is blinded by grief for the dead faun who should have won her. Faulkner's blatant mockery of man's alienation from meaningful and mature sexual love is apparent in Jones's final soliloquy.

Male and female created He them, young. Jones was young, too. 'Yet ah, that Spring should vanish with the Rose! . . . 'As autumn and the moon of death draw nigh The sad long days of summer herein lie And she too warm in sorrow 'neath the trees Turns to night and weeps, and longs to die.' And in the magic of spring and youth and moonlight Jones raised his clear sentimental tenor. "Sweetheart, sweetheart, sweetheart." (*SP*, pp. 314-315)

That Faulkner himself felt the full despair of life's betrayal of man's desires is apparent in the identification of the poet's voice with the voice of the marble faun. That to his despair over the nature of existence was added a bitterness over the nature of man is made apparent in *Soldier's Pay* by the harshness of his treatment of Cecily Saunders, whose natural beauty blinds man to her inner evil, by his objectivity and lack of complete sympathy for any character in the novel, and by the cruelty of the triumph of Janarius Jones over Emmy. The full identification of the author with his subject comes only with the last page of the novel when he moves away from bitterness at man's failures and returns to despair over the nature of the human condition.

The satirically presented spire of the rector's church, always reaching idealistically to white clouds in a blue sky, is replaced by the "canting travesty" of a spire of a shabby Negro church. Within the dark, sad passion of the Negro "thick with the imminence of sex after harsh labor along the mooned land" Gilligan, the rector, and presumably the author find a last momentary hope in the face of complete pessimism.

> It was nothing, it was everything; . . . Feed Thy Sheep, O Jesus. All the longing of mankind for a Oneness with Something, somewhere . . . . no organ was needed as above the harmonic passion of bass and baritone soared a clear soprano of women's voices like a flight of gold and heavenly birds. (*SP*, p. 319)

Cecily's physical beauty, Margaret's understanding of human needs, and Emmy's idyllic devotion to Donald suggest the promise life offers for fulfillment, beauty, and love. Faulkner asserts that despite the mocking realities of Cecily's vicious use of her sexuality, Margaret's disillusionment and inability to love, and the destruction of Emmy's potential for love, man's longing for "oneness," for fulfillment and wholeness, is so powerful that even in the face of the despair that "sex and death and damnation" bring him, he cannot deny completely the hope which the positive qualities of women offer him. Through his characterization of Cecily, Margaret, and Emmy, Faulkner presents in bold relief, even in this apprentice work, the essentials of his view of both the promise and the despair of the human situation.

CHAPTER II

The Failure of the Romantic Ideal

It is perhaps unwise to identify an author too closely with his works, but it seems obvious that Faulkner's early novels display a man in search of a perspective on life which would enable him to accept its discrepancies. The poet has glimpsed an eternal beauty and an ideal love through his imagination, or perhaps in some experience of life. But, the vision is lost, and he is in search of relief from the pain of the seeming futility of life and the signs of death. *Mosquitoes*, for example, is an intensely personal work; Faulkner does not even fictionalize a plot for the working out of the problems confronting him. He simply creates a set of deadly sterile characters, suspends them in space, and allows his "artist" characters to talk about the problems of art and love and death. The conversation abounds with comments that are frequently duplicated in other Faulkner novels, and one can only conclude that Dawson Fairchild, the Semitic man, and Gordon portray at varying times and to different degrees the private struggles of the young novelist. (Although Fairchild is generally, and probably accurately, regarded as a portrait of Sherwood Anderson, his comments also reflect Faulkner's own opinions which appear in other works.)

27

In *Mosquitoes* the motif of sexual sterility is counterpointed by the artists' visions of an ideal feminine beauty, the avenue of escape from the limitations of mortality. The apprentice novelist, who discovered with *Soldier's Pay* that he could make characters "cast a shadow," has become the artist in *Mosquitoes* asserting the value of art as a stay against sterility and mortality. If real women are to betray man's search for beauty and truth and immortality, then man can become the artist and create his own ideal woman to be his salvation.

The three artists — the Semitic, Fairchild, and Gordon — represent three facets of the artist's life. The Semitic man is the artist detached from art, man alive. He is the objective critic of art, and he is the criticizing, balancing, supportive companion of the novelist Fairchild and the sculptor Gordon. Fairchild is the artist working; the artist detached from life. He has attempted to replace life with the words of his art. Though he recognizes that art is a substitute for fertile life, he argues that since the latter is an impossibility for man, art is his only means of asserting life.

> "Well, it is a kind of sterility — Words," Fairchild admitted. "You begin to substitute words for things and deeds, like the withered cuckold husband that took the Decameron to bed with him every night, and pretty soon the thing or the deed becomes just a kind of shadow of a certain sound you make by shaping your mouth a certain way . . . . Words are like acorns, you know. Every one of 'em won't make a tree, but if you just have enough of 'em, you're bound to get a tree sooner or later." (*M*, p. 210)

Fairchild identifies man's desire to create life in art with the natural creative powers of woman. Man's alienation from the feminine process of creating real life drives him to the creation of imagined life in art.

> "Women can do without art — old biology takes care of that. But men, men . . . A woman conceives: does she care afterward whose seed it was? Not she. And bears, and all

the rest of her life — her young troubling years, that is — is filled. Of course the father can look at it occasionally. But in art, a man can create without assistance at all: what he does is his." (*M*, p. 320)

Fairchild is not only envious of woman's creativity, but he recognizes also that man's need to create life through art is a derivative of her mysterious powers.

". . . I believe that every word a writing man writes is put down with the ultimate intention of impressing some woman that probably don't care anything at all for literature, as is the nature of woman. Well, maybe she ain't always a flesh and blood creature. She may be only the symbol of a desire. But she is feminine." (*M*, p. 250)

Or, as the Semitic remarks, "Dante invented Beatrice, creating himself a maid that life had not had time to create, and laid upon her frail and unbowed shoulders the whole burden of man's history of his impossible heart's desire" (*M*, p. 339).

Gordon is the artist without words, the sculptor who envisions. He creates a marble image of the feminine ideal, describing her as "a virgin with no legs to leave me, no arms to hold me, no head to talk to me" (*M*, p. 26). Gordon finds in Patricia Robyn a physical replica of his ideal woman. She possesses "the sweet young curve" of shanks "brittle as the legs of a bird," a "clean young odor . . . like that of young trees," and she is "grave and quiet and curious, grave as a poplar."

This imagery recalls the presentation of the physical appearance of Cecily Saunders. Pat, however, is without any of Cecily's viciously selfish use of sex. She is child-like, and so totally without sexual drives that she maintains a position of superior self-control in comparison to all her male admirers. She is more nearly than Cecily the duplicate of the innocent slender poplars of *The Marble Faun*. She is, though, a flesh-and-blood creature and there is a real discrepancy between the Pat of reality and the virgin of Gordon's imagination. However, he gains a momentary satisfaction in identifying the two. The experiences they share are ideal moments in the imagination of Gordon, and for the reader the scenes are moments of beauty in the midst of the petty bawdiness of the other characters. Gordon envisions Pat as "an ecstasy in golden marble," "a swallow hard and passionate with flight," "a flame among stale ashes . . . who gone, was thinly and far away, as remembered surf on a rock coast at dawn . . ." (M, p. 187).

Gordon's last encounter with Pat is paralleled by an italicized tale, presumably the inner monologue of Gordon, which describes a king's request that his servant find for him his "heart's desire," a "true thing."

> *It is dawn, in the high cold hills, dawn is like a wind in the clean hills, and on the wind comes the thin piping of shepherds, and the smell of dawn and of almond trees on the wind . . . I desire a thing that, had I not been at all, becoming aware of it I would awake; that dead, remembering it I would cling to this world though it be as a beggar in a tattered robe . . . Find me this, O Halim. (M, p. 272)*

The servant replies, *"Ah Lord, in the Georgian hills I loved this maid myself, when I was a lad. But that was long ago, and she is dead".* (M, p. 273)

At the end of the novel is another italicized tale describing a dead beggar lying beneath a high stone gate, his body explored by swarms of rats. The narrative is significant:

> *Spring is in the world somewhere, like a blown keen reed, high and fiery cold — he does not yet see it; a shape which he will know — he does not yet see it . . . . Above the hushing walls, a thing wild and passionate, remote and sad; shrill as pipes, and yet unheard. Beneath it, soundless shapes amid which, vaguely, a maiden in an ungirdled robe and with a thin bright chain between her ankles, and a sound of far lamenting . . . . Then voices and sounds, shadows and echoes change from swirling, becoming the headless, armless, legless torso of a girl, motionless and*

virginal and passionately eternal before the shadows and
echoes whirl away. (M, pp. 335, 337, and 339)

Intertwined with this narrative is Fairchild's sudden discovery
of the definition of artistic Genius:

> "It is that Passion Week of the heart . . . that passive state
> of the heart with which the mind, the brain has nothing to
> do at all, in which the hackneyed accidents which make up
> this world — love and life and sex and sorrow — brought
> together by chance in perfect proportions, take on a kind
> of splendid and timeless beauty." (*M,* p. 339)

And, also intertwined with this sequence is the Semitic's
declaration, "I love three things: gold, marble and purple — . . .
form solidity color" (*M,* p. 340).[1]

Each man is expressing devotion to the same ideal — the
Romantic vision of beauty and truth expressed most famously
by the thin, sad pipes, "the unravished bride of quietness," the
still moment of eternity of Keats's "Ode on a Grecian Urn,"
whose images Faulkner has incorporated repeatedly into his
own works. Faulkner recorded his admiration of Keats's "Ode
on a Grecian Urn" as early as 1925 in "Verse Old and Nascent:
A Pilgrimage,"

> "I read 'Thou still unravished bride of quietness' and
> found a still water withal strong and potent, quiet with its
> own strength, and satisfying as bread. That beautiful
> awareness, so sure of its own power that it is not necessary
> to create the illusion of force by frenzy and motion."
> (*Early Prose and Poetry,* p. 117)

---

[1] Joyce Warren in "Faulkner's 'Portrait of the Artist' " identifies this description of
the artistic experience with James Joyce's epiphany concept. For Joyce and
Faulkner, Warren notes, the young girl represents the "forces of life" in contrast to
"the sterility of the artist's surroundings" (p. 126). It should also be added that for
both Faulkner and Joyce woman was a symbol of artistic inspiration and a very real
and troubling physical being. In *Portrait of the Artist* and in the early works of
Faulkner there is a painful awareness that woman represents both the vision and the
"nets"; woman is a merger of the ideal and the real.

The natural world of the Golden Age in *The Marble Faun*, Donald and Emmy's idyllic mating scene in *Soldier's Pay*, and Gordon's marble statue of virgin perfection in *Mosquitoes* are the images which reveal Faulkner's commitment to the Romantic vision. The Romanticist's transcendent world is revealed and symbolized by nature and for Faulkner by woman as well. The pure virgin is the ideality, for her beautiful, unviolated form suggests absolute beauty and eternity itself. The goal of the Romantic search is unity with the golden, perfect world glimpsed through the imagination — the capture of the maid, the "heart's desire."

The brief essay "The Hill" published in 1922 (*Early Prose and Poetry*, pp. 90-92) is another expression of Faulkner's vision of the Romanticist's idealized world. In the essay Faulkner describes a young man who, fatigued from a day of routine manual labor, climbs a hill above his town and there senses through the natural setting a momentary feeling of transcendence. Because of "the faint resistless force of spring in a valley at sunset" the young man has been troubled for the first time by the "devastating unimportance of [his] destiny." The moment of deep and serious thought combined with the beauty of the sunset provokes an experience of release and elevation.

> Here, in the dusk, nymphs and fauns might riot to a shrilling of thin pipes, to a shivering and hissing of cymbals in a sharp volcanic abasement beneath a tall icy star. ***Behind him was the motionless conflagration of sunset, before him was the opposite valley rim upon the changing sky. For a while he stood on one horizon and stared across at the other, far above a world of endless toil and troubled slumber; untouched, untouchable; forgetting, for a space, that he must return.***

Faulkner's early, painful realization of the discrepancy between the ideal vision and the actualities of man's life on earth is but an indication of the fullness of his devotion to the ideal. *The Marble Faun, Soldier's Pay, Mosquitoes* and *Sartoris*, his third novel, are in a sense elegies written for the loss of an ideal that is perpetually mocked by the realities of existence. *Soldier's Pay* and *Mosquitoes* are bitterly satiric because the idealist has turned cynic in the face of the fact that spring does fade, that the momentary glimpse of the ideal in nature's rich beauty is destroyed by the mutability of the seasons. Man's sexual longings, the sign of the universal emotional need for unity with timelessness and beauty, yield only frustration, the ever-present reminder of his inevitable and ultimate impotence in the face of death. The discovery of the real nature of woman makes her a flaunting mockery of the ideality her beauty seems to represent.

The young student of "Study" feels the tension of opposites — the facts of reality and the "desire of the heart." The experiences of the "artists" at the end of *Mosquitoes* are grounded in an ironic and much more complex vision of the same tension. The desire of the heart demands expression; it directs the Romantic to art through which he can, theoretically, recreate the ideal vision. Simultaneously, however, the desire of the heart directs man to sexuality. At the close of *Mosquitoes* the "heart's desire," envisioned as the idealization of art and symbolized by the marble virgin, is juxtaposed with the three artists' drunken visit to the brothels. The scene indicates that the "desire of the heart" is symbolized and disgraced by the artists' physical desire for woman; the ideal is eternally mocked by its inevitable merger with the sordidness of reality and the debasement of death.

The spring in *Mosquitoes* is "decked out with little green, necklaced, braceleted with the song of idiotic birds, spurious and sweet and tawdry as a shopgirl in her cheap finery, like an idiot with money and no taste . . ." (*M*, p. 8). Spring *is* the mosquitoes; the heart's desire for the ideal is reduced to the plaguing insect bite of lust. Faulkner's struggle with Romantic idealism, explicitly presented in *Mosquitoes*, explains his characterization of woman both in *Soldier's Pay* and in *Mosquitoes*. Because of her physical allure and her capacities for creativity and serenity woman is the embodiment of the Romantic dream;

simultaneously, however, her human limitations make her a mockery of the ideal.

Near the end of *Mosquitoes* Fairchild suggests that to watch a creature like Gordon's marble statue "from a distance on a May morning, bathing in a pool where there were a lot of poplar trees" is "the way to forget your grief." Gordon responds angrily, "Only an idiot has no grief; only a fool would want to forget it. What else is there in this world sharp enough to stick to your guts?" (*M*, p. 329). *Mosquitoes* reflects not only Faulkner's realization that real life mocks the Romanticist's vision, but also his realization that the Romanticist's devotion to an unattainable ideal inevitably burns itself out. The Romanticist's own sexuality betrays his vision of ideality. The desire literally destroys the vision; the virgin cannot be captured and remain virgin. Gordon, the Romantic who seeks ideal communion, is driven to isolation and marble purity or else to the harlots. He experiences the failure of Romanticism, the discovery that not only must desire fade, but also bitterness and despair. When for Faulkner only grief remained, ironic satire, the mode of both *Soldier's Pay* and *Mosquitoes*, was transformed into ironic tragedy.

Sartoris, Faulkner's third novel, represents his first fictional attempt to present his despair with the seriousness and sincerity that characterize *The Marble Faun*. The trace of authorial sympathy that appears at intervals in his first two novels are momentary exceptions in works pervaded by the satiric mode. In *Sartoris*, however, the satire is slight, and the sympathy is central. Young Bayard Sartoris is another marble faun; the structural framework of the novel, the movement of the seasons from spring through summer into winter and the season of death with a return to a second spring, is the same as that of *The Marble Faun*. The novel's superb portrayal of the serenity and beauty of nature makes it comparable in atmosphere and tone to the poems. The Sartoris inclination to die gloriously in a moment of wild adventure is another expression of man's search for an escape from the dullness and sterility of being marble bound in an age of mortality. The descriptions of nature and the women characters in the novel present the feminine alternative to man's disillusionment and despair.

Sartoris springs from a full acceptance on the part of Faulkner that those first "springs before the world grew old" is a lost and irretrievable ideal. The hero of *Sartoris* is not the faun or the artist, but the soldier; the failure of both love and art as avenues of escape pushes the Faulkner hero to the opposite extremity of life — death. If the transcendence of the marble bonds that occurs in the first six poems of *The Marble Faun* is impossible either through love or art, then to persist in the search for it can yield only increased frustration and futility. Joe Gilligan, Donald Mahon, and Gordon find that there is no alternative to accepting the fact of the corruption of the pure, even that the vision of the pure itself, symbolized by the already impure woman, will fade and after a time be no longer moving or meaningful. In *Sartoris* it seems that the only alternative to the marble bonds, the heart of winter snow, and the death-in-life existence, is a radical defiance of the sterility of life in some wild and frenzied adventure that produces a brief ecstatic moment of escape, simply because it is literally a defiance of the powers of the final death. Bayard Satoris, born into a tradition of men who have thus escaped their marble bonds, is caught between the compulsion to do as they have done and his suspicion that the glory of this escape also fades — that his brother John, whom he loved and for whom he grieves, died a fool and not a hero.

In *Sartoris*, as in *The Marble Faun*, the despairing male must exist in a natural world which is characterized by beauty, serenity, and creativity. Significantly, the novel opens in late spring when the wisteria has already bloomed and fallen — the persistent reminder of man's mortality. Bayard's tale of John's violence and speed and death is counterpointed by descriptions of the stillness and beauty of nature. Though Bayard attempts to escape the emptiness of his own existence in dare-devil drives, he is able neither to destroy himself nor to find contentment. Bayard is temporarily calmed when he becomes engrossed in the spring sowing of the farm, for he participates briefly in the reproductive process of nature. However, when this task is completed, he finds that there is simply no meaningful action of life in which he can participate, and he can only loiter on the periphery of existence in the dull heat of summer and watch the movement of the seasons into the winter of death. The cold serenity that defines the atmosphere of his visit with the McCallums is the same still "grace" of "quiescence" which allows the marble faun a momentary identity and peace with nature. When spring comes again, Bayard can no longer bear the despair of his marble existence which allows him no hope of renewal; in desperation he commits suicide.

In contrast to the inclination of the Sartoris man to die gloriously or to give in to despair, the Sartoris woman is unwilling to surrender to despair, to death, or to sterility. Significantly, the feminine ideal of *Mosquitoes*, the pure virgin, is replaced in *Sartoris* by a wise and domineering old woman who has done no more than endure in good humor several generations of dying Sartorises and to insure indirectly that the line will survive. Miss Virginia Du Pre is the representative of the feminine force of life in the novel and is at one with the reproductive process of nature.

Miss Jenny's flower garden is the parallel of the garden of *The Marble Faun*, the sign of nature's eternal renewal with which the woman can identify. Throughout the novel the desperate acts of Bayard are counterpointed by Miss Jenny's devoted cultivation of her garden. The periodic changes from planting, to picking, to watching the death of the last rose of Indian summer, punctuate the pattern of the seasons and the structural movement of the novel. Miss Jenny is obviously not the young mother spring experiencing the joyous pangs of birth; she is the old mother earth watching the inevitable passing of her many "children." She affectionately protects, instructs, and "mothers" her Sartoris men, and she possesses the wise practicality, the limited optimism, the sense of humor, and the spiritual endurance that Faulkner identifies with the mature woman. Yet, Miss Jenny emerges more a comic figure than an heroic one. She is a Sartoris herself, and her blustering ire, her cocksureness, her stubborn determination, and her personal independence prevent her from becoming identified with the tragic, grieving, pain-stricken mother earth figure of *The Marble Faun*. Essentially, Miss Jenny is incapable of that kind of grief, and it is impossible for her to assuage Bayard's despair.

Narcissa Benbow is the young virgin in *Sartoris* who assumes the role of lover to Faulkner's hero. She is not at all like the marble purity of Gordon's statue to which Bayard's first wife is compared — "a girl with a bronze swirling of hair and a small supple body in a constant epicene unrepose, a dynamic fixation like that of carven sexless figures caught in moments of action" (*Sartoris*, p. 55). Narcissa is a large woman of twenty-six with dark hair and violet eyes who dresses in gray and white. Faulkner's attitude toward her seems to waver between admiration for the calm tranquility of her femininity — "her face was that tranquil repose of lilies" — and disdain for her very feminine weaknesses. The former quality is predominant in the last pages of the novel when Narcissa, pregnant with the last Sartoris, emerges as a figure of strength and power in comparison to the aging and confused Miss Jenny and the futile Bayard. However, throughout most of the novel Narcissa is more like Faulkner's earlier heroines, Cecily Saunders and Pat Robyn, who prove to be most inadequate embodiments of a feminine ideal.

The comparison of Narcissa to Cecily and Pat, who are to a certain degree her prototypes, indicates, however, the increased complexity of Faulkner's characterization of young women in his fiction. Narcissa is like Cecily in her desire to attract the attention of men; yet the presentation of this trait is much more subtly envisioned with Narcissa than with Cecily. Narcissa cannot quite admit to herself that she keeps Byron Snopes's letters because, as Miss Jenny puts it, women "are all convinced that men feel that way about us, and we can't help but admire the one that's got the courage to tell us, no matter who he is" (*Sartoris*, p. 69).

Just as Cecily screams and faints at the sight of Donald's scar and Pat Robyn clings to David at the onslaught of the mosquitoes, Narcissa cannot bear the sight of physical danger or physical pain. She cringes at Bayard's dare-devil drives, his cries of pain, or the thought of blood. She is incapable of understanding the spiritual despair behind Bayard's actions and though she is awed by his wild daring, she is as angered and repulsed by the signs of his futile suffering as by the "horror" of her cat catching a bird or the possum hunt. This distaste for physical suffering is seemingly a harmless trait, but it is significant that Faulkner endows some of his later heroines with the capacity to endure extreme suffering and ugliness.

Like Cecily and Pat, Narcissa is unable to fulfill the spiritual needs of the hero for renewed life, but Bayard Sartoris never seems to expect this from her. It is obvious that Narcissa has had difficulty experiencing love for men; there is every indication that she views sex as something repulsive and that her natural sexual drives have been repressed. Very early in the novel she declares that she will never marry and that she hates all men. She clings to Horace, whom she can love without sexual intercourse. She is unreasonably afraid of Bayard's first advances, and even he is sufficiently normal to sense that she is cold and unnatural. Narcissa is intensely repulsed by her brother's physical attraction to Belle, whom she can describe only as "dirty." Simultaneously, Narcissa is capable of engulfing Bayard in a frantic embrace at the end of their desperate automobile ride, and of treasuring Byron Snopes's letters. The hypocritically lily-white and sexually thwarted Narcissa of *Sanctuary* and "There Was a Queen" is very much alive in *Sartoris*.

Though she is incapable of assuaging Bayard's despair, Narcissa is the feminine ideal for her brother Horace, who is, significantly, not the hero of the novel. Though some of the characters call him a poet, Horace is merely a lawyer, and his only art is glass-blowing and the composition of wordy letters. Horace, like Bayard, recognizes the futility and sterility of his existence, but he is able to imagine a contentment in a decadent ideal. The epiphany of art in *Mosquitoes* has stagnated in *Sartoris*; Gordon's statue of marble purity is transformed into Horace's glass vases — "Sheerly and tragically beautiful. Like preserved flowers, you know. Macabre and inviolate; purged and purified as bronze, yet fragile as soap bubbles. Sound of pipes crystallized" (*Sartoris*, pp. 171-172). Horace worships his one almost perfect vase, along with his sister, as the symbols of his "realization of the meaning of peace and the unblemished attainment of it as 'Thou still unravished bride of quietness,' " naming the two, significantly, Serene.

Actually Horace's inner idealization of peace and serenity is no more than an intellectual-emotional game, an affirmation of a feeling which he cannot sustain in experience. Even he is aware that Belle, whom he cannot resist physically, is a very decadent version of the ideal Serene. "Her hand was warm, prehensile, like mercury in his palm exploring softly, with delicate bones and petulant scented flesh. Her eyes were like hothouse grapes and her mouth was redly mobile, rich with discontent" (*Sartoris*, p. 183). Horace knows that what he feels is only lust, but he cannot resist Belle nor can he give up the illusion that he is faithful to his ideal. Melvin Backman (*Faulkner*, p. 10) describes Horace as an "unfulfilled poet and idealist willing to deceive himself and willing to purchase peace at the expense of life." Intellectually and spiritually Horace engages in a dishonesty with himself that proves in Faulkner's fifth novel, *Sanctuary*, to be more deadly than the Sartoris game of glamorous fatality.

At the end of *Sartoris* the promise of new life which Narcissa holds in her body seems but another mockery of man's efforts to transcend the limitations of his mortality. Narcissa's beautiful serenity, like the still evening twilight in which the novel closes, seems momentary, a "windless lilac dream, foster dam of quietude and peace." It is, however, significant that the novel ends with the double vision of the futilely heroic Sartorises, existing only in memory and in the dead marble of the cemetery, and of the unheroic, largely unadmirable, Narcissa Benbow Sartoris experiencing the inner tranquility and peace of prospective motherhood.

Bayard Sartoris is the epitome of the defeated Romanticist whose idealism turned to cynicism has isolated him and driven him to self-destruction. Throughout Faulkner's fiction the horse is suggestive of masculine virility. Bayard's beautiful, but chaotic ride on the stallion is the symbolic act which declares his utter reliance on his own masculinity, a reliance which automatically cuts him off from the compromise of life—marriage to Narcissa. His love of John, stronger than his devotion for his first wife or Narcissa, his masculine devotion to hunting, and his friendship with the male family McCallums are indicative of his commitment to maleness.

Similar to Bayard is the male would-be poet of the short narrative "Carcassone." The protagonist of this brief sketch lies asleep between layers of tar paper in an attic room provided by his patron, Mrs. Widdrington of Standard Oil. The dream which sustains him is the famous passage, "*me on a buckskin pony with eyes like blue electricity and a mane like tangled fire, galloping up the hill right off into the high heaven of the world*," (*CS*, p. 895) which has been identified by William Van O'Conner (*The Tangled Fire of William Faulkner*) as Faulkner's vision of himself as artist. Bayard, this poet, and in a sense Faulkner himself are the defeated but sincere Romanticists defying life's mockery to the last possibility of defiance. Betrayed by the impossibility of the achievement of the ideal in real life, they will escape entirely alone, on horseback, accepting death rather than the compromise of life's limitations. Each is the isolated male achieving an instant of romantic escape in a brief ecstatic moment of splendor on galloping horses with manes that swirl with fire. It is a vision, however, to which Faulkner's own temperament did not allow total acquiescence.

The authorial comment in *Sartoris* about John, who committed the defiance with joy and confidence, is that he "had not waited for Time and its furniture to teach him that the end of wisdom is to dream high enough not to lose the dream in the seeking of it" (*Sartoris*, p. 74). Bayard's defiance lacks either joy or confidence, and though he persists in his pursuit of death his end is like that of the poet of "Carcassone."

> Steed and rider thunder on, thunder punily diminishing; a dying star upon the immensity of darkness and of silence within which steadfast, fading, deepbreasted and grave of flank, muses the dark and tragic figure of the Earth, his mother. (*CS*, p. 900)

Man on his buckskin pony in glorious fire, the vision of the instant of romantic self-transcendence, inevitably fades into nothingness; but the earth, motherhood, endures.

The defeating dilemma of Romanticism, the discrepancy between the ideal and the real which isolates and destroys the idealist, is dramatized in Faulkner's early fiction by his portrayal of man's response to woman. It is the magnetically powerful attractiveness of woman that symbolizes for man the ideal beauty; simultaneously the humanity of woman is the idealist's reminder that his vision is perpetually denied him in human existence. Though the idealist may seek in sexual union the dream of communion with the beautiful and the eternal, he discovers that sex is in actuality defeating and frustrating for him, for inevitably it serves to remind him of his finitude and his ultimate impotence in the face of death. Indeed, his own sensuality can transform the "heart's desire" into mere physical lust. Most ironically, the Romantic who commits himself totally to the visionary ideal, refusing the corruption of human existence, is precisely the male who is doomed to absolute sterility, to isolation, and to self-destruction — the exact opposites of his vision of creativity, union, and immortality. The lover-poet-idealist-male is a dying star on a dark horizon; the earth, the mother, endures. The quest for the virginal ideal in *Mosquitoes* is replaced in *Sartoris* by a limited acceptance of the hope that is offered by the very imperfect woman who, despite her human failures, is capable of achieving serenity through her submission to the reproductive process of human life.

Woman plays an extremely important role in Faulkner's early works. The vision which concludes *Sartoris*, the antithetical worlds of the male and the female, is identical with Faulkner's view of the nature of the human condition presented in his first published work, *The Marble Faun*. The male world is characterized by idealism and is symbolized by the perfection of marble beauty; but it is a world of isolation, coldness, impotence and death. The alternative to the male pattern of existence is exemplified by woman. The qualities which Faulkner attributes to the major women characters in his first three novels suggest both the potentialities and the limitations of human existence. The physical beauty and sexual allure of Cecily Saunders, Margaret Powers, and Patricia Robyn and the commitment to the nourishment, sustenance and reproduction of human life displayed by Emmy, Miss Jenny, and Narcissa indicate the potentiality of the human condition for achieving the idealist's goals of beauty, union, tranquility, creativity, and immortality. On the other hand, woman's imperfections and the perversion of her natural role indicate the plaguing limitations of human existence.

Through imagery and specific women characters Faulkner creates in *The Marble Faun, Soldier's Pay, Mosquitoes*, and *Sartoris* a sense of the power and omnipresence of the feminine alternative to male despair. It is an alternative for which the male yearns but because of its imperfections, an alternative which he also flees. This is the basic tension out of which Faulkner's early works were created; it is a persistent theme in much of his subsequent fiction. Faulkner's early works provide the basis for evaluating the meaning of his characterization of woman throughout his fiction.

Though Faulkner's major female figures in *Soldier's Pay, Mosquitoes*, and *Sartoris* may be said to assume symbolic significance in his dramatization of his themes, it must be noted that for the most part they represent convincing and effective characterizations. It is appropriate and meaningful that Faulkner associates with each female figure imagery which suggests the meaning he attributes to her character. In these early works the imagery is at times extravagant; nevertheless, it creates a visual portrait of the character which is vivid, individualized, and significant. Appearance and gesture convey the sense of the character's dramatic presence and simultaneously reveal Faulkner's themes.

PART II
WOMAN: THE IMAGE OF
MORAL ORDER

CHAPTER III

The Ideal of Motherhood:
The Sound and the Fury

Sartoris is a transitional work in the Faulkner canon not only because it is the first of the Yoknapatawpha novels but also because it represents a change in Faulkner's attitude toward woman. The emphasis on the quality of serenity which permeates Narcissa Benbow Sartoris's character at the close of the novel suggests that Faulkner saw a solution to the idealist's dilemma in woman's submission to the natural reproductive process. *The Sound and the Fury* and *Sanctuary* indicate Faulkner's recognition that the yearning for ideality must be replaced by an acceptance of reality. As a result the idealization of virgin beauty is replaced in *The Sound and the Fury* and *Sanctuary* by the idealization of motherhood. However, "idealization" is a pointedly inappropriate term for describing Faulkner's mother figures. In the bulk of Faulkner's fiction the self-giving love of the mother does symbolize the most ideal way in which man can adjust to the limitations of the human condition, but these mother figures are, like their prototypes Emmy, Miss Jenny, and Narcissa, limited and imperfect human beings.

45

Through motherhood the Romantic ideals of creativity, self-transcendence, and union with the nature of existence can be achieved without evil or destructiveness. The role of motherhood fosters communication and self-transcendence, for child-bearing unites the woman with the ultimate purpose of nature and enables her to defy her own isolation and to create relation through the establishment of the family. The ideal of self-sacrifice on which effective motherhood is based provides mankind with an ethic that can bring moral order to the chaos of existence. Further, the mother is quite literally the only means by which man can achieve his limited immortality – the survival of the human race.

This vision of woman is of central importance in *The Sound and the Fury* and in *Sanctuary*. Indeed, these novels are most basically about man's need of this kind of woman. In each novel the three main women characters (Dilsey, Caddy, and Mrs. Compson in *The Sound and the Fury*; Ruby, Temple, and Narcissa in *Sanctuary*) symbolize the moral choices available to humanity. The limited nature of the human choice is indicated by the very limited and human nature of woman. The moral confusion which the central male protagonists experience is the result of their false identification of virginity and feminine beauty with inward purity. The failure of both Horace and Quentin to understand the nature of woman is indicative of their inability to understand the nature of the human condition. It is the flaw that precipitates the tragic outcome of both novels. The Compson family is destroyed because Quentin measures Caddy by her physical purity, her virginity, rather than by her capacity to love and because the perspective of Mrs. Compson, rather than that of Dilsey, rules the household. In *Sanctuary* justice becomes an impossibility because Horace and his society confuse respectability and virginity with goodness and are controlled by the selfish desires of Temple Drake and Narcissa Sartoris rather than the sacrificial love of Ruby Goodwin.

This kind of interpretation suggests by its very nature that Faulkner's women characters in these two novels may be more symbolic than real, more allegorical perhaps than believably human. Faulkner's real genius, however, is his capacity to create such individualized and convincing characters that despite the character's assumption of symbolic roles, his novels remain successful primarily because they are forceful reproductions of life. The following discussion of *The Sound and the Fury* and *Sanctuary* is designed not only to demonstrate the importance and meaning of woman in these two novels, but also to indicate the masterful methods employed by Faulkner in creating individual women who emerge as powerfully convincing and effective fictional characters.

The thematic meaning of *The Sound and the Fury* is grounded in man's need of the emotional and moral order which is created by motherly devotion. The importance of the theme of motherhood in the novel is indicated by the centrality of the role played by the major women characters, Mrs. Compson, Caddy, Quentin, and Dilsey. Mrs. Compson, Caddy, and Quentin are the driving forces behind every thought and action of the Compson brothers, who narrate the first three sections of the novel. Dilsey is the subject of its fourth section. The Compson family is dying because Mrs. Compson is incapable of loving or caring for her children; she is a total failure as a mother. As a result, the affectionate child Caddy assumes the false role of playing "mother" to her brothers. Caddy's mothering love fulfills the need of her idiot brother Benjy. Since Benjy remains a perpetual three-year-old, the potential problems created by Caddy's assumed role are limited; only her absence can hurt him. However, Caddy's false role of motherhood tragically complicates her relation to Quentin and results in confusion and frustration for herself and a disastrous incestuous love on the part of her brother. When Caddy is destroyed, the full burden of motherhood in the Compson family falls upon the Negro servant Dilsey. Sections one and two present Mrs. Compson's rejection of Benjy and Quentin and their need of Caddy as a substitute mother. Section three depicts the chaos and decay of the Compson household without a mother. Section four focuses on Dilsey's heroic effort to hold together the family's last remnants by her sacrificial assumption of the responsibilities of motherhood to a family that is not her own.

The Sound and the Fury is a novel of extreme technical complexity and thematic multiplicity. However, Faulkner asserted on numerous occasions that this masterpiece was created from a single stirring image — Caddy with her muddy drawers climbing the pear tree to peek in at Damuddy's funeral. Faulkner repeatedly emphasized the importance of Caddy's character to the novel.

> One day I seemed to shut a door between me and all publishers' addresses and book lists. I said to myself, Now I can write. Now I can make myself a vase like that which the Old Roman kept at his bedside and wore the rim slowly away with kissing it. So I, who had never had a sister and was fated to lose my daughter in infancy, set out to make myself a beautiful and tragic little girl.[1]

> To me she was the beautiful one, she was my heart's darling. That's what I wrote the book about and I used the tools which seemed to me the proper tools to try to tell it, try to draw the picture of Caddy. (Faulkner in the University, p. 6)

In the light of the importance of woman in Faulkner's apprentice fiction, it is not surprising that a character like Caddy should emerge as the focus of interest and emotional attachment in his fourth novel. Indeed, its central characters, its imagery, and its themes relate The Sound and the Fury very closely to Faulkner's earlier fiction. Caddy is a symbol of man's "heart's desire," the image of the woman whose mysterious beauty provokes man's yearning for the ideal. However, The Sound and the Fury, unlike Faulkner's earlier fiction, is a powerful indictment of the idealization of virgin purity and a moving portrayal of the destructiveness this idealism precipitates. Quentin's effort to limit Caddy's existence to symbolic

---

[1]Quoted in Michael Millgate, The Achievement of William Faulkner, p. 26.

ideality destroys her. Caddy's character is much more compelling than the ideal "heart's desire" of Faulkner's earlier works, for she is tragically human. That Faulkner should imagine his "heart's darling" as a very fallible and human woman indicates the shift in his attitude that makes *The Sound and the Fury* a contrast to his earlier works. Man's need of woman remains the primary theme; however, man does not need virgin purity, a Caddy of perpetual childish innocence, but in the midst of the chaos of reality man needs the ordering power of committed human love. Caddy is a central character in *The Sound and the Fury* because the Compson family desperately needs her feminine qualities of warmth and responsiveness, her aggressive courage, and her ability to assess realistically life's possibilities and limitations.

Though she is always seen through the "haze" of her brothers' attitudes toward her, the striking descriptions of Caddy's appearance and gestures, which accompany their recollections of her, serve to make her physical presence felt throughout the novel. Out of the unchronological disorder of the brothers' individual recollections of their sister, there emerge a number of powerfully dramatic pictures of Caddy in which she assumes some significant pose that captures the essence of her character at the different stages of its development. Caddy in her muddy drawers climbing the pear tree and Caddy with her arms about Benjy are memorable representations of the nature of her childhood character. In Quentin's section the picture of Caddy enraptured by love, her clothes soaked with the branch water, her arms hugging her knees, and her face looking skyward and the picture of Caddy in her bridal gown running to the bellowing Benjy are unforgettable. The tragedy of Caddy's life is made acutely visual by Jason's recollection of her in the black cloak standing over her father's grave in a drenching rain.

These pictures of Caddy make her a convincingly life-like and individual fictional creation. At the same time they render in a manner which is almost symbolic the nature and significance of her character. However, the full importance and complexity of Caddy's character are revealed completely only by an examination of her relationship to the two brothers who love her. Faulkner indicates the intensity and the complexity of man's need of woman through his portrayal of Benjy's and Quentin's need of Caddy and their devotion to her.

The opening pages of *The Sound and the Fury* make it immediately apparent that Benjy's mother has rejected her idiot child, while Caddy's whole childhood has focused on her mothering love and care for her idiot brother. Benjy recalls a cold day shortly before Christmas when he eagerly awaited Caddy's arrival from school. His frantic effort to communicate to someone his desire to get outside to meet Caddy is countered by his mother's cruel verbal attacks which are framed in the language of "motherly" discipline but are grounded in her desire to be rid of Benjy or to use him as an excuse for her privilege of always evading the responsibilities of motherhood. His moaning provokes only threats, "If you don't be good, you'll have to go to the kitchen." She insists that he wear his overshoes outside because she does not want him ill at Christmas time "with the house full of company." When at the end of the sequence she draws Benjy to her and laments, "My poor baby," it is obvious that her pity is not for Benjy but for herself. Caddy's beautiful and moving response is, "You're not a poor baby. Are you. You've got your Caddy. Haven't you got your Caddy?" (*SF*, p. 8).

The scene superbly demonstrates that Benjy is not a "poor baby" because he does possess the complete devotion and love of his sister. When Caddy returns from school and sees Benjy at the gate, her walking changes to running. She joyfully greets him, thrilled that he has come to meet her. Caddy's presence creates the overpowering joy of love in Benjy, an emotion which he compares to "bright rustling leaves." Mrs. Compson's rebuke of Caddy that closes the sequence is painfully ironic. "You must think . . . . Someday I'll be gone, and you'll have to think for him" (*SF*, p. 8). It is tragic that Benjy's mother has never thought "for" him, and that it is not she he loses, but Caddy.

The pattern of this opening scene is repeated at the end of section one in another dramatic presentation of the contrast between Caddy's and Mrs. Compson's treatment of Benjy. The scene demonstrates Caddy's competence as Benjy's "mother" by portraying her thorough understanding of his needs and her skill at preserving his sense of security. On the other hand, Mrs. Compson's ineptness as a mother is indicated by her unrealistic insistence that Benjy be disciplined as if he were a normal child and by her cruel and unreasonable scolding of Caddy which reveals her blindness to the fact that Caddy's attitudes should be her own. The fire and the soft red and yellow cushion symbolize love, comfort, and security to Benjy. When Mrs. Compson orders Caddy to bring Benjy to her, Caddy wisely recommends that she wait until he "finishes looking at the fire." Mrs. Compson refuses, and Caddy lifts Benjy to take him to his mother. The love and understanding of Benjy's needs which provoke Caddy's action are incomprehensible to Mrs. Compson, who rebukes her daughter for ruining her carriage. Caddy skillfully smooths over Benjy's loss of the fire by giving him the cushion, but she is immediately scolded for "humor-[ing] him too much." Mrs. Compson takes the cushion away because "He must learn to mind," but she collapses in tears at the onslaught of Benjy's bellowing. Caddy must take command, pacify Benjy, and usher her mother off to bed. Caddy is not only a willing mother to Benjy; she is also a skillful and intelligent one.

Numerous other scenes in section one depict Caddy's love for Benjy, her loyalty to him, and her skill in caring for him. She tries to communicate with him and to teach him. By outwitting the other children, she procures for him whatever he desires. She fights Jason in order to protect him. She directs Versh in caring for him, feeds him herself, and sleeps with him. Caddy's assumption of the role of mother to Benjy makes it natural that she should play the same role with her other brothers. She is their natural leader; her personality is more aggressive than theirs, and she possesses the feminine self-confidence and sense of personal fulfillment that are the consequence of being needed as a mother. She has a meaningful role to perform, and her outgoing personality makes it inevitable that she will beg that her brothers be made to "mind her," and that her father and Dilsey will not only acquiesce to her childish demand but also rely upon her for Benjy's comfort and care.

Since Caddy performs the task of mother to Benjy, it is apparent that he would regard her as his real and only mother. Benjy's painful "present" depicts his childish longing not so much for the absent sister as for the lost mother. In *The Marble Faun* and *Soldier's Pay* Faulkner relied quite heavily on "tree" imagery to depict the graceful physical beauty of young virgins. Benjy's repeated "Caddy smells like trees" suggests that she possesses this attractiveness. However, the imagery in the earlier works is extensive and picturesque, emphasizing the physical appearance of girls, whereas the physical descriptions of Caddy are much less elaborate. Since Caddy is primarily "mother" to Benjy, it is probable that the "tree" motif in *The Sound and the Fury* is meant to suggest that Caddy is a "mother of life" figure. The "tree" smell of Caddy is Benjy's reassurance of the presence of the security of a mother's love. When Caddy dons her cheap perfume, when she is embraced by Charlie, and when she engages in illicit sexual relations, Benjy weeps not so much because he is an "innocent" who senses his sister's immorality, as because he is a child who senses that the new odors signify the severing of the bonds of Caddy's motherhood. He is wholly comforted on the first occasion, for Caddy immediately washes herself and gives her perfume to Dilsey. On the second occasion Caddy is overcome by confusion, flees Charlie, and clings to Benjy, weeping. On the third occasion Caddy can no longer comfort Benjy, for the bond between them has been broken.

Caddy's willingness to be a mother to Benjy and his responsive devotion to her are virtually the only acts of natural love in the Compson family. Their relationship, however, cannot be indefinitely sustained. Caddy plays an honorable and worthy role, but one which her own need for growth and fulfillment must eventually nullify. Caddy is not Benjy's mother; she is his sister. As soon as she begins the natural process of seeking love outside her family, she is faced with a frustrating problem of identity — the confusion of her real self with the role she has assumed. It is impossible for Benjy's love to be anything but possessive, for he is as entirely dependent upon Caddy as is any three-year-old child upon its mother. Caddy is torn between her love and loyalty for Benjy and her natural drive to become a real mother. When the inevitable break occurs, Benjy becomes a pathetically lost and motherless child. Luster's search for the lost quarter, whose mandala shape suggests wholeness, coherence, and order, is paralleled by Benjy's wandering search for the security, wholeness, and order wrought by the love of Caddy. Every call of the golfers reminds Benjy of his loss, and he clings to the comforting symbols of that love — the dirty slipper he caresses, the blazing fire that signifies love's warmth and vitality, the grave that offers security, and the progression of the bright shapes in their ordered place.

Quentin Compson's obsession with his sister Caddy, the subject of the second section of *The Sound and the Fury*, is the most intense and complex of all of Faulkner's portrayals of man's need of woman. Like Benjy, Quentin forces Caddy's life into unnatural patterns because of his need of her, but his desire for Caddy is much more subtly expressed than Benjy's and is both more irresponsible and more destructive. Quentin's obsession with Caddy is the result of his devotion to her as a Romantic ideal, but it is also the result of his sexual need of her. Further, it is the expression of his unconscious desire that Caddy fulfill the role of mother to him.

Caddy as the youthful pure virgin represents for Quentin the ideality which he imagines would enable him to transcend spiritually the decadence, lovelessness, and immorality of his family. Caddy's virginity, for Quentin the symbol of innocence, is the one pure thing in his environment. This idealization of Caddy is, however, the most unreal and impossible ideality that any of Faulkner's searching heroes project. Statues of marble purity and sheer glass vases can be "practical" symbols of ideality, but the virginity of human and mutable woman is an ideal inevitably doomed to destruction. From his childhood Quentin struggles to "isolate her out of the loud world," but

Caddy's very humanity continually mocks his dream.[1] Quentin's effort to actualize his yearning for ideality by the preservation of Caddy's virginity is self-deceiving, selfish, and evil, for it entails the destruction of Caddy's humanity. The second section of *The Sound and the Fury* depicts the defeated Romanticist mourning the loss of the ideal. The section elicits from the reader the tense and painful response of juxtaposed sympathy and judgment, sympathy for the yearning idealist, but judgment on Quentin's lack of concern for Caddy as a separate and human person.

At the opening of section two Quentin's ideality has been destroyed; therefore, the symbols of his idealization are constantly tempered by the realization that his dreams are already defeated. Thus ideality is constantly counterpointed by reality. The motionless gull glimpsed high above the glinting waters represents the ideal deflated by the mockery of "willy nilly" reality. "A gull on an invisible wire attached through space dragged. You carry the symbol of your frustration into eternity. Then the wings are bigger Father said only who can play a harp" (*SF*, p. 129).[2]

Mr. Compson, who is himself an idealist turned cynic, serves as Quentin's constant reminder of the mutability of life. Though his comments are cloaked with despair, his point of view is practical and reasonable in light of the facts of the human condition.

---

[1]Quentin's Romantic dilemma is well expressed by Robert M. Slabey in " 'The Romanticism' of *The Sound and the Fury*," pp. 153-155: "Quentin's ideal is likewise [like Shelley's ideal, visionary woman, the Epipsyche] embodied in a woman, in Caddy as virgin and as a symbol of family and traditional honor — with unhealthy undertones of eroticism and incest. When the ideal is spoiled and soiled, Quentin is disillusioned and desolate . . . . His love was a love of childhood, of innocence, an impossible thing in the adult world; Caddy's pregnancy irrevocably removed the possibility of a return to childhood innocence . . . . Fundamentally, the position of the Romantic is fallacious; his 'philosophy' is inadequate in coping with reality; because of this he cannot bear the human condition, and he is defeated by it . . . ."

[2]The beautiful trout which Quentin watches flitting in the stream is another image of ideality. Lawrence E. Bowling in "Faulkner: The Theme of Pride in *The Sound and the Fury*," p. 130, writes: "The big fish symbolizes ideality, which all his life Quentin has been dreaming about but which, as the boys express it, 'cant anybody catch' . . . . Quentin's ideal of perfection, like the big fish, is not only unattainable to 'anybody' and unattempted by any positive action on the part of himself: it also has driven out of his life all achievable goals."

> And Father said it's because you are a virgin: dont you
> see? Women are never virgins. Purity is a negative state and
> therefore contrary to nature. It's nature is hurting you not
> Caddy and I said That's just words and he said So is
> virginity and I said you cant know. (*SF*, p. 143)

Though Mr. Compson has accepted this reality intellectually
and advises his son, he remains defeated emotionally and, like
Quentin, unable to react positively to the demands of life in the
"temporary." Despite his insistence that virginity is unnatural,
Caddy feels that her "sin" will kill him. His despair is as
extreme as Quentin's.

> He said it was men invented virginity not women. Father
> said it's like death: only a state in which the others are left
> and I said, But to believe it doesn't matter and he said,
> That's what's so sad about anything: not only virginity,
> and I said, Why couldn't it have been me and not her who
> is unvirgin and he said, That's why that's sad too; nothing
> is even worth the changing of it. (*SF*, p. 96)

Quentin suffers painfully over the sight of the roses of
Caddy's wedding and the lush and passionate scents of June, the
month of brides. He prefers virgin-white dogwood and milk-
weed and the path out of life — death. The escape from time by
entrance into the eternity of death makes Quentin's suicide, like
that of Bayard, the final expression of his total commitment to
ideality. Quentin's idealism is, however, so decayed that just as
he in life envisions the ideal not in terms of creativity and
communion, but as virginity and isolation, so with death he
equates ideality with the destructive flames of hell. "*If it could
just be a hell beyond that: the clean flame the two of us more
than dead. Then you will have only me then only me then the
two of us amid the pointing and the horror beyond the clean
flame*" (*SF*, p. 144). This image of escape, isolation, and fiery
purity aptly portrays the ultimate destructiveness of Quentin's

idealism. He would gladly doom Caddy to the eternity of hell flames in order to possess his ideal completely.

Quentin's willingness to sacrifice his life in order to achieve the ultimate isolation and timelessness of death is in no sense heroic. His father urges him to realize that his ideal is impossible to achieve because of the very unheroic and ignoble nature of man.

> You wanted to sublimate a piece of natural human folly into a horror and then exorcise it with truth . . . . you are still blind to what is in yourself to that part of general truth the sequence of natural events and their causes which shadows every mans brow even benjys you are not thinking of finitude you are contemplating an apotheosis in which a temporary state of mind will become symmetrical above the flesh and aware both of itself and of the flesh. (*SF*, p. 220)

Complete transcendence is impossible because humankind is by nature unable to comprehend fully the real motivations behind its actions.

Just as the idealizations of art in *Mosquitoes* must be juxtaposed with the artists' visit to the brothels, Quentin is aware that his idealization of Caddy is in part an expression of his sexual desire for her. Gordon in *Mosquitoes* is able to separate the ideal from the real by visualizing the former as a marble statue and by ridding himself of sensual desire by visiting the prostitutes. In *Sartoris* Horace avoids the dilemma by refusing to deal honestly with his true feelings. Quentin's moral idealism eliminates either of these outlets for his feelings, and he is overpowered by an emotion which partakes of both the transcendent and the sensual. Even as a child Quentin plays the role of "lover-protector" to Caddy. In the first branch scene he is embarrassed when she takes off her dress and muddies her drawers; when she rebukes and ignores him, he lurks behind the others, jealous and hurt, a reaction which is paralleled during their adolescence by his jealousy and hatred of her lovers. On several occasions Quentin expresses his outraged emotions by slapping and fighting Caddy, another action which is paralleled during their adolescence when Quentin points his "phallic" knife at Caddy's throat.

For Quentin as for the protagonists of Faulkner's earlier works, the lush odors and colors of spring and summer symbolize sexual desire. In the second branch scene Quentin becomes increasingly haunted by the rich odor of the honey-suckle. His inability to separate his idealized love and his sexual desire is indicated by the repeated phrase "getting the odour of honeysuckle . . . all mixed up in it." During his last day he is continually reminded of his "honeysuckle" desire by the orchard pinks and whites of the Massachusetts spring and the steady buzz of the honey bees. Quentin's lie to his father — that he has committed incest with his sister — expresses not only his effort to "isolate her out of the loud world," but also his actual, though perhaps unconscious, desire to commit the incestuous act and achieve physical union with his sister.

There is, however, another dimension of Quentin's obsession with his sister which is a dominant though unconscious motivation of his suicide, a dimension that is movingly revealed through Faulkner's imagery and which makes the portrait of Quentin a profound insight into the nature of man's need of woman. Carl Jung in his *Psychology of the Unconscious* shows that the intense longing for ideality is an expression of the archetypal search for the mother, a yearning which, because of the nature of man, can be paradoxically either creative or destructive.

> The longing of the moth for the star [symbolic of man's yearning for the highest things] is not absolutely pure and transparent, but glows in sultry mist, for man continues to be man. Through the excess of his longing he draws down the divine into the corruption of his passion; therefore, he seems to raise himself to the Divine; but with that his humanity is destroyed. (Jung, p. 121)

Jung states further, ". . . the libido, after having seen a 'Helen in every woman' for so long a time, sets out on a search for the difficult to obtain, the worshipped, but perhaps unattainable goal, and which in the unconscious is the mother" (Jung, p. 255). The imagery and action of the second section of *The Sound and the Fury* make it clear that Quentin's internal conflict is intensified by his psychological drive to achieve the renewal afforded by the "thought of becoming a child again, of turning back to the parents' protection, of coming into the mother once more in order to be born again" (Jung, p. 251).

The yearning for rebirth and immortality is expressed most primitively and instinctively as the desire for incest. Because of the incest prohibition, man must either repress his natural drives or else sublimate them so that his unconscious energies will be directed toward meaningful and creative actions. The pattern of repression inevitably entails self-deception and ultimately self-destruction. On the other hand, the pattern of sublimation requires a conscious recognition of the mixed nature of human motivations, a sacrifice of the incestuous desire, and the transfer of the life energy to the natural creative process of reproduction which does result finally in rebirth through others. Quentin is unable to adapt his sexual drives to this natural process of life. He clings to Caddy as a substitute mother, unwilling to make the necessary sacrifice of selfish desire which would enable the two of them to make a creative adjustment to reality. The imagery of the narrative of Quentin's last day portrays the omnipresence of his repressed longing for the maternal.

There is, of course, no evidence to prove (though there is none to disprove it) that Faulkner made conscious use of Jungian symbolism in his portrayal of Quentin's dilemma. Jung's point, however, is that the symbols are universal and that they arise from the subconscious of the artist. The parallel between Faulkner's imagery in the Quentin section and Jung's symbols for the subconscious expression of the universal yearning for the mother indicates (whether Faulkner consciously or unconsciously created the device) the source of the intense emotional power of the second section of *The Sound and the Fury*.

The events of the Quentin section are given unity by the progress of the sun across the heavens. The sun represents life, and its passage toward sunset is the movement of life toward death. Throughout the section Quentin is intensely aware of the sun's light and of its slow, constant movement. Though he destroys the hands of his grandfather's watch, Quentin cannot escape its ticking, no more than he can flee the sun's movement toward dusk. His shadow, the symbol of his subconscious self, is but the recorder of the inescapable passage of time.

Quentin's last day, measured out piece by piece by the movement of the sun, is the psychological metaphor of his whole life. It is spent in attempts at tricking and trampling his shadow and in idle, purposeless wandering. At the opening of his interior monologue Quentin thinks briefly about his father's warnings against idle habits. Jung writes,

> Nothing brings the relentless flight of time and the cruel perishability of all blossoms more painfully to our consciousness than an inactive and empty life. *Idle dreaming is the mother of the fear of death,* the sentimental deploring of what has been and the vain turning back of the clock. (Jung, p. 434)

Quentin's day's walk is twisting and without precise destinations. "The wandering is a (symbolic) representation of longing, of the ever-restless desire, which nowhere finds its object, for, unknown to itself, it seeks the lost mother" (Jung, p. 231). Periodically, Quentin wanders to streams of cool water and shadowy groves of lush trees. The maternal symbolism of both water and trees is obvious, and it is significant that these occurrences naturally bring Quentin moments of physical and psychological release from the heat of the sun, the sign of reality.

The final release from the light and the heat of the sun, and from the demands of life in time, is darkness.

> All that is living rises as does the sun, from the water, and at evening plunges into the water. Born from the springs, the rivers, the seas, at death man arrives at the waters of the Styx in order to enter the 'night journey on the sea.' The wish is that the black water of death might be the

water of life; that death, with its cold embrace, might be the mother's womb, just as the sea devours the sun, but brings it forth again out of the maternal womb. (Jung, p. 245)

When night comes, Quentin's life ends with death by water, his symbolic and literal submission to the peace of inaction that comes with the acceptance of the fate of the "terrible mother." To "not be" are for him the "peacefullest words." Jung describes the desire for drowning as a desire to be re-absorbed into the mother, a death which is "a deep personal longing for quiet and for the profound peace of non-existence, for a dreamless sleep in the ebb and flow of the sea of life" (Jung, p. 390). Quentin's inability to achieve renewal by adapting himself to life forces him to seek the maternal waters of death, to wish for the fulfillment of his incestuous desire in death.

Both at the beginning and at the end of Quentin's inner monologue, he laments, ". . . if I'd just had a mother so I could say Mother Mother." Faulkner skillfully juxtaposes the symbolic presentation of Quentin's torturous psychological journey with those recollections of past events which are the climactic experiences of Quentin's life — his rejection by his real mother and his betrayal by his substitute mother, Caddy. Quentin recalls with pain the occasions when his mother openly declared that she loved only Jason. Her discovery of Caddy's "sin" elicits a verbal assertion of her total rejection of her other children, an attitude no doubt apparent to them throughout their lives.

> Jason you must let me go away I cannot stand it let me have Jason and you keep the others they're not my flesh and blood like he is strangers nothing of mine and I am afraid of them I can take Jason and go where we are not known I'll go down on my knees and pray for the absolution of my sins that he may escape this curse try to forget that the others ever were. (SF, p. 128)

Mrs. Compson effectively damns all her children into non-existence by her total incapacity to love them. Quentin's introverted search is provoked by this total absence of natural motherly love in his childhood. His hatred for his mother is intense, for she is a despicable person, and yet by nature he is doomed to yearn for her approval.

Quentin's recollections of his mother superbly develop the image of Mrs. Compson's character that is established in section one. The habits and routines of her life reveal that she is entirely selfish and self-pitying. Her constant retreat to her dark sickroom and its camphor odor shows that she prefers turning to death to accepting the responsibilities of life. She is emaciated, whimpering, petty, useless, and hopelessly withdrawn. When Caddy makes the first step into the natural process of life and kisses a boy, her mother signifies her disapproval by dressing in the attire of mourning. It is tragic that despite Quentin's conscious hatred of his mother his suicide is an unconscious affirmation of his mother's terrible love of death and decay.

Since he has spent his life with an unnaturally unaffectionate mother, it is not surprising that Quentin's attention is attracted by an unnaturally affectionate one. Faulkner's portrait of the mother of Gerald Bland illustrates the perverted nature of the love Quentin has come to desire for himself. Gerald Bland possesses precisely what Quentin longs for — absolute devotion and attention from a mother figure. Mrs. Bland takes an apartment in Cambridge in order to be near Gerald while he is at Harvard. Her conversation consists entirely of praise for her son's appearance, his drinking abilities, and his talent at the seduction of women. Though he mocks both Gerald and his mother, it is obvious that Quentin is envious of his friend. When Quentin's mind turns to the image of his symbolic gull, he recalls also the image of Gerald, rowing up the river in the boat race with his devoted mother driving along the highway beside him. While Quentin's gull remains in frustrated motionlessness, Gerald, who has a mother, is able to achieve in Quentin's mind the "apotheosis" which is denied himself.

He [Gerald] would be sort of grand too, pulling in lonely state across the noon, rowing himself right out of noon, up the long bright air like an apotheosis, mounting into a drowsing infinity where only he and the gull, the one terrifically motionless, the other in a steady and measured pull and recover that partook of inertia itself, the world punily beneath their shadows on the sun. (*SF*, p. 149)

Quentin's inner struggle reaches climactic and tragic intensity because, unlike Jesus and St. Francis, he has a sister, and upon Caddy is projected all his futile longing. Because she exists, and as a child is willing to love and mother him, it is possible for Quentin to possess momentarily the love his mother has denied him. However, because Caddy's naturalness and the maturing process constantly threaten to break the bonds between them, Quentin clings unnaturally to her affection. He posits her virginity as his ideal because that alone would assure his lifetime possession of her, and when that is lost, he permits himself to speak the hidden and forsaken desire for incest which would make her entirely his own.

Two poignant scenes depict Quentin's dependence on Caddy as a mother figure. The first, Quentin's childish sexual experimentation with Natalie, is significantly accompanied by a drenching rain. Quentin's guilt about his behavior makes him desire that Caddy will fulfill the role of mother by disapproving of his actions, disciplining him, and thus relieving his feelings of shame. When Caddy's response is, "I don't give a damn what you were doing," he violently attacks her to force the blows which he dreadfully needs and to "make" her care.

Caddy's love of Dalton Ames and her illicit relations with him are for Quentin an outright betrayal not only of his vision of ideality but, more crucially, of his son-like love for Caddy. The second branch scene, when Caddy confesses her love for Ames, is an intense portrayal of Quentin's child-like need of Caddy as a mother and of his severe and torturous sexual love for her. Throughout the scene he weeps pathetically, a broken distraught child, and Caddy holds him, hushes him and comforts him as if he were a child: "then I was crying her hand touched me again and I was crying against her damp blouse" (*SF*, p. 188). Quentin does not weep for Caddy, but for himself and his loss of her. The nature and intensity of Quentin's desire for Caddy is powerfully suggested by the repeated descriptions of the water, the dampness, the trees, the shadowy night, and particularly, the omnipresent honeysuckle odor. That his love is the perverted, serpentine longing for the "terrible" mother is indicated by the references to twisted things such as the "matted" vines and briers of the ditch and the "crisscrossed" twig marks on Quentin's palm, as well as by the murderous phallic knife.

Two symbolic phantasies at the end of his inner monologue indicate that Quentin faintly senses the truth of his psychological condition. The first is the picture-book dungeon with "a single weak ray of light" and "two faces lifted out of the shadow" at which Quentin gazes until "the dungeon was Mother herself she and Father upward into weak light holding hands and us lost somewhere below them without even a ray of light" (*SF*, p. 215). Quentin's unconfessed, repressed longing makes him the victim of the "terrible" mother and dooms him to eternal darkness and isolation.

The second phantasy is the recalled childhood experience of rising at night to get water; the repetition of the word "door" suggests the possibility of escape from darkness and isolation and the achievement of the life-giving waters. In real life Quentin is incapable of reaching the door, of breaking the chains of his repressed desires and achieving rebirth through the normal processes of life. Unlike the symbolic trout which rises like an arrow, plunges into the water, and persistently arises again, Quentin suspects that when he is called to "Rise," the flat irons will hold him in the peaceful idleness of repression and eternal death. His life has not been characterized by sacrifice and renewal and neither will be his death. Quentin's complex need of Caddy shapes the pattern of her life, forcing her at a crucial moment to withdraw from the natural life process and dooming her to a lifetime of the serene deadliness he chooses for himself.

There is a contrast throughout the second section of *The Sound and the Fury* between Quentin's unnatural desire for Caddy and her normal devotion to him. Caddy's openness and responsiveness to her brothers' need for love and affection is well developed by the portrayal of her devotion to Benjy in section one. That she refused to give Quentin this kind of attention during their adolescence is indicative of her very natural adjustment to the realistic demands of maturity. She feels regret at severing the bond of her motherhood to Benjy because he remains in effect a child and his continued need of her is inevitable. Though she is patient with Quentin's demands on her, she is emotionally detached from him. Caddy considers him her equal and expects him to face life and its responsibilities independently.

As a child Caddy defies Quentin's efforts to correct and control her, and she likewise refuses to exercise any power of "parental" authority over him. It is most appropriate that she does not "give a damn" about his relationship with Natalie. It is abnormal and unnatural that Quentin does care intensely about Caddy's relationship with Dalton Ames. In the portrayal of her entrancement with love during the second branch scene, she gazes always up and beyond Quentin, soothing his childish sorrow but well removed from him in emotional attachment. Caddy's realistic acceptance of her fate enables her calmly to "mother" Quentin, who in contrast is child-like in his grief and anger.

Quentin: I wish you were dead
Caddy: do you you coming now

* * *

Ill kill you do you hear
lets go out to the swing theyll hear you here

* * *

Im not crying do you say Im crying
no hush now we'll wake Benjy up
you go on into the house go on now
I am dont cry Im bad anyway you cant help it
theres a curse on us its not our fault is it our
    fault
hush come on and go to bed now
you cant make me theres a curse on us. (*SF*, pp.
    195-196)

Caddy's response to Dalton Ames is the natural outgrowth of the warm affection she has given her brothers. She acts according to the normal and inevitable process of life; she is born to be both wife and mother. She responds to love when it is given, and it is the abnormal absence of genuine and natural love in her home that makes her submission unrestrained. That Ames's seduction is not altogether irresponsible is suggested by Quentin's recollection of the embracing lovers. "I could see her face a blur against his shoulder he held her in one arm like she was no bigger than a child . . ." (*SF*, p. 192). Quentin's clumsy and furious attack on Caddy's seducer is preceded by Ames's concerned inquiries about Caddy's welfare — "listen save this for a while I want to know if shes all right have they been bothering her up there" (*SF*, p. 198). Ames extended his hand to Quentin; had Quentin urged Ames to fulfill his responsibility to Caddy, to love her and help her escape the Compson decay, her life might not have ended in tragedy. Instead, Quentin attacks Ames verbally, though he is incapable of doing so physically, and drives him away. Caddy's plaintive gasps, "let me go Ive got to catch him and ask his let me go Quentin please let me go . . . . yes I can tell him I can make him believe anytime I can make him" (*SF*, p. 202), are her first cries of death, her apprehension that love and the hope of a normal life may be lost.

Because of her family Caddy loses the man she loves; her resulting promiscuity is her despairing cry at the loss of life. The deadly serenity that is born in her is the sign that the naturally responsive and loving child has been sacrificed to the unnatural — sex without love. Her mother's subsequent demand that she submit herself to a hypocritical marriage seals her doom. Quentin and Mrs. Compson succeed in destroying Caddy's humanity; by scorning her grasp at life and depriving her of a normal outlet for creativity, motherhood, love, and freedom, they kill the real Caddy and create a deadly serene lost woman.

After the death of her father Caddy's concern for her daughter Quentin forces her to submit herself to the control of Jason's cruelty and greed. Her several appearances in section three of the novel reveal the pathos of her hopeless condition.

She loves Quentin and longs to see her, but Jason responds to every attempt with extortion or threats that he will fire Dilsey, send Benjy to Jackson, and take Quentin and go away. When Caddy grasps the inevitability of Jason's hardness, she begs to have her child back. Jason, however, mocks Caddy's "occupation," and she is immediately forced to recognize that she cannot keep Quentin without destroying her every chance "to be like other girls." Caddy's exasperation with Jason makes her like "a toy that's wound up too tight and about to burst all to pieces." As Jason puts it, Caddy does have nothing at stake and her realization that she has lost everything breaks her. " 'No,' she says, then she began to laugh and to try to hold it back at the same time. 'No. I have nothing at stake,' she says, making that noise, putting her hands to her mouth, 'nuh-nuh-nothing,' she says" (SF, p. 260). Had Caddy been allowed to return home to care for Quentin and Benjy and thus to fulfill the destiny of her nature, the Compson history might have been different. Instead, the tragedy of Caddy's life is repeated by her child.

The content of Benjy's and Quentin's sections is based on their obsessed love for Caddy; the content of Jason's section is based on his obsessed agitation with Quentin. His day is spent in attempts to catch her whoring and in designs to swindle away the money her mother sends her. Quentin is trapped by the circumstances of her life; Jason's treatment of her destroys her.

"It's his fault," she says, "He wont let me alone, and I have to. If he doesn't want me here, why wont he let me go back to —."

* * *

"Whatever I do, it's your fault," she says. "If I'm bad, it's because I had to be. You made me. I wish I was dead. I wish we were all dead." (SF, pp. 323-324)

Faulkner skillfully indicates the extensive emotional despair that engulfs both Caddy and her daughter in the face of Jason's cruelty by descriptions of their nervous gestures. Caddy twitches her upper lip, raising it higher and higher as her anger with Jason mounts. Quentin frantically crumbles her biscuit while Jason mocks her, "her eyes cornered, kind of jerking her arms against her sides."

Though *The Sound and the Fury* is characterized by continuous individual dying, the novel affirms that life itself does continue. Despite the tragedy of Quentin's ruined life, she is ultimately victorious over Jason, who is anti-woman and anti-life. Jason has no feeling for any human being, but he is particularly inhuman to women. His treatment of Caddy is criminal; he shoves and beats Quentin; he slams the door in Dilsey's face and ridicules her; he constantly sasses and mocks his mother; and his mistress, Lorraine, is merely a business proposition. Marriage, family, and the reproductive process of life which are offered by woman do not interest Jason in the least. It is altogether understandable that he is never able "to learn that a woman will do anything." When Jason pits his impotent masculinity against the vitality of woman and of life itself, it is inevitable that he will be defeated. This is the basis of the comic tone that pervades the third section of *The Sound and the Fury*. Though Quentin's life is tragic, she does outwit Jason by slipping down the blossoming pear tree. Jason's destructive masculinity is overcome by the comic principle — the inevitability of the on-going process of life.

It is in the context of this view of human existence — that life despite its tragedies does continue — that the character of Dilsey assumes its full significance in the novel. It is the mother who fosters life, and Dilsey is the protecting, serving mother of the Compson household which Mrs. Comspon ought to be. Dilsey assumes the practical duties of motherhood, and by her devotion to the routine tasks of cooking for the Compsons and serving their basic physical needs, she imposes an order on their family life which would be entirely chaotic without her. Throughout the novel Dilsey is constantly engaged in actions of service, but it is with the fourth section, when her duties have become painfully burdensome because of her old age, that the heroic dimensions of her character are made fully apparent. In Faulkner's appendix to the novel he wrote of Dilsey and her kind, "They endured." It is this quality of endurance that emerges in *The Sound and the Fury* as Faulkner's highest ideal.

In his development of Dilsey's character Faulkner relies heavily on descriptions of her appearance, gestures, and routine activities to suggest the quality of her life. Repeatedly in the fourth section Faulkner presents Dilsey's laborious mounting of the stairs to answer Mrs. Caroline's whims, her hand on the wall to steady herself as she goes slowly up and down. Dilsey's whole life has been characterized by continuous physical effort to provide for the needs of others, who significantly wait at the top of the stairs. Though she is physically drained herself, she continues to respond faithfully to every demand. On the Sunday morning of the fourth section Dilsey has struggled in the rain to get in firewood, a task Luster neglected, and has prepared breakfast despite Mrs. Compson's persistent interruptions. The reader feels astonished disgust to discover that Mrs. Compson has unnecessarily forced Dilsey up the stairs once again by implying that Benjy is awake and needs attention, but Dilsey merely lowers her face and stands for a moment "like a cow in the rain" enduring Mrs. Compson's self-pitying complaints, saying nothing, then descending the stairs again, "lowering her body from step to step, as a small child does, her hand against the wall" (*SF*, p. 339).

Faulkner's portrait of Dilsey does not, however, emphasize only the pathos of her servant's role. Instead, he wisely and skillfully tempers the presentation of her hardships with humor, humor which springs from the very nature of Dilsey's character. Dilsey not only endures, but she endures with sound mind, compassion, and a sense of the comic foolishness of human life. Faulkner's description of Dilsey at the opening of the fourth section is a superb combination of the effects of the tragic and the comic, the noble and the farcical.

When Dilsey first steps out of her door on the rainy Easter Sunday morning in 1928, she wears an outlandish outfit which in its total effect evokes the comic. Her black straw hat is "perched upon her turban"; "mangy and anonymous fur" rims her cape; and her skirts "balloon" about her legs. Nevertheless, there is a touch of dignity, Faulkner suggests, even regality, in her appearance which is conveyed by the "maroon velvet cape" and the "dress of purple silk." She is "gaunt," her flesh loose and dropsical, a skeleton with "unpadded skin" as if "muscle and tissue had been courage or fortitude which the days or years had consumed until only the indomitable skeleton was left rising like a ruin or a landmark above the somnolent and impervious guts" (*SF*, p. 331). Dilsey views the gloomy weather with a "child's astonished disappointment," and re-enters the cabin to replace her Sunday garments with a blue gingham dress, "a man's felt hat and an army overcoat." Next she struggles with the umbrella which nearly blows away, "precariously" balancing the wood she collects while she contrives to open and close the umbrella. The minute the wood falls into the box in the kitchen, Mrs. Compson begins calling her.

Dilsey struggles; every action requires her entire concentration and excessive physical effort. Yet, the sense of the comic is maintained, for she is never overcome — her spirit seems unlimited and indomitable. Despite the depressing weather, Luster's negligence, and Mrs. Compson's unreasonable demands, Dilsey sings as she prepares the breakfast food, at first something "mournful and plaintive, austere," but gradually as the fire heats the room, "she was singing louder, as if her voice too had been thawed by the growing warmth . . ." (*SF*, p. 336).

Dilsey is a striking contrast to Faulkner's earlier presentations of a feminine ideal. She is, indeed, the exact opposite of the pure virgin girls who attracted Faulkner during his apprentice writing. Comically attired, she is merely an old and ugly Negro house-servant. She is despised and rejected by those who need her most, and she is in a real sense powerless to direct or control events. Yet, Faulkner makes it clear that Dilsey's pattern of life is the noblest response that mankind can make to the limited and evil nature of human existence. Indeed, it is precisely because of his recognition of man's inability to achieve transcendence that he posits Dilsey's endurance despite despair at the burdens of life's evil as his highest ideal. Her belief is not illusory; it is simply the best one can do in the face of life's limitations. Dilsey's perspective on life is splendidly realistic, uncynical, and self-forgetful. She pampers and protects Quentin because she recognizes that the girl is the victim of life's circumstances. She openly criticizes Jason's inhumanity and senses the humor of Quentin's triumph over him. Most significantly, she is not ashamed of Benjy, for, unlike the poor white trash, she knows that he is "God's own child," as she is herself.

The Compson family is blighted by the very real limitations of human life, its evils and its curses; however, they multiply the chaos of their existence because each to different degrees devotes himself to selfish aims. On the other hand, Dilsey creates order out of chaos by her love of and service to others. Indeed, as Lawrence Thompson ("Mirror Analogues in *The Sound and the Fury*," p. 88) has suggested, the "life-injuring forces versus the life-encouraging forces" do define evil and good in *The Sound and the Fury*, not only in this novel but throughout the bulk of Faulkner's fiction. As Faulkner said of her, "Dilsey, the Negro woman, she was a good human being. That she held that family together for not the hope of reward but just because it was the decent and proper thing to do" (*Faulkner in the University*, p. 85). Dilsey represents Faulkner's highest ethical vision because she endures the burden of all those activities which, both physically and spiritually, nourish and sustain human life. The matriarch of her own large Negro family, and of the white Compsons, she is the full embodiment of the "mother earth" figure of *The Marble Faun*. Because of her very nature Dilsey, like the earth, endures. Faulkner effectively conveyed his sense of the astonishing irony and mystery of human life when he chose an old Negro servant to embody his new vision of the ideal woman.

CHAPTER IV

The Ideal of Motherhood:
Sanctuary

The Sound and the Fury depicts the tragedy and chaos of a family whose mother has refused the responsibilities of motherhood and has thus destroyed her children's capacities for normal affection and creative living. The Compson children do not mature; they fail to assume the human responsibility for the reproduction and nourishment of life and thereby commit themselves to death. Dilsey's character illustrates those qualities of maturity, unselfishness, and devoted service to the sustenance of life which the Compson family lacks. In *Sancutary* Faulkner portrays the decay of a whole society which has refused the responsibilities of maturity. *Sanctuary* demonstrates that not only individual families but also society as a whole desperately needs the moral order wrought by the unselfishness that characterizes motherly love. The bitterness that pervades the novel reflects Faulkner's impatience with human beings who, like Quentin, refuse to accept the burdens of maturity. Evil flourishes in *Sanctuary* because men and women cling to their childishness, their selfishness, and their naïveté. Ruby Goodwin is the only character in the novel who is able to bear

71

the responsibilities of maturity. She recognizes the evil nature of man and accepts the limitations of the human condition; nevertheless, she is wholly devoted to nourishing and sustaining human life.

Sexuality is of major importance in *Sanctuary* as it is in *The Sound and the Fury* and Faulkner's earlier fiction. The natural sexual process represents the vitality of life. When this normal process is thwarted and sexuality expresses lust and selfishness, sex becomes destructive. Evil in *Sanctuary* is revealed through Faulkner's portrayal of irresponsible sexual behavior. Popeye's corn-cob rape is merely a graphic image of the perversion of sexuality that is apparent in Narcissa's hypocritical propriety, Temple's lust, and Horace's confused, incestuous desires. Man's irresponsible use of sexuality is equivalent to his irresponsible use of life. Ruby Goodwin is the only character in *Sanctuary* who displays mature and responsible sexual behavior. The evil of her past life of prostitution has been negated by her loyal devotion to her common-law husband, her loving care of her frail child, and her effort to maintain the semblance of a home. Her submission of herself to the demands of the natural sexual process requires self-forgetfulness and a responsible bearing of the needs of others. She provides a striking contrast to the other characters in the novel, whose immaturity and selfishness result in the destruction of life.

As in Faulkner's earlier fiction the women in *Sanctuary* represent the extremes of the human situation. Temple Drake is the young virgin whose beauty and sexuality suggest life's potential for creativity and fulfillment. However, in *Sanctuary* the virgin is totally corrupted. Temple's perverted use of her sexual powers is symbolic of man's utter corruption of the natural process of life through his evil, his selfishness, and his naïve misunderstanding of the nature of reality. Narcissa Sartoris represents conventional society which, in its effort to hide its inner corruption, is led to regard outward respectability more highly than inward purity. In contrast to Ruby Goodwin both Temple and Narcissa are aligned with the forces of evil and destruction.

Sanctuary depicts Horace Benbow's struggle to understand the nature of woman as he encounters her in his sister Narcissa, in Temple Drake, who is the mirror image of his step-daughter Belle, and in Ruby Goodwin. Horace's need to understand woman is symbolic of his need to comprehend the nature of the human situation. However, he is a very limited human being; he is confused by woman's nature and is unable to discern the evil in her from the good. He does not anticipate the extent of Temple's or Narcissa's capacities for evil, nor does he comprehend the nature of Ruby's goodness. Like his society, Horace mistakes respectability and virginity for inward purity. Because of his naïveté about woman, indicative of his ignorance about life, his efforts to halt the rampage of evil in *Sanctuary* are defeated. Horace and his society desperately need the moral order which is embodied in Ruby Goodwin's sacrificial love, but they fail to recognize her virtue. The initial scene of *Sanctuary* presents Horace Benbow's encounter with the gangster Popeye, who is the personification of evil in the novel. Immediately afterwards Faulkner introduces Ruby Goodwin; her character provides a striking contrast to the villainy which Horace encounters at the Old Frenchman's Place. Her appearance and her response to the evils of humanity that surround her reveal the extent of her self-sacrifice and, simultaneously, her realistic comprehension of the nature of evil and the limitations of human life.

The three-sentence description which introduces Ruby into the narrative identifies precisely her place in life. "A woman stood at the stove. She wore a faded calico dress. About her naked ankles a worn pair of man's brogans; unlaced, flapped when she moved" (*S*, p. 8). Ruby's extreme poverty is apparent immediately; she is the cook, and the brogans suggest the heavy weight of the burdens she bears. Popeye's taunts reveal that she is an ex-prostitute who has fallen from the wealth of her Manuel Street business to cooking. To his mockery, Ruby responds, "Yes. I cook. I cook for crimps and spungs and feebs." There is bitterness in this remark, but the reader also senses that this woman's willingness to serve is an act of courageous maturity. In the midst of the moral and physical decay that the first chapter of *Sanctuary* presents she alone acts constructively to serve a human need. As the narrative progresses, her actions indicate her humility and pride as she renders her service and her spiritual and intellectual superiority to all the men that surround her at the Old Frenchman's Place.

In chapter two the calmness, orderliness, and cleanliness with which Ruby serves the evening meal are indicative of her spiritual nature. Her movements are characterized by slowness and calmness, details which suggest her inner stability. (Later in the novel Horace observes her in similar moments of stillness which seem to him to suggest a quality of transcendence.) As soon as the meal is completed Ruby clears the dishes, eats herself, immediately washes the dishes and puts them away. Later Horace recalls the look of those "clean, spartan dishes," and they also become a detail that is suggestive of Ruby's character.

Though Horace watches the gestures that indicate Ruby's cleanliness and orderliness, the scene which is more nearly the real measure of the extent of this woman's devotion is simply too much for his stomach to bear. The blind old man with eyes "like two clots of phlegm" must be fed, and Ruby does it. The reactions of Ruby and of Horace to this sign of the horror of life signify their contrasting responses to the sickening, horrible evil that flows through the remainder of the novel.

> The woman served his plate from the dish . . . . He fumbled at the plate with a diffident, shaking hand and found a small piece of meat and began to suck at it until the woman returned and rapped his knuckles. He put the meat back on the plate then and Benbow watched her cut up the food on the plate, meat, bread and all, and then pour sorghum over it. Then Benbow quit looking. (*S*, p. 12)

When the meal is ended the men sit on the porch and drink and talk. Ruby stands stationary just inside the door listening to Horace tell of the experience with Little Belle that drove him from home. The tale is filtered through Ruby's consciousness.

Her perspective is interspersed throughout Horace's narrative, and it helps the reader make an appropriate judgment of him. " 'He better get on to where he's going, where his women folks can take care of him' .... 'He's crazy,' the woman said, motionless inside the door. The stranger's voice went on tumbling over itself rapid and diffuse." Finally, when his story ends, she thinks, " 'The poor fool.' " Horace flounders in the face of life, incapable of understanding either himself or Little Belle; Ruby sees how ridiculous he is, but she also pities him.

By presenting Ruby through Horace's consciousness and then Horace through Ruby's consciousness, Faulkner prepares for the scene of their direct confrontation that climaxes chapter two. Horace's respect for Ruby has already been established, and she has felt sympathy and pity for him. Barriers are removed; Horace is able to face the fact that his problem is that he lacks courage, and Ruby's self-protective shield of coldness and sullenness is dropped. She apologizes to Horace for her appearance, and she shows him her child asleep in the box behind the stove. In a final gesture her honest acknowledgment of the shame and ugliness of her position in life and yet her heroic acceptance of this role are dramatically rendered. Throughout the scene she has kept her hands hidden, wrapped in her dress, fearful perhaps that they, too, might be too much for Horace to bear. Horace offers to help her, perhaps to send her something from Jefferson. "She removed her hands from the fold of the dress in a turning, flicking motion; jerked them hidden again. 'With all this dishwater and washing . . . You might send me an orange stick,' she said" (*S*, p. 18). Later, Horace recalls this scene and the hands flung out in a "gesture at once spontaneous and diffident and self-conscious and proud."

The men at the Old Frenchman's Place are aimless, foolish, mocking, and addicted to drink. It is as if Ruby is the only grown-up person present and must, therefore, take care of them all. She cooks, serves, and accepts in stride the ugliness of life. She also possesses a "worldly" knowledge of men and of their weaknesses. Faulkner's descriptions of her gestures and her appearance and his presentation of the sordid and burdensome routine of her life enable him to render sharply and effectively the force of goodness she represents.

In chapter three of *Sanctuary* Faulkner presents Ruby's social and moral opposite, Narcissa Benbow Sartoris. The contrast between the two women is given emphasis by the description of their respective physical surroundings. The Old Frenchman's Place once had been set amidst ordered lawns and gardens, but now the gardens are jungles and the house is "gutted," "gaunt," and "stark" because it has been torn down piecemeal as firewood for the neighborhood. Instead of a "faded calico dress," Narcissa wears her "customary white" as she strolls leisurely in the gardens of the Sartoris mansion with a young man "in flannels and a blue coat." A servant prepares a dinner which is announced by the ringing of a "small bell" and accompanied by "roses on the table." The scene is almost a stereotype, is even meant to be, but its significance lies in its ironic similarity to the previous scenes of the novel.

Narcissa's white dress and the roses on the table are a part of the outward facade of an existence which is tainted by the same evils that haunt the Old Frenchman's Place. Her gentleman friend is Gowan Stevens, whose "plumpish," "swaggering," "vaguely collegiate" appearance is decidedly disagreeable and whose pride over his Virginia alma mater, his gentlemanly drinking, and his "jelly" in Oxford is plainly juvenile and hypocritical. The comments of Aunt Jenny, Horace, and little Benbow, which Narcissa attempts to keep submerged, continually reassert that bickering, drinking, and promiscuity are in reality as present in the Sartoris mansion as they are at the Old Frenchman's Place. Paradoxically, Narcissa courts evil, while Ruby is the only sustaining power for good in the midst of the outward decay that evil inevitably accomplishes.

This scene, along with Horace's "Little Belle" narrative in chapter two, prepares for the presentation in chapter four of Temple Drake, the main character in the novel. Socially, Temple is the peer of Narcissa and Little Belle. Like them, she is spiritually the opposite of Ruby Goodwin. In contrast to the sense of motionlessness that pervades the presentation of Ruby, Temple Drake's life is characterized by frantic motion.

Two brief but "loaded" passages indicate almost metaphorically the nature of Temple's character. Temple is seen sneaking out on week nights with town boys.

> a snatched coat under her arm and her long blond legs running, in speeding silhouette against the lighted windows of the Coop . . . vanishing into the shadow beside the library walls . . . and perhaps a final swirl of knickers or what not as she sprang into the car. (*S*, p. 28)

On weekends the town boys spy on her through the gymnasium windows as she participates in the college dances, "vanish[ing] in a swirling blitter upon a glittering swirl of music with her high delicate head and her bold painted mouth and soft chin, her eyes blankly right and left looking, cool, predatory and discreet" (*S*, p. 29). As they watch, the town boys mockingly repeat Temple's obviously habitual shielding comment, "My father's a judge." Just as in the passages that depict Little Belle and Narcissa, promiscuity merges with the respectability of the socially prestigious. The excitement, the mystery, the glamorous escapades, the very appearance of Temple – the spiked heels and blond legs, her tight dress and slightly open coat, her painted mouth, her blank eyes and curled red hair – create a stereotyped image of the popular, beautiful, wealthy girl whose "sex appeal" is the measure of her prestige and worth. Equally apparent, however, is Faulkner's implicit condemnation of a way of life which warps human values and fosters duplicity, hypocrisy, egocentricity, and artificiality.

For Temple Drake sex is an awful game in which desire is over-stimulated, but because of the demand for the hypocritical sign of purity there is never any fulfillment. Her most typical actions are dressing and applying make-up. The central activity of her life is "dating," but her courtships are not aimed at establishing meaningful relationships. She makes herself as physically enticing as possible and exploits her "sex appeal" in the most exciting ways available – sneaking out with town boys, appearing late at dances where her presence is eagerly awaited, and jumping from trains to run off with a Gowan

Stevens. Being caught in a dark and dangerous bootlegger's household surrounded by lustful men is a circumstance almost to be desired. Temple's "act" is a lie, for she will inevitably cry out, "My father's a judge." Just as "it" is about to happen, Temple stops it, so that the absence of the act, whatever the apparent intentions, will preserve her respectability and theoretically her purity.

Temple is so devoted to the game she plays that when circumstances change and polite conventions are dropped, she is incapable of making any adjustments. The role she has assumed is suitable only to Manuel Street. It is ironic that though Temple's life has been oriented toward sexual promiscuity, the whole force of family and society has taught her to fear, above all else, rape by men from outside her social group. Her ridiculously excessive fear of rape is an outgrowth of Southern culture where "womanhood" is the "most sacred" treasure. The rapist mentality is idolatrous of the "sacredness of woman," but the "sacredness" is mere sentiment, as the whole action of *Sanctuary* demonstrates. Virginity is a false measure of purity, but as long as it is the only measure, true purity becomes unnecessary. Thus Temple Drake's habitual "sex appeal" merges with her excessive fears to produce the constant "aching rigid grimace" which invites her own rape, an event she has unknowingly prepared herself to require physically and which she consciously desires to be accomplished so that her excessive dread of the disaster can be ended.

As Temple prepares for bed at the bootlegger's house, she neglects none of her routine care of her appearance.

> She opened the raincoat and produced a compact from somewhere and, watching her motions in the tiny mirror, she spread and fluffed her hair with her fingers and powdered her face and replaced the compact and looked at the watch again and fastened the raincoat . . . . The voices had got quiet for a moment and in the silence Tommy could hear a faint, steady chatter of the shucks inside the mattress where Temple lay, her hands crossed on her breast and her legs straight and close and decorous, like an effigy on an ancient tomb. (*S*, p. 69)

It is important to Temple that her face be "right" even though this checking on her sexual enticement is here ironically juxtaposed with a physical position that will protect her from rape. She removes her dress, for it must be kept neat even though it is her best defense against her "attackers." Her actions are mechanical; she is child-like and frightened, but she is methodically, though unconsciously, preparing for the final idolatrous worship of her "sacred womanhood" – her rape.

What Temple has chosen to be is not adequately signified by the tiny watch and compact mirror, or the tight dress and loosely open coat. When she goes to bed in the Memphis brothel, the room, the clock, the mirror, and the garments are blown-up. Put where she belongs, setting becomes the symbolic equivalent of Temple's inner self. The Temple who was protectively covered by her coat, the raincoat, and a quilt at the Old Frenchman's Place is now transformed into a Temple clad in "a too-large gown of cerise crepe," black against the white linen of the brothel bed; her hair is in a "black sprawl," "her face and throat and arms outside the covers were gray." In "a dim mirror, a pellucid oblong of dusk set on end," Temple glimpses herself "like a thin ghost, a pale shadow moving in the uttermost profundity of shadow." An elaborate "flowered china" clock is stopped at the hour of 10:30 – the hour when college couples stroll to church and the approximate hour of Temple's corn-cob rape.

> She watched the final light condense into the clock face, and the dial change from a round orifice in the darkness to a disc suspended in nothingness, the original chaos, and change in turn to a crystal ball holding in its still and cryptic depths the ordered chaos of the intricate and shadowy world upon whose scarred flanks the old wounds whirl onward at dizzy speed into darkness lurking with new disasters. (*S*, pp. 146-149)

It is apparent that Temple's evil is a part of all the lusts of the past that are reflected in the mirror of the brothel room. The description of the clock suggests that her evil is part of the original chaos which she has chosen to perpetuate by her perversion of sexuality. The outer garments that Temple dons in the course of the novel — the flower-splotched Chinese dressing gown, the glittering dancing frock, and the black garments of the trial scene — signify the progressive inner decay of her soul. Each time she gazes at her image in a mirror — the mirror of the brothel room, the mirror in the Grotto bathroom, her compact mirror in the last scene — there is reflected the outward appearance which indicates her betrayal of the normal feminine role and her compact with evil.

However, the vile, debauched Temple Drake is only seventeen; her childishness and inexperience are effectively revealed during her encounter with Ruby Goodwin. Temple's amazement at Ruby's past is the shock of an inexperienced, sheltered adolescent. Despite her own elaborate sex games, Temple identifies much more easily with Ruby's baby than with Ruby herself. " 'Jazzing?' Temple whispered, holding the child, looking herself no more than an elongated and leggy infant in her scant dress and uptilted hat" (S, p. 57). Ruby's judgment on Temple is absolute, but it is a judgment not unmixed with a pity that recognizes Temple's childishness. "You poor little gutless fool . . . . Playing at it." Temple has tried to play at the kind of life Ruby had led without knowing or caring about the implications of the game. Just as her interest in Ruby's baby is only self-comforting child-like play, she has used sex as exciting, ego-boosting child's play.

During the early sections of the novel especially, Faulkner's descriptions of Temple emphasize her childishness.

> Temple was sitting on the bed, her legs tucked under her, erect, her hands in her lap, her hat tilted on the back of her head. She looked quite small, her very attitude an outrage to muscle and tissue of more than seventeen and more compatible with eight or ten. (S, p. 67)

Not only do descriptions suggest Temple's childishness, but her behavior is childish; she is unthinking, naïve, and easily frightened. She is intensely upset by the rats which invade her sanctuary in the barn at the Old Frenchman's Place, and at the sight of them she childishly hurls herself upon Ruby, "flinging her arms about her, trying to snatch both feet from the floor." Childishly, she asserts that the governor's soldiers will be called in to save her from "the bad men," and, appropriately, the dreaded rape finally occurs in the corn "crib."

The nature of Temple's childishness is especially well indicated in her relationship with Popeye. Instead of fear, Popeye inspires in her a childish impudence. At the Old Frenchman's Place she sneeringly insults him and secretly dares his assault — "Come on touch me, you coward." As they drive to the Grotto on the evening of Red's death, Temple subjects Popeye to repeated childish taunts; "You're scared to . . . . He's a better man than you are! . . . You're not even a man!" Temple naïvely underestimates Popeye's power. She assumes he will do as she says until she suddenly discovers the gun in his pocket. Only then does she realize the inevitability of Red's death. Yet, she is so overcome by her own selfish desires that she persists in actions which will assure that end.

The disasters that envelop Temple are the result of a combination of her cruelly selfish lust which makes her completely disregard the well-being of any other person and her childish naïveté which makes her incapable of anticipating the extent of the evils in which she is involved. It is obvious that Faulkner does not intend that Temple's "childishness" should indicate her innocence; instead, the motif signifies Temple's dangerous naïveté, her selfishness, and her unthinking and at times intentional cruelty — qualities which are also characteristic of children.

Temple's "childishness" makes her a more believable and fully developed character, but, also, it is the key to the pattern of symbolism which reveals the basic theme of the novel. Two brief scenes indicate that Temple's careless disregard for the needs and feelings of others, her cruelty, and her vain pride in sexual power are typical of adolescent behavior. During her first evening at the Memphis brothel, Temple recalls her "innocent" experiences at the university. Particularly vivid to her is an evening when she and other girls were dressing late for a dance.

The girls cruelly compared one another's naked bodies. In an agony of self-defense the ugliest girl in the group declared that boys thought "all girls were ugly except when they are dressed." The whole group was immediately upon her, forming a vicious circle about her demanding, "How do you know? until she told them and held up her hand and swore she had." It is typical of the adolescent world that status is determined by sexual powers and experiences. It is, nevertheless, a grossly immature and cruel way of judging persons. The girl is forced into lying, swearing that she has experienced the "initiation," in order to escape momentarily the ridicule of a group from which she is already excluded because of her physical ugliness. It is certainly the harshness and cruelty of the older girls' behavior which make sex seem so horrible that the youngest girl in the group runs out of the room, locks herself in the bath, and vomits.

During his train ride to the university in search of Temple, Horace becomes acutely aware of the harshness and cruelty of adolescent behavior.

> When the train came they pushed gaily forward, talking and laughing, shouldering aside older people with gay rudeness, clashing and slamming seats back and settling themselves, turning their faces up out of laughter, their cold faces still toothed with it, as three middle-aged women moved down the car, looking tentatively left and right at the filled seats. (S, p. 164)

Some of the students ride without tickets, teasing and confusing the conductor, then mocking him and laughing loudly at their own obscenities. Horace watches them block the aisles, touching each other with "casual and puppyish pawings," while "beyond the group a countrywoman with an infant in her arms stood braced against a seat. From time to time she looked back at the blocked aisle and the empty seats beyond." The disturbing uproar of their "thin, bright, raucous laughter" drowns out all other voices and their "voluptuous, purposeless" motion tramples over all other people.

The scene is an impressionistic replica of the treatment of Ruby Goodwin, the lower-class woman in calico with the infant in her arms, by Narcissa Benbow Sartoris and "her kind." Narcissa, the churchwomen of Jefferson, Judge Drake, his daughter Temple, and Horace Benbow represent a childish "in" group which selfishly preserves its prestige, exclusivism, and respectability at the expense of the lives and well-being of those outside of the group.

Narcissa's attitude toward the plight of Ruby Goodwin is as childishly selfish and callous as the behavior of Temple and her peers. Her arguments against Horace's helping Ruby are based entirely on her selfish effort to preserve her own respectability.

> "I don't care how many women you have nor who they are. But I cannot have my brother mixed up with a woman people are talking about . . . . I don't see that it makes any difference who did it. The question is, are you going to stay mixed up with it?" (*S*, p. 178)

When Narcissa finds arguing with Horace useless, she simply betrays his trust; justice is totally irrelevant to her. It is horribly ironic that Narcissa's insulting refusal of Gowan's marriage proposal probably precipitated his outrageous behavior with Temple on the following day which resulted in Temple's rape and the murder of Tommy.

The mob whose members can declare, "She was some baby, Jeez. I wouldn't have used no cob," and simultaneously burn a man to death for violating the "most sacred thing in life, womanhood," is the embodiment of the vicious destructiveness of false "innocence." Narcissa and "her kind" are in a terrible sense children — adolescents who condemn and crucify those who can not measure up to their own shallow values. The sheltered world of the socially prestigious has kept them "children" in evil, blind to the nature of the force of evil in the world and to the evil implications of their own actions. The innocence which they assume is, therefore, not only false, but disastrously destructive.

It is through the motif of "childishness" that Faulkner makes it clear that the evil of the fantasy underworld in Sanctuary is only a reflection of the less obvious but more insidious evil of the real world.[1] The private discoveries that Horace makes about himself, as he participates through Temple, Narcissa, and Ruby in the action of the novel, inform and complete this pattern of meaning.

Horace's failure to secure justice for his client, Lee Goodwin, is the result of his childish naïveté about reality. His "innocence" is indicated by his inability to comprehend the true nature of woman; he fails to anticipate the evil actions of Temple and Narcissa because he does not admit the reality and the extent of evil in human nature. Because he is one of the sheltered, Horace believes in the natural innocence of creation symbolized by the innocence of young virgins. When this belief is undermined, he relies on "law, justice and civilization" for man's salvation. However, Narcissa demonstrates that respectable society is a dangerous enemy to justice and virtue. Through Little Belle and Temple and through his sister Narcissa, Horace discovers evil and his own guilty involvement in it.

Through his experiences with Little Belle Horace learns that nature is not pure, but "pure dissimulation"; that childhood is not innocent, but depraved. Throughout the novel Horace wishes to interpret the luxuriant richness of spring as a sign of the ethereal innocence and goodness of creation. He wants to keep Little Belle in her white dress in the grape arbor where leaves and blossoms are still growing to fullness. He wishes to preserve her as the "still unravished bride" – to preserve her virginity as the sign of her innocence. However, Horace knows that spring ends; not only do the grapes blossom, but the blooms eventually die.

---

[1]Douglas Cole in "Faulkner's Sanctuary: Retreat from Responsibility," p. 296, suggests that Miss Reba's pride that her "house" is frequented by lawyers and policemen and her desire to protect the "good name" of her business are meant as direct parallels to Narcissa's pride in the "house where she was born" and her desire to protect her "good name" among the people of Jefferson. The parallels can be extended: Uncle Bud's beer drinking makes him a parallel of the childish Gowan Stevens; Red, who is sacrificed by Temple's evil, is the parallel of the lynched Lee Goodwin; and the wake scene in its wild chaos is a parallel of the mob scene.

Just as he is imagining that Little Belle weeps as he does for the "slain flowers, the delicate dead flowers and tears," he glimpses her face in the mirror.

"There was a mirror behind her and another behind me, and she was watching herself in the one behind me forgetting about the other one in which I could see her face, see her watching the back of my head with pure dissimulation. That's why nature is 'she' and Progress is 'he'; nature made the grape arbor, but Progress invented the mirror." (*S*, pp. 14-15)

The mirror reveals to Horace the truth about woman's nature. Though he wishes to equate Little Belle's virgin beauty with innocence and purity, he discovers that she is not spontaneous and unself-conscious but is, instead, consciously using her sexual powers to control him.

Like the marble faun Horace lives in an age in which the grape arbor has been corrupted; nevertheless, he clings unrealistically to the ideal of virgin purity. He cannot bear to watch Little Belle's maturation and resulting loss of innocence even though it is obvious that she herself is devoted to bringing about that end. Though Horace suspects Little Belle's capacity for evil, he refuses to admit its reality until after his encounter with Temple Drake. Horace has sought purity and goodness in the myth of virgin innocence; his experiences with Little Belle and the utter corruption of Temple literally explode the myth for him. Horace suffers because the fallen, trumpet-shaped blooms of the heaven-tree are lying dead all over the street; the passing of spring signifies for him the death of innocence.

Faulkner makes it clear, however, that Horace clings to his idealized view of woman to escape the reality of his own evil nature. Horace is upset not only because spring fades, but also because he has not had his "spring." He has desired an innocent woman, but because of his lust he married "somebody else's wife." Denied the innocent love he has sought, he allows himself to idealize his step-daughter's virginity. Horace is aware that his yearning for Little Belle is actually sexual, but he persists in idealizing his feeling. He engages in a dangerous dishonesty with himself, for in order to escape the reality of his own guilty desire, he must refuse to admit the virgin's capacity for evil. Because he clings unrealistically and hypocritically to the myth of innocence, Horace is totally unprepared for Temple's perjury. His failure to face the reality of the evil in himself, in Little Belle, and in Temple makes him partially responsible for the disastrous injustice to Lee Goodwin he has sought to prevent.

Horace also fails to comprehend the true character of his sister Narcissa or the forces of evil she represents. His faith that law and civilization are inevitably just is as fallacious as his belief that innocence is represented by girls in white dresses, virgins, spring flowers, and church bells. Even though he is willing to indulge in paying off Clarence Snopes for information, he simply cannot believe that in the high office of district attorney Eustace Graham would do the same. Horace is so busy carrying on his petty rebellion against his sister's authority, believing boyishly that he will have his way, that he is totally incapable of imagining the measures Narcissa is willing to take to be sure he fails.

In his inability to recognize and cope with evil, both his own and the evil of others, Horace is like a child. Lee Goodwin's judgment of him is entirely accurate: "What sort of men have you lived with in your life? In a nursery?" Horace's declaration, "My Lord, sometimes I believe that we are all children, except children themselves," is the truth, but in a horrible sense which Horace is never able to comprehend until after the trial and the mob scene. Horace is so blinded by the belief in the possibility of innocence that he does not grasp the significance of the merger of his own image with that of Popeye in the spring in the opening scene of the novel. Horace mistakes sexual innocence, childhood, for moral innocence when, in truth, it is the point of the novel that it is man's childishness which he must overcome if he is not to be destroyed by evil.

The full horror of the childishness of Temple, Narcissa, and Horace is personified by Popeye who, significantly, is also described as a child. Popeye is small in stature, thin and childlike in appearance. Horace comments, "He wouldn't drink . . . he wouldn't stay and talk with us; he wouldn't do anything: just lurking about, smoking his cigarettes, like a sullen and sick child" (*S*, p. 105). Paralyzed by his impotence, Popeye is horribly pathetic when he visits Temple at the brothel. "Watching his face, she saw it beginning to twitch and jerk like that of a child about to cry, and she heard him begin to make a whimpering sound" (*S*, p. 154). Popeye is the physical image of the real nature of society's cruel childishness; significantly, he is both created and destroyed by acts of irresponsibility and immaturity.

The underworld in *Sanctuary*, the world of Popeye and Red, of Miss Reba's brothel and Uncle Bud, is a fantasy world created to symbolize the evil that is rampant in the real world of Jefferson — in the foolishness of Gowan Stevens, the vulgar greed of Clarence Snopes, the petty ambition of Eustace Graham, the deadly drive for respectability in Narcissa Sartoris, the debauchery and senseless perjury of Temple Drake, and the blindness and naïveté of Horace Benbow. The final disastrous miscarriage of justice in *Sanctuary* is the result of the childish, immature, and irresponsible behavior of the people of Jefferson who knowingly and unknowingly align themselves with Popeye. The alternative to Popeye's evil is to be found in the qualities of responsible motherhood which Ruby Goodwin embodies.

Ruby's character indicates that man can achieve virtue if he is willing to accept his inevitable involvement with evil and to replace his childish selfishness with maturity and self-sacrifice. With each successive appearance of Ruby in the novel there is an increasing sense of the dignity and pathos that surround her figure. After Lee's arrest she no longer wears the faded calico dress, but, instead,

> . . . a dress of gray crepe, neatly brushed and skillfully darned by hand. Parallel with each seam was that faint, narrow, blazed imprint which another woman would recognize at a hundred yards with one glance. On the shoulder was a purple ornament of the sort that may be bought in ten cent stores or by mail order; on the cot

beside her lay a gray hat with a neatly darned veil . . . . (*S*, p. 112)

The description effectively establishes a new sense of Ruby's character; she has ceased to struggle against the overwhelming forces of evil, but she is determined to endure her fate with dignity. The neatness of the garment and the mended veil are the signs of Ruby's self-respect and pride; yet, the gray dress and veil suggest her humility and sense of true propriety.

The garments also signify Ruby's poverty, a poverty which is shamed by the sneers of the women who would notice that her dress is made-over. As the novel progresses, the "respectability" of Jefferson society forces Ruby into a series of increasingly degraded dwellings — from Horace's home, to the hotel, to the jail and finally to a rat-infested lean-to shed room owned by another outcast white woman. Ruby's superiority to Horace is indicated by her anticipation of each of these moves and her ability to cut through his pretentious explanations with the truth about the situation. She knows that Horace is controlled by his kinfolks, "women that used to live in this house," and she accepts their persecution as punishment due her for past involvement with evil. She accepts Horace's aid also as a part of that punishment, for there is nothing else she can do. Her commitment to her vision of goodness forces her, for the sake of Temple herself, to follow Horace's advice, even though she must have guessed the inevitable outcome of her testimony.

On the evening before her husband's conviction, Horace brings Ruby some chocolates. He insists that she partake of the worthless sign of affluence and childishness. As she tells him the tragic story of her past, she fingers the candy, mussing her hands and throwing away two before one is eaten. Horace offers her his handkerchief, but Ruby refuses and instead wipes her hands with a soiled diaper. Essentially, such actions serve to establish the realism of the scene, but they are also superbly meaningful. Horace has forced on Ruby his useless aid which, ironically, leads to the tragic outcome of her life. But her humility, her sense of the inadequacy of her social position, forbids that she even allow him to clean up after the mess he has made.

Ruby Goodwin is clearly the noblest character in *Sanctuary*. Her devotion to Lee Goodwin and her willingness to be servant even to the vileness of creation — blind Pap, the idiot Tommy, the villain Popeye — make her an effective contrast to the proud, disdainful, and disloyal Narcissa. Her knowledge of men and her capacity for self-giving love make her the counterpoint of the superficial, naïve, and selfish Temple Drake. Her "feminine reserve of unflagging suspicion of all peoples' actions which seems at first to be mere affinity for evil but which is in reality practical wisdom" (*S*, p. 194) makes her far superior to her presuming helper, Horace Benbow. Because of her devotion to her illegitimate family Ruby possesses a quality of transcendence, of peaceful feminine immobility, which Horace observes is as apparent, yet intangible, as electricity.

Throughout the later parts of *Sanctuary* Ruby is constantly engaged in the realistic activity of caring for her sick baby; she warms bottles, changes diapers, and scrubs the ragged blankets until they are white. She is devoted to the preservation of the life of the helpless infant. The constant protective motions of her hands about the child's face express her intense concern and affection. The child represents human life; its frailty suggests the sickness of humanity. It can survive only if it is nourished by a responsible mother. Ruby's selfless devotion to the sustenance of life is the quality which humanity requires if it is to escape moral disaster.

The Sound and the Fury and *Sanctuary* demonstrate that the idealization of virginity leads to moral chaos and death. When Quentin and Horace cling to that ideal, they are refusing to face their own involvement in evil and the inescapable reality of evil in human existence. Horace and Quentin — mankind — desperately need the qualities which are embodied in responsible motherhood. The mother's self-forgetfulness, her service to man's basic needs, and her commitment to the sustenance of life represent Faulkner's vision of the most noble way in which man can cope with the evils and limitations of the human situation. The women in *The Sound and the Fury* and *Sanctuary* are strikingly vivid, fully realized characters who convey powerfully and effectively woman's capacity both for destroying life and for sustaining it.

PART III
WOMAN: THE IMAGE OF DEATH

CHAPTER V

Sexual Perversity and Sterility

In *The Sound and the Fury* and *Sanctuary* Faulkner makes it clear that in the face of familial and social decay the only source of moral order and endurance is woman's ability to fulfill the creative and sustaining role of motherhood. Woman's purpose is the bearing of children and in her submission to that process she achieves serenity and virtue. This submission to the natural sexual process is a response to the need of human life for the nourishment supplied by love and security. It symbolizes the woman's moral decision to act for the good of others without regard for herself. For Faulkner the perversion of sexuality is a destructive force in human life and is equated with death itself because it is indicative of evil and selfishness. The destructive nature of perverted sexuality is powerfully conveyed by Faulkner's characterization of Mrs. Compson and of the adult Caddy in *The Sound and the Fury* and of Temple Drake in *Sanctuary*.

A considerable number of the works of the middle years of Faulkner's career elaborate this theme by demonstrating that woman's failure to achieve sexual fulfillment through physical love and motherhood initiates her own decay. Woman's loss of the feminine role or her inability to live it with satisfaction results in her loss of life itself either through an actual death or a death-in-life existence. In the short stories, "Elly," *Miss Zilphia Gant,* "A Rose for Emily," "Dry September," and *Idyll in the Desert,* and in the novels, *As I Lay Dying* and *The Wild Palms,* Faulkner moves the emphasis away from the decay of society or the family to the decay of woman herself, though the effects of the one upon the other are never neglected. With the force of the negative, Faulkner reasserts the proper role of woman. Nevertheless, the women in these works are treated more with sympathy than with judgment. Faulkner is careful to delineate the way that environment and circumstance as well as their own private drives have determined the pattern of these women's lives.

Some of the women characters who are "images of death" are foreshadowed in Faulkner's earlier fiction. The family and social circumstances and the resulting sexual repression and decay of Mrs. Maurier in *Mosquitoes* make her much like Emily Grierson, Minnie Cooper, and Rosa Coldfield. The despair over the failure of love and the resulting introspection of Margaret Powers in *Soldier's Pay* make her a prototype of Addie Bundren. The perversion of physical love exhibited by Cecily Saunders and by Temple Drake is paralleled by the character of Elly and to a lesser degree by Zilphia Gant. Yet, these comparisons make it obvious that each character is distinctly herself, unique in physical appearance, gesture, routine, and outward circumstance. Though their doom is the same, the variation of individual character and situation makes each tragedy different.

In several of his short stories and in the case of Rosa Coldfield in *Absalom, Absalom!* Faulkner stresses the way that the circumstances of environment have forced a repression of a woman's natural drive for love and motherhood and have thus created in her an unnatural and perverted expression of sexual desire. In the two novels *As I Lay Dying* and *The Wild Palms* Faulkner presents heroines whose idealistic drives for complete fulfillment in physical love result in the isolation and death characteristic of the idealistic male heroes such as Bayard Sartoris and Quentin Compson. Addie Bundren and Charlotte

Rittenmeyer are doomed to death because they remain inflexible in the face of life's demand for adaptation. These two women are among the most interesting, complex, and fully rounded of Faulkner's female characters.

The short stories, "Elly" and *Miss Zilphia Gant*, present two women who are plagued by perverse sexuality. During their youth, both are controlled by women who condemn sexual desire and, in effect, deny the reality of its existence. In rebellion Elly and Zilphia over-indulge in sexuality which, in a perverted form, becomes the single driving force of their existence.

Though not among his most effective short stories "Elly" demonstrates well Faulkner's ability to arouse sympathy for a female character whose behavior makes her less than admirable. Focusing entirely on Elly's own emotional-intellectual awareness of herself and her predicament, Faulkner enables the reader to identify with her despite her extreme sexual perversity. Though the effects are greatly diminished by the limited scope of the short story, Faulkner's presentation of Elly makes her quite similar to Temple Drake. However, by repeatedly calling attention to the grandmother, whose cold sternness motivates Elly's actions, Faulkner makes even more apparent the direct relationship between cause and effect in this story than he does in the novel.

Elly's decay is already accomplished at the opening of the narrative. The sex act is for her a wild defiance of her grandmother's stern prohibitions and is performed solely to avenge herself upon this implacable woman. Elly engages in sexual play nightly though, like Temple Drake, she consistently refuses the final act which would make her unvirgin. Nightly, Elly returns to her room hating the acts but exulting in her revenge upon her grandmother, who sits up each evening until the young men leave never speaking the words of condemnation Elly expects but staring after her with "inescapable cold eyes." Elly's final defiance is intercourse with a man she and the grandmother believe to be part Negro. At their first meeting Elly finds herself at the brink of physical surrender to Paul yelling, " 'I wish she were here to see!' " (CS, p. 211). Suddenly, she senses the grandmother's presence; ready at last to sin completely, Elly is infuriated that she has been condemned " 'without even having time to sin.' "

Elly begs Paul to marry her so that she may bring the final outrage to the tradition the grandmother represents. Paul consistently refuses Elly, aware that she is using him sexually just as he is willing to use her. Repeatedly denied the fulfillment of her revenge, Elly commits a wild and criminal act: she pulls the steering wheel of the car in which she, Paul, and the grandmother are riding, causing it to careen over the edge of the road. Elly is thrown free of the wreck, but Paul and the grandmother are crushed to death. The final scene of the story reveals that Elly, like Temple Drake, remains essentially a child, naïvely unaware of the consequences of her act, whimpering in self-pity, "They [the cars passing overhead] won't even stop to see if I am hurt" (CS, p. 224).

Throughout the story the grandmother is a mysterious and foreboding figure, rarely speaking, but with the power of her stare seeming to determine totally Elly's extreme emotions and her senseless acts. Because little is known about the grand-mother's real attitude toward Elly's behavior, whereas much is known about Elly's interpretation of her grandmother's view of her, the reader is led to identify with Elly and to accept with her the grandmother's silent rebukes as the motivation for Elly's perverse behavior. Actions which would ordinarily arouse only harsh judgments because of their perversity become understand-able and pitiable. It is an indication of Faulkner's comprehen-sion of the complexity of human nature and of his great sympathy for humanity despite its failures that, as with the story of Elly, he is able to arouse sympathy and understanding even for those women whom he considers in the bonds of perversity, decay, and death.

Miss Zilphia Gant was published in a limited edition by The Book Club of Texas in 1932 and has yet to receive any wider circulation. Nearly all of Zilphia's life is traced in this rather lengthy narrative beginning with her mother's vengeful murder of her husband when Zilphia is only two years old and ending with Zilphia's half-peaceful adjustment to life in her late adulthood. Relying almost entirely on a chronological line as his narrative method, Faulkner fails to render Zilphia Gant's story as masterfully as he does the tales of Emily Grierson and Minnie Cooper. However, the story does accentuate a theme which is a major one in "A Rose for Emily" and "Dry September," which is that the fulfillment of woman's natural drives for physical love and motherhood is of extreme importance, not only to the private well being of the individual woman, but also to her ability to establish herself as an accepted member of her community.

Zilphia, like Elly, is the victim of a woman with perverse attitudes toward sexuality, but the prohibitions which this woman inflicts upon Zilphia are far more extreme than the grandmother's cold stare. Zilphia's mother is almost as important a character in the story as Zilphia herself. She possesses an intense hatred of men because her husband has run off to Memphis with a lover he met in a tavern. Acting with the "serene imperviousness of a vestal out of a violated temple," the mother goes to Memphis and murders her husband and his lover. Accompanied by her daughter, she moves into Jefferson and establishes a dressmaker's shop. There she rears her child in utter isolation, fearful that any contact with another human being may lead the child to the disaster that engulfed her own life.

The mother's treatment of Zilphia is horrendous. Bars cover the windows of the room where she sits idle throughout the day while her mother works. On one occasion she beats Zilphia until the child vomits. Zilphia becomes ill from "anemia and nervousness and loneliness and actual despair." When at a doctor's urging Mrs. Gant is forced to allow Zilphia to play with another child, the mother hides in a nearby cedar grove constantly watching over the children. On her thirteenth birthday Zilphia is told the story of the murdered father; thereafter, she is forced once each month to remove her clothing so that her mother can examine the growth of her body. Shortly afterwards, Mrs. Gant catches Zilphia lying in a ditch with a boy. The girl is taken out of school, and for twelve years she sits at the window of the shop while the other girls of the town marry and have children. Zilphia's fate seems irrevocable; the sense of inescapable doom surrounds the figure of the young woman barred from normal living.

However, Zilphia is suddenly, and rather coincidentally, freed from her bonds. A young painter comes to redecorate the shop. Since her mother is ill, Zilphia is left alone in the shop with the young man for several days. He falls in love with her, and they marry. However, before they are to leave Jefferson and consummate the marriage, Zilphia insists upon returning to see her mother once more. The husband hides for two days in an adjacent vacant lot waiting for Zilphia to emerge from the house. On the third day Mrs. Gant dies. For six months Zilphia continues to expect the painter to return for her, but he never returns. Unaware of the mother's death, he is convinced that Zilphia has permitted herself to become again enslaved. Until she is forty-two Zilphia Gant lives in a terrific struggle with her unfulfilled procreative drives.

> She would think about Christ whispering "Mary did it without a man. She did it;" or, rousing, furious her hands clenched at her sides, the covers flung back and her opened thighs tossing, she would violate her ineradicable virginity again and again with something evoked out of the darkness immemorial and philoprogenitive: "I'll conceive! I'll make myself conceive!" (ZG, p. 24)

When Zilphia discovers through a newspaper that her husband has remarried, she hires a detective to report on all his activities. For a time she lives a painfully unfulfilling vicarious marriage to the man which ends with an attempt at suicide when she learns that the new wife is pregnant. When both man and wife are killed in an accident, Zilphia leaves town for three years and returns with a child and a plain gold ring. Whether or not Zilphia actually married and gave birth to the child remains a mystery, for the reader is led to presume that the child is the orphan of Zilphia's dead husband, whereas the town, ignorant of her marriage to the painter, assumes that the child is Zilphia's own.

However, possession of the child proves sufficient to enable Miss Zilphia Gant to grow old peacefully. Gradually her furious and perverse dreaming subsides, and the onset of menopause frees her from physical desire. Keeping the little girl in a pleasant "day nursery" in the mother's sewing shop, the bars still at the windows, Zilphia at last assumes a normal life. Though the abnormality of her past clouds the serenity of her relationship to the child, its presence breaks Zilphia's isolation and initiates her acceptance into her community. The story concludes with the town's view of this strange woman: "She looked better; black became her. She was plump again in the wrong places, but to people in our town that and more is permitted a woman who has served her appointed ends" (ZG, p. 29).

This last line of Miss Zilphia Gant indicates Faulkner's insight into the role the community plays in the life of woman. In Faulkner's fiction the woman who is unable to serve her "appointed ends" is frequently denied a place of respect within her community, and her exclusion from the social group contributes to her personal decay. In "A Rose for Emily" and in "Dry September" the town's attitude toward the spinster women is of major importance in molding their lives toward the tragedy of isolation and sterility.

Both Emily Grierson and Minnie Cooper are the victims of an exclusive, depersonalizing society. Miss Emily is denied normal participation in the life of the community because she represents a traditional aristocracy of a higher social class than the norm. This situation, created by her ancestry and a father who refused to allow her a normal social life as a girl from the fear that she might marry beneath herself, is perpetuated by the community, which denies Miss Emily's humanity by thinking of her as their symbol of the past. Miss Emily is "a tradition, a duty, and a care"; the town prefers that she remain intact within her old mansion, an idol, "dear, inescapable, impervious, tranquil, and perverse" (CS, p. 128). Jefferson is smugly pleased at possessing a relic of a dead but honorable time; when Miss Emily dies, she becomes their "fallen monument."

Miss Emily is the source of mystery and intrigue for the community. Though she makes little or no effort during her adult life to become a part of the community, it is apparent that the people of Jefferson prefer that she remain a separated object, for upon her they can vent their feelings of hostility and inferiority, and at her expense they can enjoy their feelings of self-righteousness and success. The community experiences a self-comforting and self-vindicating pity when Emily reaches thirty and is still unmarried and when her buggy rides with Homer Barron convince them that she is a fallen woman.

Minnie Cooper is excluded from Jefferson society because she is of a social class slightly below the norm. As a youth she enjoyed full participation in her society; she was, indeed, one of its brightest "flames." Yet, when the age for marrying arrived, she became the victim of "the pleasure of snobbery — male — and retaliation — female." Miss Minnie even more than Miss Emily is a possession, not a member, of her community, and she is, as John Vickery ("Ritual and Theme in Faulkner's 'Dry September,' " p. 6) has suggested, its scapegoat. The young women can relish their success at marrying and producing children by observing Miss Minnie's failure. The town can vindicate itself by relegating her into adultery by public opinion when she makes her grasp at life by riding with the bank cashier in his red roadster. Like Emily's, Minnie's homelife is abnormal and debilitating. She lives with "a gaunt aunt" who runs the household, denying Minnie even that feminine role, and a mother who is totally an invalid. As a result her existence, like Emily's, becomes a "furious unreality" as she strives to express the human drives that her social situation has forced into repression.

Faulkner's description of Minnie Cooper's physical appearance conveys expertly the fragile illusions of her life. Her lace boudoir cap that she wears during her idle morning hours in the porch swing, the bright voile dresses that she dons on summer afternoons for window shopping, and the "sheerest underthings and stockings" and new pink dress that she wears to the movies

on the Saturday evening after Will Mayes's lynching suggest that
the forty-year-old woman is clinging to her lost adolescence.
Further, the garments provide an excellent pictorial parallel to
the fairyland "silver dream" of the picture shows, the unreal
but solitary outlet for Minnie's repressed dreams of love. The
constant "bright haggard" look of her face indicates the deathly
despair of her useless, sterile, and meaningless existence.

Miss Minnie's ultimate denial of reality is, of course, her
accusation of Will Mayes, an assertion which is, as Hawkshaw
the barber suggests, an expression of her repressed desires. The
implicit violence in Jefferson's denial of Miss Minnie's womanhood and in her accusation of the Negro as rapist is transformed
into the explicit and direct violence of the lynching of Will
Mayes. Momentarily, Minnie Cooper becomes again the center
of social attention, but she is unable to sustain this role.
Invaded by the horror of the reality of her life, she collapses in
hysterical laughter before the false image of the "passionate"
world that is forever lost to her in any creative and fulfilling
form.

Minnie Cooper is both victim and criminal, and her death-in-
life existence is the microcosm of the Jefferson "wasteland" of
sterility and violence. Throughout the story the "eternal dust"
remains inescapable, and at the denouement ". . . the dark
world seemed to lie stricken beneath the cold moon and the
lidless stars" (CS, p. 183). This image of cosmic death is
reminiscent of the cold world of reality faced by Faulkner's
marble faun; in "Dry September" there is no image of feminine
fertility to redeem the scene.

Faulkner's description of Emily Grierson's physical appearance is as revealing as his presentation of Minnie Cooper's. The
slender girl in white, the young woman who after her father's
death resembled "angels in colored church windows — sort of
tragic and serene" (CS, p. 124), becomes in her later years a
living image of decay and death.

> . . . a small, fat woman in black, with a thin gold chain
> descending to her waist and vanishing into her belt, leaning
> on an ebony cane with a tarnished gold head. Her skeleton

was small and spare; perhaps that was why what would have been merely plumpness in another was obesity in her. She looked bloated, like a body long submerged in motionless water, and of that pallid hue. (CS, p. 121)

Like Minnie Cooper, Emily is forced to become engaged in a defiance of time and reality. She refuses to live in the real world, ignoring the tax office, the post office, the law, and even death itself. She can hold her lover only if he is dead; her "marriage" is a horrible, grotesque opposite of normal physical love and wedlock. It is productive only of further signs of death — the "stubborn and coquettish decay" of the old mansion's exterior, the dark shadows that engulf its interior, and the persistent dust, the sign in this story as in "Dry September" of the omnipresence of mortality. Both Minnie Cooper and Emily Grierson lead idle and useless lives. Both women are driven to criminal acts in desperate attempts to simulate something of love's fulfillment. Their acts are neither life-giving nor redeeming; on the contrary they lead the two women further into frustration, perversion, isolation, and decay.

"Dry September" and "A Rose for Emily" reiterate Faulkner's theme that if woman is prevented from achieving the normal fulfillment of her sexual drives, she will become engaged in a denial of reality in which she clings to an illusory view of life in order to overcome her sense of the inadequacy and abnormality of her real existence. Engulfed by this death-in-life existence such women may be driven to perverse expressions of their sexual desires to the extent of performing criminal acts which are direct expressions of their sexual needs. The woman gradually becomes so entrenched in decay that her very appearance reveals her inner tragedy. Rosa Coldfield in *Absalom, Absalom!* is the most extensively developed woman of this type in Faulkner's fiction.

Like Emily Grierson and Minnie Cooper, Rosa Coldfield is a woman who has been excluded from the normal female role of marriage and motherhood. As a result she becomes in her middle years a character enshrouded by the signs of death. Like Emily and Minnie, Miss Rosa is dominated by unrealities and by a furious rage at man, who has denied her the normal fulfillment of her femininity. In skeletal outline these three women are much alike in character; in context they are each quite different, each uniquely drawn to contribute to the individuality of the narratives in which they appear. Miss Rosa is much more fully developed than either Emily or Minnie; an entire chapter of the novel is devoted to Rosa's revelation of her inner self, a view which is never available for the two women in the short stories. The outrage at life's betrayal which lies latent in Emily and Minnie is outwardly and immediately expressed by Rosa Coldfield's appearance, her words, and her actions.

Like her counterparts, Rosa is the victim of an abnormal family and a social situation which mold her life from early childhood toward a frustrated adulthood. Born to her parents during their middle age, Rosa spends her youth in isolation, her only sister already seven years married to Sutpen when she is born. Mr. Compson suggests that Rosa's mother's death in childbirth was an event for which Rosa never forgave her father. Motherless and sisterless she is left to a spinster aunt who rears her in "that cold masonry of females" in which she considers Rosa's very existence

not only the lone justification for the sacrifice of her mother's life, not only a living and walking reproach to her father, but a breathing indictment, ubiquitous and even transferable, of the entire male principle (that principle which had left the aunt virgin at thirty-five). (*A,A!*, pp. 59-60)

The "indictment" proves, indeed, to be transferable, for Rosa grows up in possession of a cold and implacable hatred of her father and her brother-in-law Thomas Sutpen, the "demon" who dominates her existence. Her hatred is not entirely unfounded, but it is nevertheless heightened, intensified, and exaggerated by the "grim mausoleum of Puritan righteousness and outraged female vindictiveness" supplied by the aunt. As if the combination of the aunt's vindictiveness and the father's eccentric morality were not enough to warp Rosa's attitude toward life, she is exposed from early childhood to Thomas Sutpen. Feeling the effects of the chaos that surrounds this mammoth figure long before she can understand it, she begins as a child the life-long process of escaping life, fabricating for herself a fantastic explanation for the impact which Sutpen makes upon her and her family. In Rosa's imagination Thomas Sutpen becomes ogre and demon, a visible and actual curse upon the Coldfields.

By the age of ten Rosa has abdicated existence; in no sense does she have a life in reality that is her own. Her private life is a fantasy world built upon her purely peripheral, bystander role in the Sutpen tragedy. Yet, in all the fury of her response to the Sutpen drama, Rosa Coldfield becomes a forceful and unforgettable character. She is a "ghost," not merely as Mr. Compson suggests all Southern women became after the war, but from her early childhood; yet, she is a very active and concrete ghost fully present because of the rage that moves and controls her, a rage that is conveyed by her words, her actions and her very appearance.

In the first paragraph of the novel Faulkner expertly establishes through concrete detail all the facets of Miss Rosa's character which are developed in the novel. That Miss Rosa is a woman who cannot escape the past is suggested casually by the comment that she calls her sitting room the office "because her father called it that." The room is darkened, shaded by closed blinds because once in her youth "someone had believed that light and moving air carried heat and that dark was always cooler." This detail verges on the symbolic; in her youth Miss Rosa made the choice between the light air of reality and the dark protective air of unreality. The darkness and the "yellow slashes" of light "full of dust motes" are the images of Rosa's present death-in-life existence. The effect is re-enforced by the "eternal black" of her garment worn perhaps for her sister, her father, or her "nothusband" as Quentin thinks, or perhaps for herself. The images of death, however, are broken by the wisteria vine smelling overly sweet in its second bloom, the symbol of her fourteenth summer's "enchantment of the heart," and by the images of Rosa as an enraged and frustrated child.

The fury of Rosa's "old female flesh" is continually juxtaposed — almost with the effect of the farcical — with images that convey her child-like appearance. In the first paragraph of the novel Quentin observes that as she sits "bolt upright" in her chair, Miss Rosa's feet are "clear of the floor with that air of impotent and static rage like children's feet." Throughout the novel the Sutpens treat Rosa as if she were a child. She is continually protected from and excluded from the crisis events of the Sutpen household because she is considered too immature to understand or share in the action. At the end of the novel when Quentin imagines Rosa in her old age facing the flames of the decayed Sutpen mansion, he envisions her as a "small, furious grim implacable woman not much larger than a child" struggling "with silent and bitter fury, clawing and scratching and biting" at the men who hold her to prevent her from plunging into the flames.

The image of Rosa as an enraged and frustrated child is fitting, for the rage and the frustration are the products of the childish fantasy of romanticizing and demonizing that has dominated her life and destroyed it. Chapter five of *Absalom, Absalom!* recounts the history of the Sutpen tragedy from the point of view of Rosa. The chapter reveals much about the inner being of Rosa Coldfield; it is designed to answer a question Rosa continually asks of herself — why was she willing to marry Sutpen, a man whom she had actively hated for most of her twenty years of life? The answer lies in Rosa's utter devotion to the dream of the "might-have-been," the product of her intense longing for the normal fulfillment of herself in love and marriage. The dream is born during her fourteenth summer when she falls in love with love; it is a dream inspired by a man she was never to see, Charles Bon. The fantasy is initially harmless adolescent romanticizing, but Rosa clings to it for five years, until Bon is killed, and then within another year she is able to transfer the dream to Thomas Sutpen, whom she has feared and hated since childhood.

Rosa's self-revelation begins with the announcement that she vastly preferred the dream of love to the reality of life. "... there is a might-have-been which is more true than truth, from which the dreamer, waking says not 'Did I but dream?' but rather says, indicts high heaven's very self with: 'Why did I wake since waking I shall never sleep again?' " (*A,A!*, p. 143). Moved by the romance of Judith and Charles, Rosa becomes entranced with love; she is stirred by the scene of every rendezvous, by the trace of every step in the garden, and by Bon's photograph glimpsed in a stolen moment, a portrait which needed no human parallel but merely "vague inference of some walking flesh and blood desired by someone else even if only in some shadow-realm of make-believe" (*A,A!*, p. 147). Rosa is completely aware that her "romance" is a fairy tale, a dream fantasy. The intensity of her feeling is explained only by the fact that she does possess a powerful urge for love, not, she admits, the bloom nor even the leaf,

> But root and urge I do insist and claim, for had I not heired too from all the unsistered Eves since the Snake? Yes, urge I do: warped chrysalis of what blind perfect seed: for who shall say what gnarled forgotten root might not bloom yet with some globed concentrate more globed and concentrate and heady-perfect because the neglected root was planted warped and lay not dead but merely slept forgot? (*A,A!*, p. 144)

It is thus that Rosa Coldfield, who knows that no man will ever consider her "as not more child than woman but even as less than any female flesh," and who at fourteen knew nothing of love, not even the love of parents, became "not mistress, not beloved, but more than even love; I became all polymath love's androgynous advocate" (*A,A!*, p. 146).

Rosa is both pathetic and comic as she pushes her desire for love to its extreme. During the years of the war, when Bon and Henry are away fighting, Rosa becomes a war poet. While she faithfully feeds the father who has shut himself in the attic to protest the South's stand, Rosa writes sentimental poetry about the glory of battle and the Southern heroes of war, a pastime fed by her dream of "romance." When she is nineteen and learns suddenly of Bon's murder, she recognizes for the first time that she has spent five years in a dream world in complete self-surrender to a shadow. Rosa is shocked when Judith, who she imagines has also spent the five years in the same dream, appears "standing calmly in a gingham dress" showing no sign of dismay or grief at Bon's death. Rosa is dazed by the turn of events, but she does not relinquish her dream. Remaining at Sutpen's Hundred after Bon's death and Henry's flight, she awaits Sutpen's return, not consciously aware that she awaits a marriage proposal, but aware that Sutpen is all that is left for her if she is to survive.

For a time Rosa experiences something of woman's fulfillment as she participates with Clytie and Judith in caring for the Sutpen plantation and finally for Sutpen himself. When the proposal comes, Rosa finds herself accepting as a marriage partner a man whom she has hated most of her life and whom she presently believes to be insane. Why? because the ogre had been momentarily dispelled by the wisteria summer, the glories of war, and the necessities of female living, reasons enough to make Rosa give in to what she later calls a "deluded sewer-gush of dreaming." When Sutpen makes his second proposal — that they cohabit and, if the offspring is male, they then marry — it is for Rosa an occasion which represents "the death of hope and love, the death of pride and principle, and then the death of everything save the old outraged and aghast unbelieving which has lasted for forty-three years . . ." (*A,A!*, p. 168).

It is the pivotal moment of Rosa's life, for this outrage molds her remaining years, which are spent in hopeless virginity and furious hatred. Rosa again retreats to her child's image of Sutpen as ogre and demon, a vision now enhanced in the horror it holds for her. "He was the light-blinded bat-like image of his own torment cast by the fierce demoniac lantern up from beneath the earth's crust and hence in retrograde, reverse; from abysmal and chaotic dark to eternal and abysmal dark . . ." (*A,A!*, p. 171). At twenty Rosa Coldfield accepts virginity and a death-in-life existence of hatred and decay as the unalterable

pattern of her remaining forty-three years of life. She remains a
child whose life has been built on fantasy and dreams which
when destroyed leave her with only the child's outraged
tantrum.

Rosa Coldfield's character is part of the larger motif in
Absalom, Absalom! of the failure of the female world to halt
the destructiveness of the male drive which is embodied in
Thomas Sutpen.[1] Sutpen is consumed by his dreams and is
incapable of submitting himself to the compromise with life
that woman and survival require.[2] Not only Rosa, but all the
women who encounter him are powerless victims of his selfish
design — his Haitian wife, Ellen Coldfield, who is as weak and
ineffectual as a butterfly, and Milly Jones, who is brutally
rebuked for her failure to bear him a son. The helpless virgin
white women, the debased octoroon women, and the per-
secuted Negro slave women are the victims of a masculine world
which they cannot overpower. The result is the creation of a
world which is characterized by impotence; Sutpen fails to
establish his dynasty and his dreams come to nothing. Judith's
endurance and acts of love are heroic, but because of her father,
her life and the hope that is embodied in her character are also
doomed to sterility. *Absalom, Absalom!* portrays the death and
decay that are the result of man's perverted use of woman to
achieve his selfish goals. Woman's potential powers for life are,
as a result, negated, and she becomes an ineffective force for
countering the male's destructive drives.

Elly, Zilphia Gant, Emily Grierson, Minnie Cooper, and Rosa
Coldfield lead tragic lives because they are unable to assume the
procreative role set aside for woman by the natural processes of
life. Alienated from the forces of life, they are idle, useless
women doomed to death and to sterility, the sign of death in
life. Their tragedies are in part the product of a society which
encourages sexual repression. Elly's stern grandmother, Zilphia's
mother, and Rosa's spinster aunt are cold and perverse women

---

[1]Cf., however, Thomas Lorch, "Thomas Sutpen and the Female Principle," pp.
38-42.

[2]See Olga Vickery, *The Novels of William Faulkner*, p. 97.

who reject the normal reproductive process of life. Likewise, because of their traditions of restrictive sexual mores, the communities of which Emily, Minnie, and Rosa are a part limit the woman's freedom to escape the bonds of death. Yet, these women are the rejected victims of the general social power, thrust into complete aloneness and isolation from the rest of humanity, because they have failed to serve woman's "appointed ends."

To compensate for their failure in real life, these women indulge in fantasy and make-believe in order to create for themselves a world in which their natures can be fulfilled. Such a denial of reality, however, is disastrous, for thereby the women give up all hope of entry into the real world and the assumption of a normal role within it. As a result these women emerge as fragile, child-like figures, incapable of accepting or comprehending reality, and as figures in black who are pallid and bloated with decay and death. With these women characters Faulkner creates superbly an outward appearance which is parallel to and symbolic of the psychological and spiritual condition of their lives. Despite their failure and their decay, Faulkner is able to portray them sympathetically. Grotesque as they may be, Elly, Zilphia Gant, and Minnie Cooper are pitiable characters, and the lives of Emily Grierson and Rosa Coldfield assume something of the nobility and grandeur of tragedy because of their complete expenditure of themselves in response to the events that mold their characters.

CHAPTER VI

The Female Idealist:
As I Lay Dying and *The Wild Palms*

Addie Bundren, the central character of *As I Lay Dying,* is one of Faulkner's most fully rounded female figures. Because of the complexity of her personality, Addie's character is something of an enigma. Some critics have focused on her admirable qualities and have viewed her sympathetically.[1] Others, focusing on her failures, conclude that she is meant to be a character who arouses severe judgment.[2] *As I Lay Dying,* like *The Sound and the Fury,* is an immensely complicated work which embodies a number of richly created themes. However, as in *The Sound and the Fury,* (the nature of woman and the importance of her impact on others, especially her family, are among the novel's major thematic concerns.) When the character of Addie Bundren is examined in relation to this theme, as it is revealed in *As I Lay Dying* and Faulkner's earlier fiction, the ambiguities of her character are largely resolved.

---

[1] See, for example, Olga Vickery, *The Novels of William Faulkner,* pp. 52-55, and Edward Wasiolek, *"As I Lay Dying*: Distortion in the Slow Eddy of Current Opinion," pp. 18-23.

[2] See Elizabeth M. Kerr, *"As I Lay Dying* as Ironic Quest," p. 8, and J. L. Roberts, "The Individual and the Family: Faulkner's *As I Lay Dying,*" p. 37.

Addie possesses the natural woman's drive for sexual union and procreation; she is completely feminine both as lover and as mother. When Anse fails her, she seeks the fulfillment of passionate love with Whitfield. Nevertheless, she bears four children by Anse and devotes a lifetime to keeping his house in order and caring for her family. Yet, these assertions require qualification. Though Addie's sexuality is never driven to perversity, neither is it satisfactorily fulfilled either by Anse or Whitfield. Though Addie is faithful to the duties of motherhood, she is never able to give herself to that role with absolute devotion and self-denial. Further, Addie's character has a dimension not frequently found in Faulkner's women. Addie is an idealist whose desire for the achievement of an inner vision of perfect union and fulfillment within human reality drives her ultimately to a rejection of reality, of humanity, and of life itself.

As I Lay Dying is another dramatization of Faulkner's vision of the polarities of choice available to man — man's choice to survive, which requires a compromise of personal visions of transcendence, and man's desire for the achievement of transcendence and ideality which, as his earlier fiction demonstrates, results in isolation and death. Faulkner's variation of the theme in As I Lay Dying indicates both his comprehension of the complexity of human life and the range of mood with which he is able to portray his theme. By exchanging in this novel his typical view of the male and female roles, Faulkner heightens the presentation in his fiction of life's irony and complexity.

Anse, despicable failure that he is, represents, as does woman ordinarily in Faulkner's fiction, mankind's capacity to survive. Addie, struggling admirably with the problems of identity and meaning, expects so much from life that she, like Faulkner's searching male heroes in Sartoris and The Sound and the Fury, loses life entirely, discovering that during all her years of intense striving she has, indeed, lain dying. Like Bayard Sartoris, Quentin Compson, and Horace Benbow, Addie Bundren has Faulkner's sympathy and his admiration; yet he is compelled to display the flaw in her view of life. Addie portrays, as do these male heroes, Faulkner's sense of the tragedy of the individual man's inevitable failure to attain any kind of absolute ideal within the complexities and limitations of reality. Anse, on the other hand, is comic, the sign of Faulkner's optimism about the destiny of mankind and its ability to survive. By allowing a woman to portray the role that is typical of his male heroes, Faulkner adds a new dimension to the presentation of woman in his fiction.

Faulkner develops Addie's character from a number of different angles; the reader's view of her is a composite of her family's and her neighbors' conscious and unconscious perception of her character and of her own self-revelation. The outward circumstances of Addie's life are delineated by the direct and objective statements made about her by her family, her neighbors, and herself. Limited though these views may be, they provide a needed reminder of the nature of Addie Bundren's public life. As Vernon Tull explains, Addie has led the "hard life" of the farm woman, bearing children and working every day rain or shine. For this faithful fulfillment of woman's duty, Addie possesses the respect and admiration of her community and her family and the right, when she is tired from it all, to lie down and die.

Addie's hardships, as she herself reveals, began in her childhood. Like many of Faulkner's women characters, Addie lacked the security of normal family relationships during her youth. When Anse seeks her out for marriage, she tells him that all the family she has lies dead in the Jefferson cemetery. The father, whom she does remember, possessed a cynical view of the meaninglessness of life comparable to the philosophy of Quentin Compson's father — ". . . that the reason for living is getting ready to stay dead." On the basis of this information it is possible to view Addie's life as doomed by the circumstances of her life as a child, a view which no doubt represents one facet of Faulkner's vision of her character. Denied normal family relationships as a child, she attempts as an adult to force relationships into being. When relationships fail her, she concludes that a vital life is altogether impossible and that she is, as her father warned her, already dying.

Particularly in her relationship to Anse, Addie feels the absence of vitality and spiritual intensity. Ironically, however, it is because of her marriage to Anse that she achieves the family she desires and needs and the acceptance of the community, which gives her some sense of belonging. Her children, Anse, and the neighbors compliment the way she has fulfilled this feminine role. Anse is proud of her cleanliness and orderliness and her efforts to bring up the boys "right." Her children sense the cleanliness of her character, knowing that above all she hated deceit. Even Cora Tull, who considers Addie proud and vain, irreverent of religion, and inadequate as a mother because she prefers one child above another, believes that Addie deserves the obvious reward of her death — freedom from Anse. Addie's neighbors respect her because she has endured Anse by fulfilling her duty to him. From all outward appearances Addie Bundren's life represents woman's normal fulfillment of the role of wife and mother with its accompanying hardships and satisfactions. It is significant that Faulkner allows this view of Addie to persist throughout the novel by making it the tacit assumption of most of the characters, despite the fact that a number of them on various occasions sense Addie's unrest and inner struggle.

The discrepancy between the outward appearance of Addie's life and its inner reality is made apparent by Addie's revelation of her inner self. At the opening of her chapter she gives an account of the feelings aroused in her by nature in early spring. As a young woman she was deeply stirred by the natural beauty of a secluded spring — ". . . the water bubbling up and away and the sun slanting quiet in the trees and the quiet smelling of damp and rotting leaves and new earth . . ." (*AILD*, p. 161) — and by the haunting cries of the wild geese flying north for the summer.

> Sometimes I thought that I could not bear it, lying in bed at night, with the wild geese and their honking coming faint and high and wild out of the wild darkness, and during the day it would seem as though I couldn't wait for the last one to go so I could go down to the spring. (*AILD*, p. 162)

The emotions aroused in Addie by the beauty of the rebirth of nature in springtime are the vague tremblings of sexual desire in itself symbolic of a deep need for life's vitality and fulfillment. Addie repeatedly comments that the feeling is most intense in early spring. The emotion is the same as that aroused in the marble faun when he is called by the pipes of Pan into the world of eternal spring. Addie is possessed by the same intense yearning as Faulkner's male Romantics, an emotion which partakes both of sexual desire and the desire for self-transcendence and the achievement of absolute union and emotional fulfillment.

Because Addie possesses the Romantic's desire for union, she abhors the sense of isolation she recognizes as the very essence of her life as an unmarried school teacher. Addie beats the school children in a futile attempt to force them into a relationship of identity with her. However, they are not her children; they do not belong to her, and she cannot achieve with them the fulfillment of the need within her. The desires aroused in Addie can be fulfilled in her world only by marriage and motherhood, a pattern of life which can bring to a woman the complete physical and spiritual union with another human being that results in the ultimate denial of human isolation and mortality — the creation of new life. However, the desire and the dream that are stirred in Addie are so powerful that she is overcome by the need for an absolute fulfillment, a kind of fulfillment which proves impossible for her in real life. Like Faulkner's earlier Romantics, Addie is defeated by life's limitations. When Anse appears in the midst of her dreaming with a proposal of marriage, she finds her need so intense that she does not pause to study the nature of Anse's character but accepts him immediately as a promising alternative to her loneliness and isolation. The trick of reality is that Anse not only is incapable of fulfilling Addie's physical need for a sense of union, but also is totally incapable even of comprehending the nature of her emotions.

Addie recognizes the absence of fulfillment in her relationship with Anse only after she conceives her first child.

Pregnancy brings to her the sense of union and vital life she has been seeking:

> And when I knew that I had Cash, I knew that living was terrible and that this was the answer to it . . . . I knew that it had been, not that they had dirty noses, but that we had had to use one another by words . . . and that only through the blows of the switch could my blood and their blood flow as one stream. I knew that it had been, not that my aloneness had to be violated over and over each day, but that it had never been violated until Cash came. Not even by Anse in the nights. (*AILD*, pp. 163-164)

With Cash's birth Addie momentarily achieves a sense of absolute fulfillment; the ideal vision of unity, oneness, and wholeness becomes reality for her. That love is only a word to Anse matters not at all, for Addie's fulfillment is found in Cash alone. It is precisely this that makes the birth of Darl an outrage.

Idealist that she is, Addie makes Cash and her feelings about him into an absolute. With Darl she is forced to become not one with Cash but three; with the multiplication of the ideal it ceases to possess its unique and absolute quality. Addie's image of fulfillment is inflexible; she clings to the inner vision despite the fact that experience demonstrates that the ideal fades into the real, and pregnancy becomes an oft repeated pattern initiated, to Addie's outrage, by Anse's empty acts in the night. Compromise is impossible for Addie; she cannot discover with Darl the fulfillment she found with Cash, and she is unwilling to sacrifice her vision for the good of her child. Rather than admitting that marriage is not all she expected and accepting its limitations as a quality of living reality, Addie concludes that if marriage and childbirth do not bring the ideal fulfillment she has imagined, then being wife and mother are merely another aspect of the death of which her father warned. Anse is to her a dead body lying with her at night, and in her imagination her two sons become mere words, names which "would die and solidify into a shape and then fade away."

To Addie words represent the limitations of reality, the sign that human beings do not experience in reality the full meaning of the words they use. To Addie, Anse and her neighbors live by words alone, never experiencing the full impact of their meaning. Addie wishes to be fully alive at every moment; when life fails to measure up to her vision, she believes that she too has been tricked by words, for sex and love and motherhood bring only partial fulfillment. It is at this point in her life that she conceives of her revenge on Anse. Realizing that living is deadening, she knows that she belongs not with her live Bundren family, but with her dead family in the Jefferson cemetery.

Though she rejects the possibility that the circumstances of her life with Anse can bring her fulfillment, Addie makes peace with reality by refusing to expect more of Anse than he can give. This is to her the complete fulfillment of her duty to him. However, the yearning that stirred her before her marriage remains a powerful force in her inner life. Lying in the dark by the "dead" Anse, Addie would listen to

> the dark land talking of God's love and His beauty and His sin; hearing the dark voicelessness in which the words are the deeds, and the other words that are not deeds, that are just the gaps in peoples' lacks, coming down like the cries of the geese out of the wild darkness in the old terrible nights, fumbling at the deeds like orphans . . . . (*AILD*, p. 166)

The deeds of Addie's life seem to her no parallel to the emotions stirred in her by the cries of the geese and by the "red bitter flood boiling through the land." Therefore, she concludes that her first duty is not loyalty to Anse or her children but is instead "the duty to be alive," to her the total enactment of the meaning of the words.

The words Addie chooses to enact are sex and sin; she flings herself with complete abandon into an intense sexual relationship with Reverend Whitfield. The act stirs her emotions, for it is a secret, illicit affair, a defiance of normality and of the limitations of reality. Further, the sin is glorified in Addie's imagination by her partner's sanctity. Addie thinks of their sin "as garments which we would remove in order to shape and coerce the terrible blood to the forlorn echo of the dead word high in the sky" (*AILD*, p. 167). Addie is determined to act without deceit, and she is convinced that she has at last experienced a deed that parallels in reality the full meaning of the word men use for it. However, Whitfield proves as inadequate a lover as Anse. Once his lust is filled, he loses courage and abandons Addie. He certainly does not live up to the image which Addie projects of him. When Jewel, Whitfield's son, is born, Addie ceases her struggle with life. She watches the child's birth, and with its capping and suturing "the wild blood boiled away and the sound of it ceased." The birth of Jewel marks the end of life for Addie. The only task left to her is "to clean up after herself," a task which is the product of Addie's practical feminine logic. She gives Anse Dewey Dell to negate Jewel and Vardaman "to replace the child I robbed him of."

Addie Bundren is an admirable woman. She possesses a deep desire for a vital life; she seems created to enjoy the fullest rewards of womanhood. She is to be pitied that Anse should prove to be utterly lacking in the spiritual sensitivity and deep emotion that she possesses. Addie is a woman of intelligence, courage, and integrity. She is able to discern the crucial events of her life and to recognize where life has failed her. Despite her despair, she maintains her devotion to her inner vision and simultaneously fulfills her duty as wife to Anse and mother to her children. She lives her life with absolute sincerity and seriousness, molding her acts to the values she idealizes.

Nevertheless, Addie's life is one of negation and partial fulfillment. She does reject her children; she does burden them with the emotional turmoil that plagues her. She achieves no genuine satisfaction in her marriage and, therefore, she refuses the joy she might have found in giving herself to her children. She suffers because she is not loved, but she herself proves incapable of loving either her husband or her children. Life has failed Addie, but also Addie fails life. By refusing to enter life on its own terms, Addie loses it completely.

Faulkner's characterization of Addie is enriched by his portrayal of her relationship to each of her children. A number of critics have demonstrated in varying ways that the personalities and problems of the Bundren children are to a large degree the product of their mother's personality and her inner struggle.[1] It is certain that particular characteristics of each of the children do assist in reinforcing and re-interpreting the many facets of Addie's character. As a result, their characters offer a final judgment upon hers.

Dewey Dell is much like Addie in her intense response to the physical sensations of pregnancy. Though she appears quiet and simple-minded, she possesses much of Addie's sensitivity to the power of nature over her, and she reacts to the "seed" within her with strong emotions.

> I feel my body, my bones and flesh beginning to part and open upon the alone, and the process of coming unalone is terrible .... The dead air shapes the dead earth in the dead darkness, further away than seeing shapes the dead earth. It lies dead and warm upon me, touching me naked through my clothes .... I feel like a wet seed wild in the hot blind earth. (*AILD*, pp. 59 and 61)

Though Dewey Dell fears giving birth to her child because of its illegitimacy and, therefore, actively seeks abortion, she is comically defeated in her efforts. The child survives in her womb. Like Dewey Dell herself, who is the true child of her father, the child is certain to survive. By the end of the novel Dewey Dell has accepted her fate.

It is important to note also that though Dewey Dell is immensely concerned with her physical condition throughout the novel, she is not the egoist many critics accuse her of being.[2] Like Addie, she faithfully fulfills the woman's role of caring for the family. She is at her mother's bedside until Addie

---

[1] See Olga Vickery, *The Novels of William Faulkner*, pp. 55-62; Irving Howe, *William Faulkner*, pp. 130-132; and Jack Goellner, "A Closer Look at *As I Lay Dying*," pp. 44-45.

[2] See for example, Irving Howe, *William Faulkner*, p. 133, and Elizabeth Kerr, "*As I Lay Dying* as Ironic Quest."

dies; though she is engulfed by her personal despair, she must prepare food for the family and care for Vardaman. Throughout the journey to Jefferson she repeatedly wipes Cash's mouth and face with her skirts when he is ill. Until the new Mrs. Bundren is acquired, Dewey Dell must provide the family with its basic necessities for physical survival. This duty she fulfills as faithfully as did her mother, though like her mother she is burdened with the turmoil of her own inner struggle.

Cash, Addie's oldest son, is considered by the community to be the most sane and responsible of the Bundren children. He is the child of Addie's momentary peace and fulfillment, a fact which perhaps accounts for his admirable adjustment to and acceptance of life with all its hardships and limitations. Cash's endurance of pain without complaint reflects this quality of acceptance, but it is also apparent in his readiness to adjust his view of ideals to the necessities of reality. Though he senses that Darl's burning of the barn is in one sense a noble act, and that there is a narrow line between the sane and the insane, he is compelled to be practical and to recognize the requirements for survival in reality. He concludes, "I dont reckon nothing excuses setting fire to a man's barn and endangering his stock and destroying his property. That's how I reckon a man is crazy . . . . And I reckon they ain't nothing else to do with him but what the most folks say is right" (*AILD*, p. 223). Thus Cash allows Darl to be sent to Jackson. Cash's morality is hardly idealistic, but it is practical and realistic. His character parallels the public character of Addie and by comparison offers another reminder of Addie's devotion to the role she could fulfill, the performance of her duty as wife and mother.

Darl and Jewel are the mysterious sons of the Bundren family, and they reveal most about Addie's inner self. Darl's inner turmoil is the result of Addie's knowledge of life and her despair. Like his mother Darl is intelligent and extremely sensitive to the real nature of human relations. He guesses the nature of his mother's character and the secret motivations of each member of the family in making the journey; thus he senses the horror of the whole macabre episode. Darl sees the truth of the limitedness of human beings in the microcosm of his own family, and because he sees sharply the discrepancy between the ideal and the real, he is, like his mother, driven to the agony of too much knowledge. Because he possesses Addie's insight into the essential isolation of the individual, he experiences her outrage, disappointment, and despair at the inevitable failure of man to achieve identity, meaning, and union. He sees in reality only insanity and absurdity, an absurdity which he is unable to bear. As a result, he is driven out of life; he loses his chance for normality when he is wafted off to the insane asylum by the sensible Bundrens, who prefer to be free from exploring themselves deeply. Darl feels too intensely the discrepancy between reality and ideality; knowing too much, he is driven to isolation and hopeless despair. His character reveals the end product of Addie's commitment to ideality.

Jewel is the product of Addie's defiance of normality, her sin with Whitfield. He is her favorite son, petted and whipped more frequently than the others because she senses an identity with him that she feels with none other of her children. Jewel is the son that Addie prophesies will be her salvation; he represents the very inner core of her selfhood. Jewel and his horse are the symbols of Addie's driving energy for vital and intense life.

> Then Jewel is enclosed by a glittering maze of hooves as by an illusion of wings; among them, beneath the upreared chest, he moves with the flashing limberness of a snake .... Then they are rigid, motionless, terrific, the horse back-thrust on stiffened quivering legs, with lowered head; ...
> They stand in rigid terrific hiatus, the horse trembling and groaning. Then Jewel is on the horse's back. He flows upward in a stooping swirl like the lash of a whip, his body in midair shaped to the horse. (*AILD*, p. 12)

As with the horse in *Sartoris*, the vitality and power of Jewel's horse signifies masculine virility. Before the birth of Jewel Addie declares that all of her children are of her alone; Addie is like Bayard Sartoris in her desire to wrest the vitality from life in isolation. Unable to find satisfaction in her relationship to Anse or Whitfield, Addie turns in upon herself, relying wholly on her own vitality to bring her fulfillment and immortality. Jewel upon his horse parallels Addie's isolation, her rigidity, and the forcefulness of her personality. Though Jewel saves Addie's dead body from flood and fire, the power he represents is finally overthrown. Jewel is forced to sell his horse and to submit himself to Anse so that his mother can be buried in Jefferson.

The comic overrules the tragic in *As I Lay Dying*. It is Addie who fails and Anse who triumphs. The irony is heavy, for Faulkner felt with bitterness the defeat of ideality; yet, he asserts the final victory of man who survives in spite of himself. Anse, the epitome of puny and faltering but comic mankind, cannot fail. His neighbors, even God himself, are bound to aid him. He achieves the fulfillment of his promise to Addie despite intense summer heat, the odor of decay, fire, and flood, and in addition he gets some new teeth and a new wife. *As I Lay Dying* demonstrates that it is impossible for man or woman to force out of life a reality that matches the idealism of an inner vision. To persist in devotion to ideality rather than to reality results in personal isolation, individual decay, and death. Submission to life, expecting no good luck in it and accepting fully the limitations of the human situation, enables man to survive.

Charlotte Rittenmeyer, the heroine of *Wild Palms,* is a character much like Addie Bundren; she possesses a great sensitivity to life's limitations and possibilities and, like Addie, she is a woman of courage and integrity. But also, like Addie, Charlotte has the fatal flaw of devotion to idealism. Harry Wilbourne is the central intelligence in *Wild Palms,* but because his mind is constantly preoccupied with Charlotte's personality, her words, and her actions, she emerges as the novel's central character, just as Addie Bundren is the central character of *As I Lay Dying* because she is the center of concern of all the other narrators. The descriptions of Charlotte's physical appearance and gestures, the portrayal of her emotions through her activities, her own comments about her concept of love, and

Harry's comments about her combine to present a character of depth and complexity.

Though their first meeting initiates a sudden and intensely romantic love affair between Charlotte and Harry, Faulkner's description of Charlotte's physical appearance is anything but a romantic presentation. Throughout the novel Faulkner emphasizes Charlotte's broad stature and blunt facial features, qualities which combine with numerous other details to suggest that her appearance is slightly masculine. Harry observes that her face "laid no claim even to prettiness" and that her art work made her hands rough and manly.

There is much that is masculine about Charlotte's character. She is the companion of males; the only girl among four brothers, she married Rat simply because he was the friend of a beloved brother. During her relationship with Harry the only other friendship she makes is with another man, McCord. There is never any feminine intimacy between her and Billie, the woman she lives with in the Utah mining camp. Charlotte possesses no fragile femininity; she is physically a hard and solid woman, capable of extensive physical activity. In her relationship to Harry it is she who assumes the male's role; sexually she is the aggressive partner; it is she who labors and brings economic support to their liaison; it is she who is the superior, dominating force in their relationship. Charlotte is independent, self-controlled, and self-determining, whereas Harry in comparison to her is passive and submissive to the power which she wields over him.

However, Charlotte's masculine qualities are continually juxtaposed with Harry's intense awareness of the power of her femininity. He is continually amazed at her feminine skill at mastering the "mechanics of cohabitation" and at making respectable a relationship that to him is criminal. When he leaves New Orleans with Charlotte on the train, he feels a momentary alignment with her husband, the man who is supposed to be his enemy, because he knows that both of them are "doomed and lost, before the entire female principle" which Charlotte embodies. Repeatedly, Harry notes that behind what appears to be a quality of masculinity in Charlotte there lies a quality of femininity. Charlotte's handwriting which at first strikes him as the "big sprawling untrained hand" of a man, he recognizes an instant later as "profoundly feminine." Harry's observation of Charlotte as she comes to meet him and McCord at the bar during the Christmas season in Chicago again combines the faintly masculine appearance with a primeval quality of femininity.

> . . . her hat of the current off-the-face mode thrust back still as if she had pushed it there herself with a sweep of the forearm in the immemorial female gesture out of the immemorial female weariness, approaching the table, her face pale and tired-looking though she moved as strongly and surely as ever, the eyes as humorlessly and incorrigibly honest as ever above the blunt strong nose, the broad pale unsubtle mouth. (*WP*, p. 124)

Though she possesses the qualities of the "immemorial female," Charlotte Rittenmeyer is not simply some symbolic representation of the primeval feminine. Instead, Faulkner quite expertly reduces her to the human and the real by making her physically unattractive, even somewhat manly. As a result her character takes on an added quality of roundness and reality. Further, the full nature of Charlotte's character and the meaning of her tragedy are made clear by Faulkner's repeated juxtaposition of her masculine and feminine qualities.

The sense of the complexity of Charlotte's character is developed through Harry's struggle to understand the nature of her personality and of the love she bestows upon him. However, Harry's view of Charlotte is greatly affected by his own self-understanding, and the reader's comprehension of Charlotte's character must surpass Harry's understanding of her. From the moment their relationship is initiated until Charlotte's death, Harry consistently feels inferior to his lover. He considers himself ignorant about love, lacking in Charlotte's courage of defiance, her daring, her wisdom, and her sensitivity. Until his decision that they go to the Utah mining camp, Harry remains dependent upon Charlotte, relying completely on the strength of her personality to save her from destruction and on her faith in love to save him.

The reader's sense of Charlotte's strength of character is continually reinforced by Harry's awareness of his own weaknesses. His dependence, his lethargy, his confusion, and his sense of inevitable failure make Charlotte's independence, activity, happy self-confidence, and intense faith in love completely admirable. Harry has drowned "volition and will in the yellow stare," and he is as powerless before the flood of her sexual passion and dominating personality as is the tall convict in the face of the yellow flooding river. In this state of eclipse from reality Harry is incapable of work or meaningful activity. It is this idleness which at last brings his dependence to a close; at the Wisconsin lake he realizes that while Charlotte is completely occupied with painting, swimming, lying in the sun, and "bitching," he is occupied with nothing and is, despite his pleasure in their sexual relationship, extremely bored.

This realization represents the climax of a vague sense of insecurity and dissatisfaction which Harry has felt since the initiation of their affair. Unable to resist Charlotte's passion, he is also unable to overthrow his own past. Throughout the first months in Chicago and at the lake Harry is constantly noting slight gestures and activities of Charlotte which he interprets as her efforts to make their relationship look respectable. Her work, her selection of apartments, her feminine efforts at rearranging the objects in their lodging are to Harry Charlotte's attempts to make their relationship into a normal marriage. Two episodes at the lake suggest that Harry is quite wrong about Charlotte in this respect. He is annoyed by their neighbor Bradley's "predatory," accusing eyes; however, Charlotte exults in it — "Don't you know yet that we just don't look married, thank God, even to brutes?" Later with their food supply nearly gone, Harry suggests that he return alone to the city to find work, but Charlotte replies, "No! No! Jesus God, no! Hold me! . . . This is what it's for, what it all was for, what we were paying for: so we could be together, sleep together every night . . ." (*WP*, p. 118).

Gradually, Harry begins to realize that Charlotte is not at all interested in marriage or respectability. Instead, the kind of love they share requires that they sever all bonds with society. In his long speech to McCord in explanation of the Utah scheme, Harry admits that his loss of virginity put him momentarily in eclipse, outside of time, and that he has floated on the periphery of reality, relying upon Charlotte to keep "balanced and intact above disaster" the "fragile globe" of their love. Harry at last realizes that he has resented the lack of respectability in their relationship. It is this that is the basis for his sense of inferiority to Charlotte; the faith he had in love was only a by-product of her faith. Only by devoting himself for a time to the pursuit of respectability does he recognize that the normal routine of respectable, economically secure marriage destroys the kind of love which he and Charlotte share. At last Harry is able to reject his past, to sever his bond with society, and to accept as completely as Charlotte has from the beginning the necessity of their isolation from the rest of the world. Harry is able to assert his own faith in love when he makes arrangements for them to go to the Utah mining camp, a setting which seems to Charlotte and Harry a suitable scene to preserve the relationship they share.

Juxtaposed with Harry's growing understanding of Charlotte and the nature of her love for him are a number of direct statements by Charlotte herself which define her attitude toward love. These comments provide the reader with an inner view of Charlotte's character; the result is that the sense of the irony and complexity that surround her character is increased, for the reader is able to perceive more about her than is Harry himself.

Until she meets Harry, Charlotte does not believe that love exists. She marries her husband not because she loves him, but because he is her brother's friend, and she cannot sleep with her brother. Charlotte's sudden emotion for Harry and his for her are mysterious, completely inexplicable except in terms of romantic love. By the time they have met for lunch several times, they are ready to admit their love for each other.

Charlotte willingly gives up her two children because she feels that she has learned

> what I had read in books but I never had actually believed; that love and suffering are the same thing and that the value of love is the sum of what you have to pay for it and any time you get it cheap you have cheated yourself. So I don't need to think about the children. (*WP*, p. 48)

For Charlotte love is no pastoral idyll; instead, she expects to pay for the love she has by hardship, labor, and starvation, a duty she is able to perform without failure or complaint. Nevertheless, her view of love is extremely idealistic; like Addie Bundren, Charlotte is determined to possess love absolutely, to be constantly, wholly, and intensely alive through the emotional force of love. Charlotte makes every sacrifice to assure that the emotion she feels for Harry does not fade. As they leave New Orleans, she demands that Harry engage a drawing room so that their love can be immediately consummated, and she can feel "Whole. Wholly lost — something." When they first settle in Chicago, Charlotte again attempts to explain to Harry her view of their relationship.

> "Listen: it's got to be all honeymoon, always. Forever and ever, until one of us dies. It can't be anything else. Either heaven, or hell: no comfortable safe purgatory between for you and me to wait in until good behavior or forbearance or shame or repentence overtakes us." (*WP*, p. 83)

Like Addie, Charlotte cannot be satisfied with life in the in-between; she sets out to defy the normal limitations of love and to preserve in an absolute form love's intensity and its vitality. When Harry realizes that she is actually in love with love, Charlotte admits that the source of her strength is not her love for Harry, but her faith and belief in the power of love itself.

> "They say love dies between two people. That's wrong. It doesn't die. It just leaves you, goes away, if you are not

good enough, worthy enough. It doesn't die; you're the one that dies. It's like the ocean; if you're no good, if you begin to make a bad smell in it, it just spews you up somewhere to die. You die anyway, but I had rather drown in the ocean than be urped up onto a strip of dead beach and be dried away by the sun into a little foul smear with no name to it, just *This Was* for an epitaph." (*WP*, p. 83)

Charlotte's commitment to the emotion Harry arouses within her is her way of flinging herself into the ocean of life. She achieves the whirling flood of life in all its intensity and vitality through "bitching" with Harry and making things with her hands.

Charlotte is an extremely creative woman who devotes herself in furious activity to the construction of the dolls, animals, and puppets which support her and Harry during their first months in Chicago. When she and Harry arrive at McCord's Wisconsin lake home, she glimpses "a narrow finger of beach with a buck standing on it, pink in the Sunday dawn, its head up, watching them for an instant before it whirled . . . ." The sight so overwhelms Charlotte that she races to the water's edge, crying, " 'That's what I was trying to make', she cried. 'Not the animals, the dogs and deer and horses: the motion, the speed'," (*WP*, pp. 99-100). This statement not only explains the intensity of Charlotte's labor in the act of creating, but it also explains more fully the motivation behind her commitment to Harry and her devotion to love. Charlotte's complete and utter dedication to love is based on her desire to possess life in all its "motion and speed." To capture life in its complete aliveness is her goal both in art and in love.

It is ironic that though Charlotte finds the fulfillment of living in two creative acts, art and sexual intercourse, she is ultimately driven to a denial of creativity in her effort to preserve the absolute fulfillment of the moment. It is significant that the figures she makes, which are "almost as large as small children," are "effigies elegant, bizarre, fantastic and perverse."

The product of her intercourse is as perverse as her works of art, for Charlotte denies life to the child within her womb because, " 'It's not us now. That's why: don't you see? I want it to be us again, quick, quick. We have so little time' " (*WP*, p. 210). Charlotte knows that a child would require a return to normality, to the demands of society, to the limitations of reality. Her love of Harry is of such a nature that to preserve its quality of absolute vitality Charlotte feels she must suffer intensely, defy social custom, embrace isolation, and live solely for the preservation of the love relationship.

Harry does not grasp the full implications of the nature of the love Charlotte has bestowed upon him until in arguing about the abortion, he realizes suddenly that precisely the wrong thing to say to Charlotte is, " 'But this will be ours'." Their love has been an effort at transcending the limitations of reality; the child would bind them once again to the obligations they have sought to escape. The kind of love to which Charlotte and Harry are committed cannot be diffused by the normal process of life, by children and the resulting requirements of economics and respectability. Charlotte's concern for the child — " 'They hurt too much'," she says — is genuine, but the hurt is part of the reality of existence which she struggles to escape.

By demanding that Harry perform the abortion, Charlotte willfully destroys the product of the creative act of love and thus denies its real meaning. It is her ultimate refusal to submit herself to the flow of life; she prefers the preservation of an ideal to the survival of life. In a courageous and noble effort to defy the limitations of human reality Charlotte commits the disastrous act of destroying life. Significantly, the novel's action is paralleled by the progress of the seasons. The idyllic Indian summer at the lake fades into the icy deadening cold of winter in the Utah mining camp, the scene of Charlotte's discovery of her pregnancy. The return to the South and the mocking rebirth of nature in the spring parallel Charlotte's slow death from Harry's attempted abortion.

The theme which is reiterated throughout Faulkner's works is central to the tragedy of Charlotte Rittenmeyer. To survive man cannot require that life be either heaven or hell, that it be some idealized vision of absoluteness. Survival requires that man submit himself to the in-between existence which Charlotte defies; in her grasp at heaven she plunges into hell, and the ocean of life spews her up onto the hot, windy shore to die. Like all of Faulkner's earlier idealists Charlotte is extremely admirable for her courage, her determination, and her expenditure of her physical, emotional, and intellectual powers for the achievement of her ideal. Nevertheless, Charlotte's idealism proves destructive.

In his admiration for Charlotte, Harry sees himself as a sparrow devoted to a falcon. The bird of prey imagery and the engulfing, deluging power of Charlotte's yellow eyes connect her to the flooded river in *Old Man*. Like the river Charlotte is the immemorial female, the source of life itself, but when the waters flood the result is death and destruction. By demanding too much of life and refusing her proper role in it, Charlotte destroys herself and is a destructive force in the lives of those who love her. The juxtaposition of masculine and feminine qualities in Charlotte's appearance and personality symbolizes the two-fold nature of her character; she is a combination of the natural and the powerful feminine capacity for creativity and procreation and of the masculine drive for transcendence and ideality which results in the opposite of life — isolation, decay and death.

Faulkner never diminishes Charlotte's heroism; she faces death with unselfish concern for Harry, and she accepts the pain and the destruction with courage and without self-pity. Nevertheless, the Charlotte Rittenmeyer of the first and last chapters of *Wild Palms* is a ghastly embodiment of death and decay. Noble and courageous though she may be, she is an agent of destruction in nature's normal process, and nature — the ocean and the chuckling, blowing palms — mocks and rejects her.

A short and not widely circulated Faulkner story, *Idyll in the Desert* (1931), is a tale of a woman whose capacity for love is comparable to Charlotte Rittenmeyer's and whose doom is the same. The woman falls in love with a man ten years younger than she, a junior employee in her husband's business. When her lover contracts tuberculosis, the woman leaves her husband and two children for a deserted canyon cabin, where she nurses the young man back to health. The setting is much like the Utah mining camp of *Wild Palms;* the woman endures intense cold and hardship to care for her lover. However, when he is cured, he deserts her, leaving her alone to fight the disease contracted from him. The woman is aided in secret by her faithful husband; she believes the money is from her lover, whom she expects to return to her. When after ten years her condition becomes hopeless, the husband gives up the deception and sends for her. As she lies in her stretcher waiting to board the train which she yet believes is to take her to her lover, she is passed by the young man and his recent bride. Whether or not she recognizes him, the narrator is unsure; but he is confident that the lover could not have recognized her, for she has aged forty years in ten winters.

Like Charlotte at the end of *Wild Palms*, this dying woman is a ghastly embodiment of physical decay. Though her sacrifice for her vision of love was utterly wasted, whereas Harry at least was able to return Charlotte's love and to suffer at her death, the tragedies of the two women are much the same. They both sacrifice not only loyal husbands but life itself in order to pursue a dream of love. The narrator's tone makes the love affair between the woman and the young man in *Idyll in the Desert* much less noble and admirable than the romance of Charlotte and Harry, but in truth the stories are much the same. The narrator of *Idyll in the Desert* comments,

> "So I guess it couldn't have been long before they had one another all steamed up to where they believed they couldn't live until they told her husband and his boss that love was im-perious or impecrious or whatever it is, and had went off to live just down the canyon from a stage settin with the extra hands all playing mouth-organs and accordians in the background."
>
> "That would have been all right. They could have bore unreality. It was the reality they never had the courage to deny." (*Idyll in the Desert*, p. 12)

The narrator's point of view in this story offers a commentary on Charlotte's view of love. Faulkner never mocks her as this woman is mocked, but the action of the novel reveals that though she had the courage to defy reality, Charlotte could not overpower it or control it. It is the painful realities of disease, of the responsibilities of childbirth, and of death itself which not even absolute devotion to love can efface.

Despite the powerful image of decay which Charlotte embodies in the first and last chapters of *Wild Palms*, Faulkner's judgment upon her would remain oblique without the counterpoint story, *Old Man*. The *Wild Palms* presents two alternatives to Charlotte's idealization of love. *Wild Palms* itself offers only a negative alternative. Charlotte's sacrifice for love is made more admirable when she is compared to the cold, stern, grey, and sterile wife of the doctor. The doctor and his wife possess such a fear of life that they have retreated from it entirely, refusing any degree of emotional or moral involvement in it. To escape the kind of tragedy and destruction Harry and Charlotte face, they have chosen to be corpses throughout their whole lives. Their pattern of life is as much a denial of the possibilities of life as Charlotte's is a denial of its limitations. Another alternative is represented by the young pregnant woman whom the tall convict saves in *Old Man*.

Like Charlotte, this young woman is cast upon the ocean of life, but not by her own choice, for she is completely subjected to nature and chance. But unlike Charlotte, this woman asks nothing of life; indeed, she seems to expect absolutely nothing from it. Without complaint and with few signs of fear she gives birth to her child under the most hideous of circumstances. Landing on the one spot of available dry ground, an Indian mound which is infested with poisonous snakes, she is her own midwife, forced to cut the umbilical cord with a tin can. Yet, the woman and the child miraculously survive because of the aid of a man who is compelled to save them even though he despises and fears them. Despite nature's turbulence and ferocity this woman and her child are preserved from repeated episodes of seemingly inevitable destruction. The nameless woman does not possess any of Charlotte Rittenmeyer's admirable qualities of intellect and emotion; yet she emerges as the heroic representation of the capacity to survive in contrast to Charlotte's embodiment of the capacity for self-destruction. Woman — and mankind — endure not by a commitment to ideality which forces one into a denial of life's limitations, but by an acceptance of life and a commitment to it which enables one to face its limitations without question, complaint, rebellion, or defiance.

Addie Bundren and Charlotte Rittenmeyer are the most fully rounded and complex of Faulkner's women, largely because he deviates from his usual method of portraying women and provides an interior view of their characters. Because they possess much sensitivity to the possibilities for fulfillment in life and a great capacity for self-assertion in the face of life's limitations, both Addie and Charlotte emerge as noble, tragic figures worthy of the central role they play in the novels in which they appear. Because of the vitality of their inner lives they are quiet different from Faulkner's women characters who lead a death-in-life existence because they have completely withdrawn themselves from life.

Nevertheless, it is difficult to imagine a more forceful presentation of the image of death than that which is portrayed by the dying Charlotte Rittenmeyer and by the decaying corpse of Addie Bundren. It is significant that Faulkner presents both these women in the thralls of death before he presents them fully alive. The haunting image of the immobility, decay, and death of Charlotte Rittenmeyer which is presented in the first chapter of the novel pervades the reader's entire discovery of the nature of Charlotte alive and in motion. The result is that her love and her defiance of reality, which are her efforts to escape the limitations of the flesh, are cloaked from the beginning with the ultimate limitation of the flesh — its mortality. The effect is the same in the presentation of Addie Bundren; the reader is painfully aware of the fact of her mortality at the moment that he discovers that Addie's life was devoted to an effort to transcend the limitations of human reality.

The deaths of these women are not simply the inevitable slipping of old age into the peaceful and everlasting sleep. Instead, Faulkner makes their deaths intense, painful, shocking, and horrifying. Charlotte is hysterical, literally on fire with infection and pain. Addie, her dead face bored with holes, is a putrefying corpse subjected helplessly to flood, fire, and decay. Throughout these two novels the force of nature is the enemy of these two women, and it mocks their deaths. Despite Faulkner's powerful and humane sympathy for them, there can be no doubt that he envisioned nature itself to be in judgment upon their defiance of life's limitations.

Woman becomes the image of death when she is unwilling to or is incapable of submitting herself to the natural process of life. Sexuality naturally fulfilled is life — creative, productive of tranquility and moral order, and the source of the survival of mankind. The natural process of life continually requires the sacrifice of private needs and individual ideals for the survival of humanity. The fulfillment of the natural drives of sexuality both in physical love and procreation is for woman the way to life and endurance. "Elly," Miss Zilphia Gant, "Dry September," "A Rose for Emily," Idyll in the Desert, As I Lay Dying, Absalom, Absalom!, and The Wild Palms, on the other hand, present forcefully Faulkner's equation of the misuse of sexuality with death itself.

For Faulkner sexual perversity is equal to the perversion of life. Woman's sexual perversity is the product of thwarted natural drives, and it is the sign of decay and death, frequently not only the decay of the woman herself, but also the decadence of the society that has nourished her perversity. The fragile unreality of Minnie Cooper and of Rosa Coldfield and the black, bloated deathliness of Emily Grierson make them the embodiments of the evil and death in the environment that produced them. When, like Addie and Charlotte, woman attempts to use sexuality as a means of escaping the reality of life's limitations rather than as a means of reproducing life, she aligns herself with the forces which destroy life, and, ironically, in her search for life's vitality she embraces decay and death.

Faulkner's emphasis upon sexuality and the atmosphere he is able to produce in his stories and novels by his use of it indicate that for him sexuality naturally fulfilled is symbolic of life, and sexuality used unnaturally is symbolic of moral decay and death.

PART IV
WOMAN: THE IMAGE OF LIFE

CHAPTER VII

The Feminine Ideal of
Light in August

Lena Grove, the heroine of *Light in August,* and Eula Varner, the heroine of the Snopes trilogy, provide a needed counterpoint in Faulkner's fiction to his image of woman as death. Unlike the women whose feminine drives are thwarted or perverse, Lena and Eula possess an immense capacity for natural life. They symbolize the possibilities for fertility, creativity, serenity, and abundance which human life offers to mankind. The two women, however, are aliens in the fictional worlds they inhabit, for their worlds are filled with characters who are devoted to death. *Light in August* and the Snopes trilogy, especially *The Hamlet,* display the conflict between the male and the female — the former representing the human drive for self-assertion and personal freedom and the latter the human need for submission to the on-going process of life. In these novels the male drive is depicted as destructive and suicidal, whereas the female drive is creative and sustaining.

In *Light in August,* as in his earlier works, Faulkner presents the male drive with great sympathy; the reader is compelled to identify with Joe Christmas just as he must identify with

139

Bayard Sartoris, Quentin Compson, and Horace Benbow. At the same time, Lena Grove's ideal serenity is diminished by the comedy which accompanies her portrayal. Similarly, Eula Varner is a mock-heroic goddess of love. The result is that Faulkner's presentation of the struggle between the male and the female forces of life is never simplistic. Lena Grove and Eula Varner play symbolic roles in the presentation of the themes, but they are also human and believable characters.

Lena Grove is Faulkner's most fascinating portrayal of woman fulfilling her natural destiny. It is with the understanding of Faulkner's view of woman offered by his earlier works — the initial despair in the face of the failure of the virginal ideal and the subsequent devotion to woman as the nourisher and sustainer of life — that his portrait of Lena Grove can best be comprehended as a wholly favorable one. Lena is presented with tenderness, humor, and profound respect. Faulkner identifies her with a pastoral and serene world. She is a "mother earth" figure very much like the beautiful young mother Spring in *The Marble Faun* who is a creature of the Golden Age. Explaining his choice of the title of the novel, Faulkner commented,

> it was just to me a pleasant evocative title because it reminded me of that time (of fauns and satyrs and gods from Greece, from Olympia), of a luminosity older than our Christian civilization. Maybe the connection was with Lena Grove, who had something of that pagan quality of being able to assume everything . . . . as far as she was concerned, she didn't especially need any father for it (her child), any more than the women . . . on whom Jupiter begot children were anxious for a home and a father. (*Faulkner in the University*, p. 199)

Further, and most significantly, Faulkner identifies Lena Grove with eternal beauty and truth, the ideals symbolized by virginal woman in *Mosquitoes* and identified in that novel and in *Light in August* with the images of Keats's "Ode on a Grecian Urn." Lena possesses the quality of serenity and purity which

Gordon concretizes in his marble statue and Horace in his sheer glass vases and which Quentin attempts to realize through his idealization of his sister Caddy. Early in the first chapter of *Light in August* Lena is described as "somthing moving forever and without progress across an urn." The adjectives which are repeatedly associated with her — "peaceful," "tranquil," "innocent," "profound," "motionless," "calm," "grave," "quiet" — continually connect Lena's person with the sense of serenity and beauty aroused by Keats's poem.

However, unlike the maiden silver poplars of *The Marble Faun* or the lithe, slender figure of Pat Robyn, the human replica of Gordon's statue, Lena's body is swollen with child. Unlike Horace's and Quentin's idealized "unravished bride of quietness" Lena Grove is not virgin. It is significant that Faulkner should endow Lena with the qualities of serenity, tranquility, and purity, which his romantic idealists dreamed were possessed by beautiful and virgin young women, despite the fact that she is unvirgin, unmarried, and very pregnant. Lena's character indicates the change in Faulkner's view of the ideal woman which took place between the composition of *Mosquitoes* and *The Sound and the Fury*. Her character makes it again apparent that he no longer idealized virginity, but asserted that woman finds serenity and fulfillment in a submission to the natural reproductive process of life.

The author's personal despair at the loss of the virginal ideal, apparent in his sympathetic portrayal of the suffering of Horace and Quentin and of the women characters who are "images of death," is absent from his portrait of Lena Grove. It must have been with both relief and pleasure that Faulkner created her, for he depicts her faults neither with despair nor with bitter satire but with the joyous triumph of comedy. He is able to present Lena's very real human limitations without diminishing the significance of her character or the value of what she represents.

Lena is an exemplar of a weak and limited humanity. She is simple-minded and ignorant, lacking in foresight or rationality. Yet, she possesses a certain shrewdness which assures that her basic physical needs will be met. She is not a strikingly beautiful woman, as is Eula Varner; rather her bulging, faded blue gingham dress and flopping borrowed brogans would make her farcical were it not for the penetrating power of her eyes and the quality of serenity which Faulkner continually associates with her. Though she has behaved shamefully in the moral context of her world by getting pregnant outside of marriage, Lena is not burdened by any sense of guilt. To marry before the child's birth is an acceptable means of correcting her fault in her culture, and she devotes herself to meeting that demand of her society.

However, as Faulkner's own comment indicates, Lena experiences little genuine concern about her unmarried state. She is burdened neither by dead moralities nor intellectual introspection. Her unthinking, unquestioning attitude toward life results in the absence of despair and a serene acceptance of whatever life brings. On the rare occasions when she pauses to ponder the alternatives life might have offered her, Lena recalls her decisions with neither shame nor anxiety but with self-mocking good humor. Climbing out of her bedroom window to begin her pursuit of Lucas Burch, Lena thinks, " 'If it had been this hard to do before I reckon I would not be doing it now' " (*LA*, p. 6).

Lena's serenity and self-confidence stem from the fact that she is fulfilling the role in life which she was created to perform. She has little concern for who planted the seed, for her life is made meaningful by her prospective motherhood. Her interest is focused upon her unborn child, and because of her condition and her obvious need the community is compelled to assist her. Because Lena expects almost nothing of herself or of anyone else, life is for her a series of astonishing and pleasurable surprises; she is continually amazed at how kind people are. Lena's journey in *Light in August* is characterized by her immense personal enjoyment of life despite the hardships it has brought her. Her presence does arouse the good in the hearts of those she encounters, for they recognize that she is engaged in the sacred act of replenishing the earth and assuring the survival of man. Her self-confidence, her inner assurance and faith, and her tranquility are the result of her immense satisfaction with the role she is performing.

Lena senses her own oneness with the order of creation, and she has no reason to fear life. She is free to allow the escape of the lesser lover Lucas Burch because she is confident of the more worthy devotion of Byron Bunch. She has endured great hardships — the early loss of parents, a poverty-stricken youth, the absence of any promise of material or family security, desertion and betrayal by her lover — yet she is free of anxiety. She has expected so little from life that disappointment is nearly impossible. When pleasure comes to her — the bearing of a child, a devoted lover, and an adventurous journey — she is able to enjoy fully the abundance of human life. She is the "good stock peopling in tranquil obedience to it the good earth."

The importance of Lena Grove's character in *Light in August* cannot be overestimated. Faulkner commented,

> that story began with Lena Grove, the idea of the young girl with nothing, pregnant, determined to find her sweetheart. It was — that was out of my admiration for women, for the courage and endurance of women. As I told that story I had to get more and more into it, but that was mainly the story of Lena Grove. (*Faulkner in the University*, p. 74)

The significance of Lena's character in the novel is fully apparent when her life-giving, life-sustaining, and anxiety-free attitude toward life is compared to the destructive and anxiety-ridden lives of the other major characters, Joe Christmas, Joanna Burden, and Gail Hightower. *Light in August* displays the tragic suffering which results from the denial and perversion of the natural process of life which Lena's character symbolizes. This dialectic of birth and reproduction versus death and destruction forms the basis of the structure of the novel.

Joe Christmas, Gail Hightower, and Joanna Burden are idealists who, like Horace Benbow, Quentin Compson, Addie Bundren, and Charlotte Rittenmeyer, cling to a static vision of an ideal and ignore the demands of reality. Unlike Lena Grove, who expects nothing from life, none of these characters are able to accept life as they find it. Each devotes himself to his private search for self-realization to the extent that he becomes almost totally isolated from other human beings. As a result they all lead lives characterized by alienation and self-destructiveness.

Were the tone of the Lena Grove sections different, it might be possible to interpret her presence in the novel as Faulkner's bitterly ironic mockery of life's betrayal of man, for the bulk of the novel's content and much of the author's sympathy are directed at the three tragic figures. The failure of their lives is poignantly felt by Faulkner, and it is their characters which the reader experiences most deeply. This is the result of the delicate, subtle balance of Faulkner's fiction, most plainly structured in *Light in August;* every imaginable device is utilized to elicit sympathy for the "driven," failing protagonists. Christmas and to a lesser degree Hightower and Burden are victims of the circumstances of their lives, but Lena Grove is also the victim of circumstances. *Light in August* presents two opposing attitudes toward life: man may either accept life as he finds it, endure its imperfections, and determine to survive it, or he may reject life as it is, devoting himself to an idealized vision of life.

The latter is the choice of the three tragic protagonists of *Light in August.* Each is obsessed by a static image of life that exists only in his mind and is unrelated and inapplicable to the real circumstances of his existence. Since the actions and attitudes of these characters are totally controlled by the dead images in their minds, none are able to live freely or to respond to life with spontaneity. It is only in the context of the counterpoint which Lena Grove's character offers in the novel that the nature of the failure of the lives of Gail Hightower, Joe Christmas, and Joanna Burden is made fully apparent.

The image which controls Gail Hightower's life is the electrifying vision of his grandfather's moment of heroic daring.

You can see it, hear it: the shouts, the shots, the shouting of triumph and terror, the drumming hooves, the trees uprearing against that red glare as though fixed too in terror, the sharp gables of houses like the jagged edge of the exploding and ultimate earth. Now it is a close place: you can feel, hear in the darkness horses pulled short up, plunging; clashes of arms; whispers overloud, hard breathing, the voices still triumphant; behind them the rest of the troops galloping past toward the rallying bugles. (*LA*, p. 424)

The action is comparable to the Sartoris defiance of death; the image and the excitement of the language recall the passage that ends "Carcassone." Similarly, Hightower's vision expresses his devotion to the ability to defy life's limitations and its mediocrity, a capacity he himself can experience only through his idealized dream. As with Faulkner's other romantic idealists, Hightower's vision of glorious defiance results, ironically, in the adoption of a passive attitude toward life. Though he acts aggressively to attain the Jefferson parish, falling into deceit and hypocrisy to accomplish his aim, once Jefferson becomes his home, he submits himself totally to the image of the grandfather without any regard for the demands of reality. He fosters evil in his congregation, and he destroys his wife because of his single-minded devotion to the thrilling image.

Faulkner demonstrates the evil of Hightower's commitment by presenting him as the perpetrator of death. Hightower destroys his wife by ignoring her need for normal sexual love, driving her to debauchery, insanity, and suicide. He assumes that his subsequent expulsion from the community is the price he pays to earn the right to isolate himself from reality and from society and to devote himself to the enjoyment of the dream vision. His life becomes a solitary death-in-life existence. His only friend, Byron Bunch, observes that Hightower's much used canvas deck chair is

mended and faded and sagged so long to the shape of Hightower's body that even when empty it seems to hold still in ghostly embrace the owner's obese shapelessness; approaching, Byron thinks how the mute chair evocative of disuse and supineness and shabby remoteness from the

world, is somehow the symbol and the being too of the
man himself. (*LA*, p. 317)

It is Hightower's preference for isolation and his refusal of
responsible involvement with other human beings that make
him deny Joe Christmas the alibi which would save them both
from destruction.

The meaning of Christmas's character is the most complex
and subtly developed aspect of *Light in August*. The ambiguities
which surround his figure suggest numerous patterns of interpretation of the novel. Yet, the central conflict of Joe
Christmas's life is in its broadest terms a struggle between the
forces of life and death; it is in this sense that he is clearly the
counterpoint of Lena Grove. Throughout his thirty odd years
Joe is continually drawn toward a submission of himself to the
needs of survival. Simultaneously, however, he rebels with
violent intensity at any subjugation of his pride and selfhood,
and in so doing he directs his life toward death. Joe's inability
to accept life on its own terms is the most admirable refusal of
life Faulkner has created, for Christmas's tragedy is the product
of his society's demand that he be either Negro or white.
Christmas is incapable of merging himself with either race; yet,
to be neither is, in his culture, an impossibility. Christmas
devotes himself to an unattainable ideal which inevitably
isolates him from other human beings and drives him toward
self-destruction.

However, the tension between black and white is actually
symbolic of the more basic conflict between the instinct for life
and the drive toward death. In *Light in August* the Negro and
the female are symbolic of the fertility of life. Were Joe able to
submit himself to either force in its natural manifestation, he
would be relieved of his alienation. However, the experiences of
his life have taught him to hate and fear both the Negro and the
female. As a result his mind and his nature war within him.
Human being that he is, he is drawn to the forces that offer him
survival; idealist that he is, he can envision the worlds of the
Negro and of woman only as subjugating and evil. He devotes
himself to fleeing and denying them in order to preserve the

sense of individual identity he does possess. His pride and his rebellion at the nature of his existence are in one sense heroic; nevertheless, the destructive, violent, and death-directed pattern of Christmas's existence is a perversion of life.

The forces of the black and of the female are omnipresent in Christmas's life; repeatedly, he reacts to both forces with fear, flight, violence, and rebellion. In his night-time walk through Jefferson's Freedman Town, Joe seeks out the artificial lights of the white world, which, ironically, persecutes and destroys him, and flees the fluid and fecund life of the Negro world with its "rich murmur of womenvoices."

> It was as though he and all other manshaped life about him had been returned to the lightless hot wet primogenitive female. He began to run, glaring, his teeth glaring, his inbreath cold on his dry teeth and lips, toward the next street lamp. Beneath it a narrow and rutted lane turned and mounted to the parallel street, out of the black hollow. He turned into it running and plunged up the sharp ascent, his heart hammering, and into the higher street. He stopped here, panting, glaring, his heart thudding as if it could not or would not yet believe that the air now was the cold hard air of white people. (*LA*, p. 100)

To Christmas the Negro world is the black abyss, the pit of evil; but, in truth, it is the dark womb of life, the force of nature with which Christmas must come to terms if he is to live.

Just as Christmas must inevitably stumble into the Negro world, he cannot escape the force of the female. Repeatedly, women offer Christmas physical sustenance and sexuality, the means of physical propagation. As long as he is alive, he cannot be free of the need for nourishment or of the need for sex; yet, in contrast to Lena Grove, who accepts offers of both with joy and serenity, Christmas can respond only with rebellion and violence.

As a youth Joe violently rejects Mrs. McEachern's offers of food, preferring his step-father's stern absolutizing to her humiliating compromise with the necessities of survival. Years later he resents the necessity of consuming the food prepared for him by Joanna Burden, and in a moment of anger he methodically crashes every dish against the wall, destroying the "woman's muck" she has set out for him. Similarly, he recalls as an adult how as a child he angrily ripped off every button patiently sewn onto his garments by some unremembered woman's hands. Joe's attitude toward sexuality is molded by his betrayal by Bobbie Allen, but his childhood experiences with sex reveal an early violent rejection of it. The nausea that accompanies his witnessing of the sex act between the dietician and the intern plagues him throughout his life. As a youth he is unable to participate with his friends in sexual experimentation, and he violently beats the Negro girl the others have accosted. When his friends explain the cycle of woman's natural reproductive process, Joe is literally made ill by the horror of that blood.

At no point in Joe's life does he experience sexuality as a healthy and normal affirmation of the goodness of life. He is constantly driven to sex because it is the force of life in him which he cannot escape; yet he clings to death by satisfying his sexual drives with women who are devoted to perverting normal sexuality. His first lover is a prostitute, and until his encounter with Joanna Burden, Joe's only sexual relations are with women who live in promiscuity and require of him no promise that he enter with them into the natural reproductive process of sexual life. Joe Christmas vastly prefers the scent of horses, the sign of the male's reliance upon his own virility, but only at brief intervals is he able to escape the power of the scent of woman. Fleeing life, yet drawn to it, he at last aligns himself with a woman whose perversion of life and sexuality draws him into a deathly "still black pool" of "gutter filth" and drives him inevitably toward destruction.

Joanna Burden is one of the most pathetic women characters in the Faulkner canon. She is an opposite of Lena Grove; her life is plagued by guilt, thwarted sexuality, and sterility. Like her counterparts, Hightower and Christmas, she is controlled by a single image which drives her into isolation from others and alienation from reality. The nature of her existence is determined by the vision left to her by her ancestors.

I seemed to see them for the first time not as people, but as a thing, a shadow in which I lived we lived, all white people, all other people. I thought of all the children coming forever and ever into the world white, with the black shadow already falling upon them before they drew breath. And I seemed to see the black shadow in the shape of a cross. And it seemed like the white babies were struggling, èven before they drew breath, to escape from the shadow that was not only upon them but beneath them too, flung out like their arms were flung out, as if they were nailed to the cross. (*LA*, p. 221)

Joanna assumes the burden of the black guilt, denying the natural female drives within her in order to perform her martyrdom to this vision. Joanna's philanthropy is not the life-giving product of love, but it is a sacrifice to alleviate her own fears and guilt. Her thwarted sexuality is the sign of her perversion of life, a perversity which Faulkner effectively conveys through his descriptions of Joanna's physical appearance: "he saw a head with hair just beginning to gray drawn gauntly back to a knot as savage and ugly as a wart on a diseased bough" (*LA*, p. 241). The horror of Joanna's appearance is matched by the violent and perverse manliness with which she yields to Christmas in the sex act.

Joanna's character forcefully demonstrates the destruction that accompanies woman's alienation from the normal process of mating and child-bearing. Normal sexuality produces new life, but thwarted sexuality as it is exemplified by Joanna Burden is characterized by lust and nymphomania and culminates in sterility and violent death. Christmas attacks Joanna with the violence that expresses his rebellion against the force of life; Joanna never sees Christmas as a man but only as a Negro, the embodiment of a lifetime of guilt against which she rebels through the sin of the sex act. Their sexual relationship is abnormal and perverse because they are devoted not to fostering life but to destroying it.

Hightower and Christmas achieve a degree of relief from the evil of their lives because each experiences a brief encounter with the beauty and serenity of the natural world. Hightower is compelled to assist Lena in giving birth to her child; the contact with her and with the act of reproduction accomplishes in him a momentary revival of the spirit of life. He recognizes in Lena the possibility for a continuing abundant life, and the realization brings about a new sense of triumph within him and a renewed communion with the natural world.

Shortly afterwards, Hightower experiences the tragedy of Christmas's murder and castration. The two events force him to reconsider the nature of his own life, and he at last recognizes himself as a man of death. His admission that he, through his grandfather, is the murderer and debaucher of his own wife raises his moral stature but comes too late in his life to effect any real salvation. Admitting his failure, he succumbs once again to "the wild bugles and the clashing sabres and the dying thunder of hooves."

During the last week of his life, Joe Christmas also submits himself briefly to the serenity of the natural world. He experiences a sense of inner peace through the beauty and tranquility of nature; he seeks the sustenance of food, and he accepts the aid of the Negro. He asks the time of day because he at last experiences momentarily the desire to be in time, to be alive. As he flees, he feels that he is "being hunted by white men at last into the black abyss which had been waiting, trying, for thirty years to drown him and into which now and at last he had actually entered, bearing now upon his ankles the definite and ineradicable gauge of its upward moving" (LA, p. 289). By accepting the Negro's shoes and assuming the identity of a black man, Christmas at last experiences some relief from his alienation, fury, and despair.

Though the forces of submission and self-assertion battle within him until the last moment of his life, Christmas's death is serene, paradoxically, both because he momentarily submits himself to the demand of the community and achieves a social identity and because he has at last overpowered his natural desire for survival.[1] When death comes to Joe Christmas, Joanna Burden, and Gail Hightower, they welcome it, for it offers not only relief from their suffering but also the fulfillment of the whole pattern of their lives.

Light in August displays the opposing forces of death and of life. Self-assertion, sexual perversity, violence, and isolation are the signs of death and the portrayal of these qualities in man makes up the bulk of the content of the novel. However, *Light in August* does not conclude with the pattern of death but with the pattern of life. The last chapter, which focuses on Lena Grove's continuing journey, is more than comic relief; it is a re-affirmation of the power of life.

Lena's new lover, Byron Bunch, discovers early in the novel that he cannot resist Lena's power over him. He sacrifices his pride, his self-image, and his moralities in order to pursue her. Aware of the perpetual comic humiliation of the man who would accept life's imperfections and endure them, Faulkner still affirms that through Lena Grove there is to be found both the fulfillment of life and the survival of humanity.

---

[1] "Joe's death, the soaring or lightness with which his peace comes, is very basically an escape from the female world which has tried to entangle him (in life itself) and the Negro world whose symbolic meaning is much the same" (Phyllis Hirshleifer, "As Whirlwinds in the South," p. 237.)

CHAPTER VIII

The Male and the Female Principles: *The Snopes Trilogy*

The dialectic of the life-nourishing female principle versus the life-destructive male principle which is basic to the structure and meaning of *Light in August* is also of central importance in the Snopes trilogy.[1] The struggle between the female and the male forces is especially prominent in *The Hamlet*, where every episode which involves both a man and a woman displays this conflict. The pattern of contrast is initiated in the opening chapter of *The Hamlet* by the seemingly digressive tale of Ab Snopes's horse trade with Pat Stomper. The episode introduces several motifs which portray the male-female conflict throughout the novel and which culminate in the parallel narrative of "The Spotted Horses" in the last book of the novel.

Ab Snopes engages in a hopelessly defeating barter for a horse which is useless to himself and his poverty-stricken family and is absolutely worthless. Ab bargains for the horse because

---

[1] "In contrast to Eula who embodies a feminine natural principle which is fertile, organic, 'eternal,' and life-giving, the Snopeses embody a masculine physical principle which is deformed, time-bound, and mechanically repeats the life cycle: a death-in-life" (Herbert A. Leibowitz, "The Snopes Dilemma and the South," p. 279).

he idolizes the animal and because the bartering excites him, offering him the opportunity, he believes, to get something for less than its real worth and the chance to prove his personal superiority at horse trading. In contrast, Ab's wife has saved diligently for four years in order to buy a separator. The wife is devoted to the cow which provides real sustenance for her family. In order to accomplish his horse trade Ab uses the money saved for the separator. When his wife discovers what he has done she can only cry out in despair, " 'Fool about a horse yes! But why the horse? Why the horse?' " The distraught wife promptly swaps the cow for the yearned-for separator.

Mrs. Snopes's furious query initiates a pattern that recurs throughout the novel. The horse in *The Hamlet* is symbolic of man's individuality and his assertion of his own self-will and freedom in defiance of his responsibilities as a domestic being.[1] Like Ab Snopes, most of the men in *The Hamlet* welcome the chance to escape the routine pattern of labor whenever events offer them an opportunity to exploit their desire for physical or economic adventure. They are enticed by the excitement of bartering, for it offers an opportunity to assert their superiority, to profit without labor, and to pit themselves against the forces of fate and chance. Horses are of no domestic value in Frenchman's Bend; yet horse trading is the most honored form of bartering.

In contrast, the women in *The Hamlet* devote themselves to the regular, unexciting and laborious pattern of family sustenance. Whereas the male rarely refuses the opportunity to barter, the female relies on her own labor, faithfully and regularly rendered, to supply her family needs. Like Ab, Mink Snopes and Henry Armstid take money their wives have set aside for family needs and squander it to satisfy their own pride. Throughout the novel the contrast of the two sexes is conveyed by the labor versus bartering motif, by the cow versus horse motif, and by the imagery of immobility or slow movement

---

[1] T.Y. Greet, "The Theme and Structure of Faulkner's *The Hamlet*," p. 343, comments, ". . . to own and trade in horses is purely a masculine prerogative: that 'bitless masculinity' which is relinquished not only in marriage, but in subjugation of any sort."

associated with the cow and with the productive labor of females and the imagery of rapid, violent movement associated with the horse and the destructive activities of the male.

All of the women characters in *The Hamlet* are notable for the hard labor that is required of them in order to provide their families with physical sustenance. Even Mrs. Will Varner, whose husband has achieved such success at bartering that her family has no unmet physical needs, experiences "an acutal physical pleasure . . . from the laying-away of ironed sheets and the sight of packed shelves and potato cellars and festooned smoke-house rafters" (*H*, p. 97). In contrast to the Snopes men who rely most heavily on their ability to barter, the Snopes women labor diligently. Lump Snopes's "ma," a thin, plain schoolteacher, spent her youth caring for a brood of younger siblings, a task that prepared her well for her marriage, which required the capacity to "wash and feed and clothe" children "without ever enough food or clothing or soap to do it with." Mink Snopes's wife is able to keep her family scantily fed and clothed on Mink's meager earnings as a tenant farmer. When he is jailed in Jefferson, she obtains work there, and by her ill-paid labors she provides for their children. The productive labor of women in *The Hamlet* is striking because their self-submissive attitude contrasts with the self-assertive attitude of the males.

Significantly, Faulkner frequently describes women at household labor in terms of immobility. For example, the daughters of Ab Snopes, in the act of drawing water from the well, are depicted as "two big absolutely static young women . . . who even in that first glance postulated that immobile solidarity of statuary." One girl, bent down to pull the well chain, is like "a carved piece symbolizing some terrific physical effort which had died with its inception . . . "(*H*, p. 20). The girls are also compared to "two cows, heifers, standing knee-deep in air as in a stream, a pond nuzzling to it . . . ."

The quality of immobility associated with woman in *The Hamlet* suggests not a peaceful serenity as it does in *Light in August*, but a sense of hopelessness and defeat. Too frequently in *The Hamlet* the hard labors of the female are brought to nothing by the pride and wastefulness of the male. Jack

Houston, Mink Snopes, and Henry Armstid display the destructiveness of male pride and the drive for self-assertion. The wife is, in each case, the pathetic and helpless victim of the male's action.

The relationship between Lucy Pate and Jack Houston is a clear portrayal of the conflict between the life-sustaining qualities of the female and the life-defying qualities of the male. From her first encounter with Houston as a schoolmate, Lucy seems determined to tame and domesticate him. Faulkner describes the couple's relationship during their school days as a "feud" between her "unflagging will not for love or passion but for the married state" and his "furious" will for "solitariness and freedom."

It is Houston's desire for individuality and freedom which makes him leave Frenchman's Bend to escape the power Lucy Pate wields over him. Though he lives for seven years as man and wife with an ex-prostitute, the woman never expects marriage of him, and he remains in effect free of the bonds of the female. At last as though the fate of marriage were inescapable, he returns to Frenchman's Bend to marry the woman he has been unable to forget. Despite Houston's thirteen years of absence, Lucy accepts his return and marriage proposal as if they were inevitable. Her years of waiting and the mass of hand-sewn domestic articles prepared and ready for marriage demonstrate her "infinite capacity for constancy and devotion."

By submitting himself to marriage Houston breaks the pattern of isolation and self-assertiveness that have characterized his life. He accepts marriage to Lucy as relief from the tension and struggle within him, and he devotes himself entirely to loving his wife and eagerly provides her with ample materials for fostering their domestic life. However, Houston cannot refrain from purchasing a stallion whose violent spirit is symbolic of "that polygamous and bitless masculinity which he had relinquished." Though she is aware of the stallion's wild spirit, Lucy does not fear him, for she feels that the married state has triumphed over the force the horse symbolizes. However, after but six months of marriage she is attacked by the stallion and killed while searching out a lost hen's nest in the barn.

Houston's own wild nature, subdued by his brief marriage, emerges again in his grief and fury at his wife's death. Though he attacks the stallion with a knife and then shoots it to death, he cannot destroy the spirit of the stallion in his own soul. The masculine self-assertiveness that made him flee marriage to Lucy is given its final expression in his pointless purchase of the wild stallion which proves to be the instrument of the triumph of his masculine nature. The doom which Houston feels is inevitable in the "trap" of marriage is the inevitable conflict of his own dual nature. Though Lucy Pate possesses enough stability and devotion to living to draw Houston into a pattern of productive and creative life, his last assertion of his masculine willfulness destroys his wife and thus his only opportunity to escape the doom to which his own nature drives him. In the fury of his grief he retreats to his old nature; he purchases another mighty stallion; he isolates himself from society; and he feeds his own pride and self-will until he provokes one as proud as himself to murder him.

Mink Snopes is of a much lower station in life than Jack Houston, but he has no less pride. Unlike Lucy Pate, who spent her pre-marital life in complete devotion to her future husband, Mink Snopes's wife is engaged in a bizarre life of prostitution before her marriage. Mink is only one of many lovers, but when the strangely masculine woman encounters the wasp-like Mink, she meets her equal in passionate love. The actual marriage which takes place six months later is more the product of the father's bankruptcy than of the woman's desire, but she is, nevertheless, devoted to Mink, a loyalty she symbolizes by allowing her short black hair to grow long and dying it a yellow blond. The poverty and hardship which she endures do not diminish her devotion to Mink both as his lover and as a wife and mother to his children.

When Mink's pride drives him to murder Houston, his wife responds with a mixture of fury and devotion. She takes the two children and leaves him, obviously hoping that her departure will sober him or at least allow him to escape the consequences of his act. When he appears at Will Varner's shortly after the news of the murder is out, she explodes at him in a fury of fear and grief. Scolding Mink for being foolish enough to commit the murder, then too foolish to eat to sustain himself in flight, and even too foolish to run, she forces upon him a ten dollar bill to aid his flight, earned, as Mink knows, by her old trade. The woman shakes Mink, wishing that she could hang and then let him loose again and again in order to teach him the consequences of his foolhardy pride and thus to save him from the inevitable destruction he faces. She is a striking contrast to Lucy Pate, for she expresses her emotions with almost as much violence as does her husband. Nevertheless, as a loyal wife and a faithful provider for her children, she contributes to the sustenance of her family's life, while her husband completely disregards her devotion and the needs of his children in order to avenge himself.

"The Spotted Horses" episode is the climax of *The Hamlet* and represents the culmination of the battle between the male and the female principles in the novel. The horses themselves are symbolic of a wild self-assertion and irresponsibility of which the men are guilty when they submit themselves to the fraud. The horses circle about the corral in fierce and rapid movement. When they are unleashed to their new owners, they dash through Mrs. Littlejohn's hotel and rampage the countryside; they are forces of chaos, wild freedom, and destruction. The spirit of the horses rules the men as they gather irresistibly for the auction, gradually submit to the enticement of a bargain, and at last enter into the wild and frantic chase of the useless ponies. Henry Armstid is the male character who gives in most completely to the force of evil which the horses represent. Driven by a false and bitter pride, he is determined to prove to the others his capacity for making a bargain. His behavior is insane as he cruelly strikes his wife to force her to submit to his wild desires. He takes their last five dollars and sacrifices it and his family to satisfy his pride.

The wife, who has labored at her weaving far into the night to earn the five dollars to buy shoes for their children, is the pitiable victim of her husband's violence and foolishness. After a brief resistance she is forced to give in to his physical power over her, to yield the money to him, and to attempt to assist him in capturing his pony. None of the others offer her any assistance or protection. When the bidding is accomplished and the money lost, Mrs. Armstid returns to the wagon; sitting "in the gray garment, motionless, looking at nothing still, she might have been something inanimate . . . now in the wagon until he should be ready to go on again, patient, insensate, timeless" (*H*, p. 298).

The immobility which Faulkner repeatedly associates with Mrs. Armstid is the sign of her hopeless defeat. She is the helpless victim of the irresponsibility of her husband and her community and of the heartless cruelty of Flem Snopes. Accepting the nickel Snopes offers instead of the promised five dollars, she departs but seems to progress "without motion like a figure on a retreating and diminishing float; a gray and blasted tree-trunk moving, somehow intact and upright, upon an unhurried flood" (*H*, p. 322). At the end of the novel when Henry has again squandered their savings on Flem's buried treasure fraud, Mrs. Armstid is still submissive to her wife's role, regularly bringing Henry's meals to him while he digs furiously, oblivious of her presence as she stands "motionless" with her "gray garment falling in rigid carven folds."

The motionless quality of Mrs. Armstid is paralleled by the presentation of Mrs. Littlejohn, whose boarding house is adjacent to the site of the auction. Throughout the day's bidding Mrs. Littlejohn's tranquil activities offer a contrast to the furious, dashing motion of the horses and the wild behavior of the men. Unlike Mrs. Armstid, whose immobility signifies defeat, Mrs. Littlejohn possesses a quality of serenity because she is engaged in useful actions which are unaffected by the male forces. The progress of the auction is punctuated by her ritual performance of household chores; repeatedly she pauses to gaze across the fence at the ponies, unmoved and unaffected by the force they represent.

In "The Spotted Horses" episode the contrast between the rapid motion associated with the horses and the men and the quality of stillness associated with the women links woman to nature and to the land which in its stillness and tranquility is strikingly the opposite of the men's wild movement as they

chase the ponies during the moonlit night. On the evening before the auction the symbolic, unreal quality of the ponies is
reinforced by their "mirage-like" appearance as they huddle in
the corral in the silver mist of the moonlight. The repeated
references to the moonlight, to the mockingbird which makes
its first appearance on the same evening, and to the blossoming
pear trees make the natural world compellingly present throughout the episode. Significantly, the pear tree is

> in full and frosty bloom, the twigs and branches springing
> not outward from the limbs but standing motionless and
> perpendicular above the horizontal bough like the separate
> and upstreaming hair of a drowned woman sleeping upon
> the uttermost floor of the windless and tideless sea. (H, p.
> 281)

The imagery of the over-lush blossoms recalls, of course, the
same pattern of imagery in *The Marble Faun, Soldier's Pay,* and
Sanctuary. As in those works the abundance of nature suggests
the possible abundance of human life in the midst of man's acts
of evil and failure. During the mad chase of the horses, Will
Varner notes the promise which the full-blossomed pear tree
offers for a productive harvest and tells a legend of fertility.
However, the chase is an impotent substitute for the male's
natural expression of sexual drives. By the time of the court
scene when Mrs. Armstid and Mrs. Tull, who is attacking not
only her husband's foolishness and Flem's evil but "all men, all
males," are defeated by the law, the rising gusts of wind have
brought "a faint snow of petals, prematurely bloomed." The
offer of life which nature holds is fleeting and momentary, and
the men of Frenchman's Bend have already sacrificed woman
and the chance for fertility to the destructive male drive of
irresponsible self-assertion.[1]

Woman, like the land, is the unthinking and submissive agent
of the natural force of life. Man, on the other hand, is engaged

---

[1]Cf. Russell Roth, "The Centaur and the Pear Tree," 199 ff., and T.Y. Greet, "The
Theme and Structure of Faulkner's *The Hamlet*," pp. 337. ff.

in a furious effort to escape the power which woman and the land hold over him and to establish his own self-sufficiency. The episodes which involve the people of Frenchman's Bend convey, largely in a realistic manner, the minor skirmishes of this battle. Eula Varner and Flem Snopes are symbolic figures who are "larger than life" and thus portray the natures of the two forces in their extremes.

Eula Varner is a source of comic joy in *The Hamlet*. She is person, but she is primarily force; her own personality and her body are subservient to the force of life which emanates from her. The feminine quality of motionlessness is so exaggerated in her that Faulkner's description of it merges into the ridiculous. As a child she refuses to walk; she sits in her perambulator until she has grown too large for it. Then she is moved about from chair to chair or carried by a manservant until she is five years old. The comic image of the over-grown, immovable child is reinforced by the description of the adolescent Eula riding to school on horseback behind Jody, mindless of the power of attraction of her half-revealed thighs, and by the description of her behavior in school – her only action is the laborious devouring of the daily sweet potatoes.

Only when Eula begins to mature are the nature and power of her immobility apparent. She is the still point of life, the source of creativity, action, and motion. By the time she is thirteen her appearance suggests "some symbology out of the old Dionysic times – honey in sunlight and bursting grapes, the writhen bleeding of the crushed fecundated vine beneath the hard rapacious trampling goat-hoof" (H, p. 95). The extravagance of the language devoted to describing Eula conveys the excessive quality of abundant life which she possesses. Jenny Steinbauer in *Mosquitoes* is the only other of Faulkner's female figures whose purely physical allure is comparable to Eula's. Eula seems to emanate an "outrageous quality of being, existing, actually on the outside of the garments she wore and not only being unable to help it but not even caring" (H, p. 102). Eula does not intend her attractiveness nor does she in any way exploit her power. The force of life itself has simply descended upon her and bestowed upon the body she inhabits a tremendous capacity for the creative abundance of life. Both comic exaggeration and extravagant language contribute to her portrayal as a figure who is "larger than life."[1] Throughout her life Eula herself and most of the males she encounters are the powerless servants of the force which flows from her. Motionless herself, she is the focal point of endless movement.

The men of Frenchman's Bend, however, can respond to the force of life which Eula embodies only with the violence of wild desire and frustrated impotence. Though her first "lover," the schoolteacher Labove, is able to appreciate the nature of Eula's attractiveness, he resists her power for so long that when he at last submits, it is with lust and violence. Labove's reveries on Eula contribute to Faulkner's symbolic presentation of her character. Eula is the queen among a swarm of bees. To Labove she transforms his bleak classroom into a "grove of Venus"; her presence brings to "the harsh functioning of Protestant primary education a moist blast of spring's liquorish corruption, a pagan triumphal prostration before the supreme primal uterus" (H, p. 114). Dedicated to the respectability of a law career and the wisdom of books, Labove cannot accept the fact that he knows is true: that the over-grown, simple-minded, potato-devouring young girl represents a force of life which is serene, tranquil, "at once supremely unchaste and inviolable," and superior to "the whole long sum of human thinking and suffering which is called knowledge, education, widsom."

Eula exists in calm repose, whereas Labove is a creature of movement and violence. He rides horseback to the university each week in order to play his frantic game of football; he beats the local boys in order to create a disciplined school. Once he encounters Eula, his mind ranges through the whole history of romantic love. Physically and mentally Labove is in constant motion, but his activities prove to be useless and misdirected. Incapable of submitting his pride to Eula's superior power, yet incapable of containing his lust, he at last attacks her in a fit of

---

[1] "That she is an anachronism, she had no place there, that that little hamlet couldn't have held her, and when she moved on to Jefferson, that couldn't hold her either .... You're quite right, she was larger than life, she was too big for this world" (Faulkner in the University, p. 31).

desire, impotence, and violence. For Labove the sex act is perverted into rape, hatred, and physical struggle. However, Eula is
both literally and symbolically a superior force, and the episode
ends comically with Eula unharmed and unmoved. Labove's
lustful and violent reaction to Eula initiates a pattern of male
destructiveness which she must endure throughout her life.

The tension between the male force of self-assertion and the
male drive for submission to the sexual prowess of woman produces the violence that erupts among Eula's teen-aged beaux. As
with Labove, none wish to marry her, but all are competitors
for the ecstatic moment of a single physical union with her.
They possess something of Jody's "invincible bachelorhood"
and are angered by the disturbance Eula arouses in them. Simultaneously, their repeated failure and their resulting impotence
frustrate them. They stampede like wild cattle and lust like
dogs. When McCarron at last wins Eula, it is because his is the
superior masculine power. However, when her virginity is destroyed all of her lovers flee in order to earn the sought-after
honor of having deflowered her, but also to escape the lifetime
of submission that would accompany marriage to her.

Eula's abundant capacity for life can endure the violent circumstances of her deflowering. Her loss of virginity is treated
comically, for it is an insignificant and inevitable event in terms
of her nature. She was born to be unvirgin and to reproduce;
that the natural process has been initiated is a source of joy and
laughter. The tragedy is that when the normal male who possesses desire flees the responsibility to submit himself to domes-
tication and reproduction, Eula is sold to Flem, the embodiment of the male principle in its most extreme and negative
manifestation.

Flem Snopes is devoted to self-aggrandizement; he is completely isolated because he is totally lacking in human
sympathy; and he is impotent. Eula is damned not by her own
act, but by the males who have set lust and rapacity above the
responsibility to create and sustain human life. When Eula is
given up to male sterility, nature and the whole process of
fertility is betrayed and perverted. It is in the context of this
event that the destructive male forces are loosed in Jack

Houston, Mink Snopes, and Henry Armstid. The oppressive summer heat fades into the dead cold of winter; the year at last turns again into spring, but man achieves no renewal of fertility. In the midst of the beauty of lush pear blossoms, men rampage the countryside to chase the spotted horses. Eula makes a brief but striking appearance in this episode:

> She was in a white garment; the heavy braided club of her hair looked almost black against it. She did not lean out, she merely stood there full in the moon, apparently blank-eyed or certainly not looking downward at them — the heavy gold hair, the mask not tragic and perhaps not even doomed: just damned, the strong faint lift of breasts beneath marblelike fall of garment; to those below what Brunhilde, what Rhinemaiden on what spurious river-rock of papier-mâché, what Helen returned to what topless and shoddy Argos, waiting for no one. (*H*, p. 311)

In *The Hamlet*, as in *As I Lay Dying* and *Light in August*, the comic prevails despite the presence of perversity, grotesqueness, and tragedy. The struggle between the male and the female forces is never-ending; the unresolved conflict is the characteristic motion of human life, and it arouses both laughter and sorrow. Eula symbolizes the creativity and productivity of life, and man cannot resist her magnetic power. However, the feminine force of life demands the total submission that Ike Snopes yields to his beloved cow.

Ike is able to lose his identity in the beauty of nature, to pursue only the life-giving force of the sun, and to devote himself absolutely to the female. The quality of Ike's devotion makes his love of the cow an ironic commentary on the loveless relation of Eula and Flem. Nevertheless, the idiot's devotion to a cow is as extreme as the sacrifice of fertility to impotence. If the idealization of the feminine is attained, it is, ironically, only in an idiot's tender love of a cow. Though Flem wins Eula, the force of his evil is diminished by the constant presence of the comic mode. In real life man is simply incapable of submitting himself completely to woman and to nature as the idiot can submit himself to the cow. Man is not natural; he is human and fallen. Yet, the self-assertive force of Flem Snopes is never completely triumphant in man. Though Eula is damned by her marriage to Flem, she is neither destroyed nor defeated. In *The Town* and *The Mansion* the feminine force of life remains an irresistible temptation to man.

As is frequently noted, *The Hamlet* is a novel of myth and legend, whereas the subsequent volumes of the Snopes trilogy are more comparable to the novel of manners. Eula in *The Town* and Flem in that novel and in *The Mansion* are less symbolic figures and more fully rounded characters. Though Faulkner sustains to some degree the mythic nature of Eula's character, he also develops much more fully her individuality and humanity. Rather than brutal country boys, Eula's admirers in *The Town* are Manfred de Spain, Gavin Stevens, and Ratliff. Since the circle of her devotees rarely includes more than these three, and since they possess far deeper insight into the significance of her nature than do any of her lustful lovers in Frenchman's Bend, the sense of the dignity of her character is increased. The comic ribaldry associated with her youth in Frenchman's Bend is deleted, and throughout *The Town* Eula is portrayed with the dignity of her momentary appearance in "The Spotted Horses" episode.

The central theme of *The Town* and *The Mansion* is the same as that of *The Hamlet;* the two novels depict the battle between the male and the female principles.[1] Flem continues to represent the male principle of self-assertion, and much of the content of both novels is devoted to his rise to financial power. His success, however, depends in part upon his ability to use his wife and her daughter for his cause and thus to destroy the

---

[1]Unlike *The Hamlet,* the minor narratives in *The Town* and *The Mansion* are unified not by the male-female conflict but by the theme of Flem's rise to respectability, entailing the necessity that he do away with all the unrespectable Snopeses. The latter is the major point of "Mule in the Yard" as it appears in *The Town.* However, in imagery and theme this episode is also an example of the male-female conflict. Mrs. Hait and her tranquil cow are attacked in the morning fog by I. O. Snopes's mules. The rampaging mules and the motionless cow symbolize the battle of the male Snopes and the female Mrs. Hait. Snopes engages in a fury of action to outwit Mrs. Hait, but she calmly outmaneuvers him. In this episode the individual female triumphs.

force of life within them. *The Town* portrays Eula's resistance to Flem's powers, and finally her sacrifice of her own life in order to free her daughter from him. In *The Mansion* the daughter, greatly injured by Flem's evil and by life itself, retaliates and indirectly but knowingly brings about Flem's death. In the end the rule by the purely negative qualities of the male principle is destroyed, but only through a compromise and sacrifice of the most positive qualities of the female principle.

Gavin Stevens is the "Greek chorus" in both novels who witnesses and participates in this drama and persistently struggles to understand it. Cleanth Brooks (*William Faulkner*, p. 217) suggests that *The Town* outlines Gavin's education about women and about reality. Gavin is like Horace Benbow in his inability to understand women or to predict their actions, a characteristic which reflects his inability to comprehend the real nature of the human condition. Though Gavin resists marriage to the two Snopes women, his life is, nevertheless, wholly submitted to them. *The Town* recounts this growing attachment. Initially, Gavin idealizes Eula; her beauty suggests to him that she is a Helen, a woman of an order of creation far superior to himself and Jefferson, Mississippi. Ratliff recognizes almost immediately that Gavin's interest in Eula is more than casual and abstract, though Gavin does not admit to himself the extremity of his devotion until after the fight with Manfred de Spain. Gavin is persuaded that Eula is chaste and unjustly scorned by Jefferson society. As a result he is the butt of much of Faulkner's comedy in the opening chapters of *The Town*, for he persists in his role of the naïve knight-protector to a woman who is obviously unconcerned about chastity. The comic mode indicates Faulkner's complete detachment from Gavin's plight, the sign of the shift in Faulkner's attitude toward the unvirgin woman that took place between the first few years of his career and the years after the publication of *The Sound and the Fury*.

Except for Gavin, the people of Jefferson recognize that the exceptional abundance of life which Eula possesses is fated to be united with a man of equal passion. That Manfred de Spain has cuckolded Flem Snopes is a fact that the town accepts and supports by its silence because it is man's instinct to approve the lovers' capacity for a vital sexual life despite the social mores which restrict it. Gavin alone insists that Eula is more than human, and he is shocked and angered during their first interview to discover that she is a very human and limited being. It is largely through Gavin's three interviews with Eula in *The Town* that her character is developed.

The description of Eula's physical appearance during the first interview is striking and significant. Rather than the overblown image of femininity portrayed in *The Hamlet*, Eula is presented as a woman whose figure appears small and slight despite the grandeur of her height. Hidden by her cloak, Eula's body is not the force which overwhelms Gavin; it is the penetrating, perceptive power of her dark blue eyes. Aware that the eyes possess as much power to engulf and control his physical being as does the blue sea itself, Gavin can only flee close contact with Eula and cry, "Don't touch me," to escape submitting himself to her physical power. To Eula, unburdened by pride or the need of it, the situation is quite simple. "You just are, and you need, and you must, and so you do" (*T*, p. 94). Gavin cannot believe that Eula offers herself to him simply out of compassion for the pain of his physical need. His pride does not allow him to admit that his aching desire could be so simply relieved, nor that Eula could act with a total lack of self-concern.[1] By the end of the interview he has persuaded himself that if it is not Manfred, it is at least Flem that she is sacrificing herself to protect. Calm and patient, Eula gazes at Gavin's antics imagining that he is a gentleman rather than the coward he himself admits that he is.

Gavin is fully aware that his refusal of Eula's offer springs as much from his sense of his impotence as from his sense of honor. He has loved Eula chaste, and her offer reveals that she is tainted. When Gavin calls her "Lilith," he is expressing his

---

[1] "By that time she had learned something of compassion for people through her determination to protect that girl, and to see someone that anguished over the need for a particular woman to her seemed foolish. That hers was more of a Hellenic attitude. That wasn't important enough to be frustrated about, and if that was going to make him feel any better she was perfectly willing to help him" (*Faulkner in the University*, p. 118).

awareness of the possible destructiveness of Eula's sexuality. Yet, as with his identification of Eula with Helen, this appellation reveals Gavin's inclination to consider her primarily a symbol and his inability to accept her as a real physical being. Yet, Gavin has known the truth and refused to admit it; he has clung to the ideal to escape the reality of his own physical failure. Though he is not literally impotent, Gavin has idealized and intellectualized love to the extent that he has enslaved the natural man and is unable to respond freely to his natural drives. He is frustrated and angered because he cannot respond to Eula with the simple physical passion with which Manfred wins her. Momentarily he is the weeping, defeated child, begging, "Papa what can I do now?" Gavin flees Jefferson for the security of a Heidelberg education. In the context of Faulkner's view of human nature Gavin is altogether the normal and typical mortal man; he is desirous of the freedom and fulfillment of the natural world which Eula embodies, but he is limited by his fallen nature, his pride, and his rationality.

Gavin, however, does not retreat permanently into unreality; he eventually returns to Jefferson to continue his struggle with the tensions of reality. Admitting his symbolic impotence, the sign of his mortality and limited nature, Gavin is able to sacrifice his male pride and submit himself to a lifetime of devotion to Eula and her daughter Linda. Gavin becomes the dedicated enemy of the male qualities embodied in Flem Snopes and the servant of the force of the female, though he is doomed to repeated discoveries that he has failed to fathom the full nature either of his enemy or of his heroines. Gavin Stevens is genuinely devoted to the force of life, but because of the nature of existence he must struggle constantly with his own limitations and weaknesses in the midst of his efforts to insure the preservation and prospering of life. Gavin never escapes the frailty and impotence of his mortality, but he never wavers in his concern for woman.

By the time of his second interview with Eula, Gavin has accepted the task of saving Linda from Snopesism by helping her leave Jefferson. However, he is still incapable of comprehending fully either Eula's character or Flem's. Ratliff, Gavin's detached mentor, perceives more accurately and quickly the nature of Flem's goal and guesses his willingness to use his daughter. Gavin, however, supposes that it is Eula who inhibits Linda's departure from Jefferson. Again, he is surprised by Eula's character. When he enters her home, Gavin recognizes immediately that Eula has submitted herself to Flem's power. Her husband's control over the household is ominously apparent in the false pretensions of the furniture. Gavin is pre- pared to face the power of Eula's beauty, but he is again sur- prised that she neither displays it nor exploits it. Despite the gloom of her surroundings, her thirty-six years, her "careless yellow bun," and her simple cotton dress, Eula still emanates a quality of serene and ample life. Though she is forced to be subservient to Flem, she has not been destroyed by him.

When Gavin discovers Flem's intentions for his daughter, he naïvely proposes that he reveal to Linda the truth about her birth, Flem's evil, and Eula's love and devotion. Eula responds,

"You dont know much about women, do you?" she said. "Women aren't interested in poets' dreams. They are in- terested in facts. It doesn't even matter whether the facts are true or not, as long as they match the other facts without leaving a rough seam. She wouldn't even believe you. She wouldn't believe him if he were to tell her. She would just hate you both — you most of all because you started it." (T, p. 226)

The passage indicates Eula's persistent concern with the facts of reality. Reality requires that a young girl have the security of a home and a name. Eula, born to create and reproduce, has spent a lifetime in a sterile marriage and a barren love affair to provide her only child with that security. She urges Gavin to marry Linda in order to save her from the disaster of Flem's using the girl's normal devotion to fatherhood to advance his evil power. Gavin cannot; he can love Linda as a child but not as a woman. He is free neither of his physical desire and devotion to Eula herself nor of his distrust of her nature. At the close of their last interview Gavin still believes that Eula asks him to marry Linda so that she will be free to elope with Manfred. He is completely unprepared for her suicide because he is still unable to fathom her character.

Before his last interview with Eula, Gavin drives to a hillside outside Jefferson and gazes at the physical beauty of the land. The landscape is engulfed in a rich darkness broken only by the stars, the fireflies, and "the faint and shapeless lambence of blooming dogwood returning loaned light to light as the phantoms of candles would" (*T*, p. 317). The scene suggests to Gavin the abundant potential of life, but also he knows that such abundance is "proffered once to the lips in youth and then no more." The tragedy of life, he concludes, is that "it must be premature, inconclusive and inconcludable in order to be life; it must be before itself, in advance of itself, to have been at all" (*T*, pp. 317-318).

Gavin Stevens was unprepared for Eula Snopes when she entered his life; throughout his lifetime of experience with her he has never fully comprehended her, nor has he been able to anticipate her actions. Though in their last interview Eula explains in full Flem's impotence, his selfish goals, and his cruel use of Linda, Gavin does not grasp the gravity of Eula's circumstance. Despite the sterility and anguish of her existence, Eula still miraculously possesses the quality of the abundant promise of life. Her eyes, Gavin notes, are "not the hard blue of fall but the blue of spring blooms, all one inextricable mixture of wisteria cornflowers larkspur bluebells weeds and all . . ." (*T*, p. 332). When Gavin returns home after the interview, he is disturbed by "the damned mockingbird . . . keeping his constant racket in Maggie's pink dogwood." The lushness of spring's renewal is disturbing to man because it is his tragic reminder of the sad waste of life's potential. The bird and the rich blossoms, ironically, foreshadow Eula's death.

Having obtained Gavin's promise that he will protect Linda to the extent of marrying her should it be required, Eula returns home and commits suicide. Gavin, again shocked and amazed by her action, weeps for the waste of her death: "To waste all that, when it was not hers to waste, not hers to destroy because it is too valuable, belonged to too many, too little of it to waste, destroy, throw away and be no more" (*T*, p. 358). However, the wreath of "black tulle and artificial flowers" which announces Eula's death was not "the myrtle of grief, it was the laurel of victory." Eula's suicide is the only act which could forestall Flem's use of Linda. It frees Linda from Flem's power and at the same time allows her to escape the shame of the public revelation of her mother's whoring. Eula sacrifices herself to preserve the security of her daughter's life. The suicide of the mother and the injured life of the daughter, which is portrayed in *The Mansion,* are the signs of the inevitable waste and destruction of life's potential at the hands of evil. Nevertheless, though Eula herself is destroyed, the force she embodies endures and at last triumphs.

As a youth Linda Snopes does not possess the overwhelming feminine power of her mother, but she is a strikingly beautiful and intelligent girl. Her eyes are the same hyacinth blue as her mother's, but her hair is dark; she is tall but lanky. Linda must encounter briefly the brutality of male desire in her affair with Matt Levitt, but unlike her mother, she has Gavin to flee to for protection. Though Gavin devotes himself to "forming her mind" in order to free her, eventually, from male violence and evil, particularly the evil of Flem, Linda's life is unalterably affected by the conflict of forces that is her inheritance.

The strange and ambiguous nature of Linda's character in *The Mansion* — the mingling of attractiveness and repulsiveness, of fulfillment and alienation — indicates that she is both the recipient of the feminine abundance of life and the victim of male destructiveness. No other of Faulkner's women is quite comparable to her. Linda's lack of physical and personal beauty and her malaise are the signs that the struggle between the forces of life and of destruction that she has endured has permanently injured her. The beautiful and innocent dark-haired girl in the wisteria dress of *The Town* has been transformed in *The Mansion* into a masculine woman with a horrible quacking voice and a streak of white hair like a "collapsed plume." Though Linda still possesses something of her mother's allure — young Charles Mallison feels her attraction, as does Gavin himself — she is in no sense beautiful nor does she possess Eula's abundant quality of creative life.

Linda's life is characterized by grief and alienation: she suffers the suicide of her mother, the discovery of her foster-father's evil and her illegitimacy, the death of her lover in war, deafness, and homelessness. Her life is given some meaning and fulfillment through her dedication to the ideals of justice, love, and compassion which Gavin fosters in her; however, her idealism is to some degree responsible for her alienation. Her experience with love is rich and rewarding; yet it is short-lived and ends tragically. Like her mother she is supported and aided by the dependable devotion of Gavin Stevens, but their relationship is not without tension and pain.

The culminating deed of Linda's life is her plot to destroy Flem. She acts because of her bitterness at his cruel use of her natural devotion to him and her desire to avenge her mother's sacrifice. Linda's deed expresses the combination of forces which have molded her life; it is an act of destruction and an act of submission to the needs of human survival. Linda is an accomplice in murder; she participates in evil and destruction. Nevertheless, the crime fosters life, for it accomplishes justice, destroys Flem, and frees Jefferson from the evil he embodies.

At the end of *The Mansion* Gavin is able at last to analyze the human situation accurately: "There aren't any morals, . . . [p]eople just do the best they can" (*The Mansion*, p. 429). The forces which mold the nature of Flem and Eula, of Mink and Linda, are the composites of reality. Man can escape neither the drive of self-assertion, death, and destruction nor the magnetic force of the power of life, submission to its natural process, and survival. This is man's nature and the nature of the world he inhabits. At the close of *The Mansion* as Mink submits himself to the pull of the earth and human mortality, he senses, despite his own frailty, his oneness with all humanity, even "the beautiful, the splendid, the proud and the brave." Man is a creature of the earth — therein lies the possibility both of evil and destruction and of creativity and sustenance. To William Faulkner man is alive and in motion and worth writing about when he is participating in this human struggle. Though the conflict of the male and the female is forever unresolved in Faulkner's fiction, the capacity for life displayed by Lena Grove and Eula Varner Snopes indicates his faith in the ability of humanity to survive and to sustain life.

CONCLUSION:
MINOR FIGURES AND
MAJOR MOTIFS

In woman's capacity for creativity and sustenance and in her capacity for perversity and destruction, Faulkner has embodied two alternative responses to the human condition. The tension between these two forces is the major thematic motif of his fiction. It is largely because of his vivid characterization of his female figures and the intricate patterns of imagery which link their characters to the meaning of the novels that Faulkner has been able to convey this central conflict with depth, clarity, and emotional power. Faulkner has made very skillful use of a basic reality of human existence; vital, life-giving sexuality is a force-ful symbol of the vitality of life itself. Faulkner's portrayal of evil and destructiveness in terms of perverted sexuality and his portrayal of the human need for order, security, and love in terms of the need for the sacrificial, life-giving love of the mother make an inevitable appeal to man's deepest emotions and his most significant experiences.

Faulkner's minor women characters perform two important functions in his fiction. They reinforce the patterns of meaning that the major female figures convey; and they, along with the minor male characters, provide the backdrop of human density

175

and variety that helps to make Faulkner's fictional world comparable to the real world. The minor female figures are variations of the major images of woman in Faulkner's fiction, but they also illustrate his superb capacity for creating a large number of characters who are unique and individual.

Faulkner's commitment to Romanticism during the earliest stage of his career resulted in the creation of a number of young women characters whose physical beauty represents the elusive but powerful dream of an idealized and perfect beauty. Faulkner was intensely attracted to the beauty of slender, youthful girls; in his early fiction he devoted much attention to the pictorial presentation of their physical allure. The imagery which conveys this physical quality in Cecily Saunders and Patricia Robyn makes them appealing and vivid characters. This quality of fragile but compelling girlish beauty also characterizes Caroline White Sartoris, young Bayard's first wife, Susan Reed of the short story "Hair," the strange girl in white of the story "Mistral," the youthful Linda Snopes, and Cecilia Farmer who appears briefly in the historical section of *Requiem for a Nun*. Melisandre Harriss, another character of this type, appears at different stages of her life in *Knight's Gambit*, *The Town*, and *The Mansion*, and she is always a slight, elusive figure. It is most significant that the "romantic" Gavin Stevens marries Melisandre instead of Linda Snopes.

These young women possess the quality of physical beauty that characterizes the slender, glistening poplar "maidens" of *The Marble Faun*, but the beauty of the fictional characters is, in most cases, deflated by Faulkner's accompanying portrayal of their human limitations and weaknesses. Though Faulkner envisioned the young virgin as the embodiment of Romantic ideality, even his earliest fiction displays his intense awareness of the discrepancy between the virgin of the imagination and the virgin of reality. Indeed, Faulkner was painfully aware that the sexual allure of the beautiful virgin gives her a power which is potentially destructive. Susan Reed, for example, possesses such an overabundance of sexual prowess at such an early age that Ratliff is provoked to comment,

"There's not any such thing as a woman born bad, because they are all born bad, born with the badness in them. The thing is to get them married before the badness comes to a natural head. But we try to make them conform to a system that a woman cant be married until she reaches a certain age. But nature dont pay any attention to systems, let alone women paying any attention to them, or to anything." (*TT*, p. 211)

Faulkner recognized the intense force of life in the sexuality of young women. Untamed and perverted, the force could erupt into the selfish use of power and the destructiveness of Cecily Saunders, Little Belle, and Temple Drake.

In Faulkner's early fiction the sexual allure of young women is identified with the male's intense desire for escape from the bonds of mortality. The inevitable defeat of this idealism is conveyed by the portrayal of the virgin's destructive powers. Just as the young girl's destructiveness is hidden by her youth, her seeming innocence, and her physical beauty, the destructiveness of the male's desire to escape reality is hidden by the grandeur of his ideals.

In Faulkner's early works there is a gradual movement from sympathy for the Romantic idealist to judgment upon him, a movement which is apparent in the characters of Gordon of *Mosquitoes*, Bayard Sartoris, Quentin Compson, and Horace Benbow. Simultaneously, there is a movement from an emphasis on man's physical need of woman to an emphasis on his emotional requirement of the qualities of maturity, self-sacrifice, and commitment to the sustenance of life which Faulkner chose to embody through the woman as mother. Faulkner conveys his implicit condemnation of self-assertion, isolation, and idealism through characters whose commitment to these qualities results in a perversion of the natural sexual process. Perverted sexuality reveals a perversion of life and a conscious or unconscious devotion to death.

It is the genius of Faulkner's fiction and the sign of his insight into the complexity of human nature that his figures of perversion and death, both male and female, are treated with fullness and deep sympathy. His least sympathetic treatment of the woman who misuses her sexuality is seen in the portraits of Belle Mitchell in *Sartoris* and of Miss Atkins, the dietician in *Light in August*. Bobbie Allen, Joe Christmas's prostitute-lover, is a ghastly embodiment of the death-like qualities of sexual perversion, but her genuine though momentary interest in Joe is at least one redeeming trait. However, most of Faulkner's women characters who are images of death are portrayed with great sympathy despite his condemnation of the pattern of their lives. Because Faulkner displays fully the combination of private drives and public circumstances which thwart the normal sexual process in the lives of women like Elly and Zilphia Gant, he is able to arouse pity for them even though their lives are characterized by perversity and decay. And, because of their complete expenditure of themselves in response to the events which mold their characters, Emily Grierson, Rosa Coldfield, and Joanna Burden assume something of the dignity of the tragic despite the horror of their sterile lives.

Faulkner devotes such great sympathy to his characterizations of Addie Bundren and Charlotte Rittenmeyer that despite their perversion of life, they are in many ways admirable women. As a result, they emerge as the most fully rounded and complex of Faulkner's female characters. They possess the feminine drive to create life, but their masculine commitment to idealism prevents their submission to the feminine role and makes them forces of death rather than of life. Laverne Shumann in *Pylon* is much like Charlotte Rittenmeyer in her masculine, violent response to the sex act. Even though Laverne is pregnant with her second child at the end of the novel, she is, like Charlotte and Addie, aligned with forces of death. Like Charlotte, she leaves her child to pursue her lover.

The mixture of masculine and feminine traits that is apparent in the characters of Addie Bundren and Charlotte Rittenmeyer is displayed in a more obvious way in Faulkner's characterizations of Linda Snopes, Judith Sutpen, and Drusilla Hawks. The circumstances of the lives of these women have forced them as young girls into masculine roles which require that they participate in acts of tragedy and destruction. That their femininity is permanently injured is signified by their alienation from the feminine role.

The force of Thomas Sutpen's masculine destructiveness is so powerful that his daughter seems to have been infected by it from childhood. It is Judith who is able to bear the horror of her father's savage fights with his Negro slaves, and it is Judith who races the horses to church. Unlike Rosa Coldfield, Judith never experiences romantic love; though she grieves inwardly over the tragedies that surround her, she preserves the outward appearance of an emotionless response to tragedy and death. Like Linda Snopes, she is crippled from birth by the destructiveness of her father, and she is forced to sacrifice the natural desire for love in the face of a force of death which she cannot overpower. The courage with which Judith endures the continual disruption of normal life that her father's ambition precipitates makes her one of Faulkner's most admirable women.

The Unvanquished, like most of Faulkner's novels, is based on the conflict between the forces of life and the forces of anti-life. The South, besieged by the North, engages in a valiant struggle for survival. The male world reacts with the same violence and destructiveness as the enemy; the female world attempts to carry on the activities of survival — the protection of the young and the preservation of the home. The women who survive the war without trauma or psychological change are those who do not waver from this feminine role. However, both Drusilla Hawks and Rosa Millard are drawn into the destructive male world because of the extensiveness of the disaster, the need for a daring response to it, and their possession of the somewhat masculine traits of pride and defiance. Both suffer as a result of their assumption of masculine roles.

Like Linda Snopes, Drusilla experiences the bitter grief of the early death of her lover. Denied the normal fulfillment of the feminine role by the tragedy of war, she casts off completely all signs of femininity; dressing as a soldier, she goes to battle against the Yankees who killed her lover. Faulkner makes it very clear that Drusilla's behavior is the product of her grief. Nevertheless, the more she is involved in violence the more she is committed to it. When the war is over, Drusilla is forced by the other women to put on her dress again, but they cannot force her to give up her masculine love of war. At the end of the novel young Bayard Sartoris sees that the time for violence is past, but Drusilla urges him into battle, for she wishes to achieve through him the only fulfillment she has ever known — the experience of the courage it takes to meet death. Bayard's decision to face his enemy unarmed marks the end of the era of violence, and Drusilla is left without any meaningful pattern of life to pursue.

As with Drusilla, Rosa Millard is drawn into the male world because of the unusual circumstances created by war. But unlike Drusilla, she is never able to live at peace with the crimes the need for survival has forced upon her. The horror of the moral and physical consequences of war is powerfully conveyed by Faulkner's portrayal of Rosa Millard's "mule stealing" and her death. The old woman is successively comic, heroic, and pathetic in her effort to help her community survive and in her attempt to subdue her grief over the compromise of her moral standards. Rosa Millard is an interesting variation of a familiar female type in Faulkner's fiction. She is the wise and courageous "mother" figure who devotes herself to the physical survival of her family and homeland. Yet, her involvement with evil and violent men results in a certain complication of characterization that makes her a more serious and a more significant figure than the other dauntless old women of Yoknapatawpha.

All of these women characters who are forced to participate in the masculine world of violence lose something of the purity, simplicity, and faith in life that characterize Faulkner's "mother" figures, but they do not lose that quality of unrelentless courage, determination, and endurance which Faulkner most admired in woman.

The Sound and the Fury is the pivotal work in the Faulkner canon, and in it Faulkner portrays most powerfully woman's capacity both for destroying life and for sustaining it. Mrs. Compson is the ghastly embodiment of the destructiveness that results from the perversion of the mother's role. The cold and serene adult Caddy is the woman whose capacities for participation in the normal reproductive process have been destroyed. Dilsey, on the other hand, embodies those qualities in woman which Faulkner most admires. She is a matriarch, the source of life for a large Negro family and the active mother of the Compsons. Despite the handicap of old age, she imposes an order upon the decayed Compson household through her faithful performance of those activities required for physical sustenance. Her endurance, her acceptance of responsibilities not her own, her devotion to the care of children, and her self-giving love make her the embodiment of the virtuous response to the evils of the human situation.

Nevertheless, Faulkner does not idealize Dilsey. She is old and ugly, and her ill-fitting garments make her appearance almost farcical. She is Negro and servant, and the faith which sustains her is an unsophisticated and unquestioning belief. It is the sign of Faulkner's realistic acceptance of the limitations of human nature that the female characters who are committed to the sustenance of life are never idealized, but instead appear briefly, with the effect of understatement, and are always deflated through a display of their unattractiveness, their old age, or their menial position in life and through the comic mockery of their weaknesses.

The view of human nobility and virtue that is behind Faulkner's characterization of Dilsey is expressed in the extreme by his characterization of Nancy Mannigoe in *Requiem for a Nun*. Nancy, another Negro maid, sacrifices her life in order to save Temple Stevens's children from suffering. Like Dilsey, Nancy is not idealized; instead, her character displays Faulkner's complete disregard for the "morality" of respectability. Nancy has participated in all sorts of human vice; she is a prostitute and a dope addict. Yet, ironically, she achieves the height of human nobility, for she overcomes the evil of her own life because of her love for little children, a love which symbolizes her commitment to life. Nancy possesses Dilsey's simple and irrational belief in the infinite love and mercy of God no matter what the extent of man's evil may be.

Nancy's murder of Temple's baby is an action designed to force Temple to accept the role of responsible motherhood to her other child. It is a symbolic act based on the idea that man can overcome his evil through sacrifice and suffering. However, Nancy is a less effective character than Dilsey and *Requiem for a Nun* is a less effective novel than *The Sound and the Fury* because Faulkner relies entirely on an extreme and totally symbolic action to convey his theme rather than on the complex, symbolically-tempered realism of most of his fiction.

The devotion to the sustenance of human life which Nancy and Dilsey embody is expressed in a variety of ways by a multitude of women characters in Faulkner's fiction. Perhaps the most appealing of these characters are Miss Jenny Du Pre, Miss Habersham (*Intruder in the Dust*), and Rosa Millard; these women are stabilizing and life-sustaining forces in the homes and communities they inhabit. They are completely content and secure in their roles as the matriarchs of their families and their communities, despite the fact that they have either borne no children of their own or are past the age of child-bearing. Because they possess a keen insight into the practical problems of survival, they are able to perform bold and daring actions to protect the lives and well-being of others. They are pleasantly domineering — no one dares to defy their authority — and they are able to endure great hardships, both physical and spiritual. Yet, they remain undaunted.

Margaret Mallison (*The Town, The Mansion,* and *Intruder in the Dust*) is Faulkner's most typical "mother" figure. She possesses the sterotyped motherly weaknesses; she is over-protective of both her son Chick and her brother Gavin, and she is immensely concerned with the routines of home duties and the proprieties of social living. Maggie and the "respectable" women of Jefferson are not outraged by Eula Snopes's immorality, but they reject her simply because her unworldly beauty endangers the stability of their social world. As Margaret puts it,

"Women are not interested in morals. They aren't even interested in unmorals. The ladies of Jefferson dont care what she does. What they will never forgive is the way she looks. No: the way the Jefferson gentlemen look at her." (*T*, p. 48)

Yet, Maggie possesses an amazing capacity to disregard completely the stereotyped female role when the well-being of those she loves is at stake. Her position in her world is so secure that she can safely defy social propriety and invite Eula to the Cotillion Ball merely to please her brother and to be kind to the outcast woman. In *Intruder in the Dust* when Chick's gravedigging helps to unravel a murder case and prevent a lynching, his mother becomes his willing accomplice. Chick recalls that

"she had been a hundred times less noisy than his father and a thousand times more valuable, yet now when all he intended was to walk to town with his uncle and sit for an hour, . . . she had completely abolished Lucas Beauchamp and Crawford Gowrie both and had gone back indefatigable to the day fifteen years ago when she had first set out to persuade him that he couldn't button his pants." (*ID*, p. 208)

Faulkner's fictional world is peopled with a host of very minor female characters whose primary function is to embody the stability of the human community. These women perform the menial tasks required for physical survival. They are resourceful and determined, and they are the willing aids of those in need. Mrs. Littlejohn and Mrs. Tull in *The Hamlet* exemplify such qualities, as do Mrs. Walker, the jail-keeper's wife in *Sanctuary;* Mrs. Beard, the boarding house proprietress in *Light in August;* and Lula Armstid and Rachel Samson, the women who offer food and assistance to the Bundren family during their journey to Jefferson.

The numerous Negro maids in Faulkner's world perform much this same function in the households they inhabit. An "Aunt Callie," who is much like Dilsey, appears in *Soldier's Pay* and another by the same name in *The Reivers.* In order to preserve the stability of the social order, Louvinia in *The Unvanquished* remains loyal to the Sartorises despite the increasing disloyalty of the younger generation of Negroes, as does Elnora in *Sartoris.* All of these Negro women are deeply loved and respected by the whites they serve. Cleanth Brooks, (*William*

Faulkner, p. 355) remarks about Minnie, Miss Reba's maid in *The Reivers,* "To hold on to good sense and good humor and yet avoid cringing and truckling servility calls for sanity, imagination and moral courage." This statement is applicable to nearly all of the women Negro servants in Faulkner's fiction.

For the most part, Faulkner shows the faults as well as the virtues which accompany woman's commitment to the sustenance of life. Martha Armstid in *Light in August* feels compelled to assist Lena Grove, but her mores demand a harsh judgment of Lena's illegitimate pregnancy. As a result Mrs. Armstid is unable to render aid with a spirit of kindness. Cora Tull (*As I Lay Dying*) is the epitome of the dutiful neighbor, and she does willingly assist the Bundrens during their family crisis. Nevertheless, she is narrow and harsh in her judgments of others and horribly self-righteous and self-assured. However, like her husband, Faulkner is compelled to accept with good humor the inevitability of Cora's dominance.

> "I reckon if there's ere a man or woman anywhere that he could turn it all over to and go away with His mind at rest, it would be Cora. And I reckon she would make a few changes, no matter how He was running it. And I reckon they would be for man's good. Leastways, we would have to like them. Leastways, we might as well go on and make like we did." (*AILD*, p. 70)

Frequently, Faulkner portrays the maliciousness of women who are excessively devoted to preserving the structures of community stability and propriety at the expense of the well-being of life. Such "good women" appear in *Soldier's Pay, Sanctuary, Light in August,* and the short story, "Uncle Willy."

Because of their commitment to life, many of Faulkner's female characters possess an amazing ability to endure extended hardships and suffering. Chick Mallison judges that "women couldn't really stand anything except tragedy and poverty and physical pain" (*ID*, p. 208). Dilsey, Ruby Goodwin, Judith Sutpen, Eula Snopes, and Nancy Mannigoe display a tremendous capacity for the silent endurance of tragic circumstances. Many women in Faulkner's fiction are forced to accept the hardships and limitations of their lives with no avenue of escape and no capacity for overcoming their plight. This is the predicament of Ellen Sutpen and Milly Jones in *Absalom, Absalom!*, of the Snopes women and of Mrs. Henry Armstid in *The Hamlet*, of Mrs. Hines and Mrs. McEachern in *Light in August*, and of Roth's mulatto mistress in *Go Down, Moses*. Molly Beauchamp, who is a superbly vivid character, possesses this same ability to endure silently the hardships of her life with the proud Lucas, though in "The Fire and the Hearth" she does at last assert a feminine power when his foolishness drives her to threaten to divorce him.

Though the woman's capacity for bearing hardships frequently makes her an embodiment of human suffering, it is precisely her ability to survive despite "tragedy and poverty and physical pain" that makes her a stabilizing and sustaining force in the human community. Hence in *A Fable* when both the old general and the young corporal have passed away, the two women, Marthe and Marya, are, at the end of the novel, still engaged in cultivating the farm, serving food and maintaining a home.

Though Faulkner displays the pathos of woman's role, it is important to note that the comic tone is abundant in his characterizations of those women who are committed to the sustenance of life. The humor that dominates Faulkner's portrayal of Miss Jenny, Miss Habersham, and Rosa Millard is a reflection of the pleasant sense of security that their wisdom and persistent devotion supply to those they love. Miss Sophonsiba in *Go Down, Moses* and Reba Rivers in *Sanctuary* and *The Reivers* are broadly comic figures, and Faulkner is immensely successful with such creations. Much of the comedy of Miss Reba's character is based on the fact that though she is the keeper of a brothel, she possesses a "motherly" devotion to her girls, a concern for the "respectability" of her house, and an intense loyalty to her "husband," Mr. Binford. The comic effect is apparent not only in the characters of Miss Jenny, Rosa Millard, Miss Habersham, Cora Tull, and Mrs. Will Varner, but it is also present in the more serious characters, Molly Beauchamp and Dilsey.

Most significantly, the comic tone is of major importance in the portrayal of Lena Grove and Eula Varner. Thematically, the comic mode is the result of Faulkner's optimistic belief that humanity, despite its imperfections, will survive. The comic in the portraits of Lena and Eula serves the dual purpose of deflating their idealized qualities so that they become more life-like figures and of asserting the joy and hope for human life which are offered by their fecundity.

The comic tone permeates Faulkner's last novel, *The Reivers*, and is a final witness to his essential optimism about human life. Through Everbe Corinthia young Lucius Priest discovers both virtue and evil. Though Lucius's learning process is not without pain and suffering, the novel demonstrates Faulkner's pleasure in this process of human life. Significantly, the novel closes with Everbe giving birth to a child and establishing a new home. The reproductive process is the means by which man achieves his immortality — the survival of the human race.

Primarily through patterns of imagery, Faulkner has established throughout his fiction a close connection between woman and nature. This identification of woman with nature is fitting, for woman possesses the beauty of nature, and her procreative role links her to the earth's natural process of reproduction. Therefore, Faulkner's women are distinguishable from the men because they have a closer identity with the sexual process, an identity which gives them their early knowledge of the nature of life which men must learn gradually. The women also possess a greater commitment to the sustenance of life than do the men, a commitment which enables them to disregard traditional morality and rationality when the preservation of the well-being of life is at stake. Further, the identification of woman with the earth accounts for her qualities of determination and endurance.

It is through his experience with nature that Ike McCaslin in "The Bear" and *Go Down, Moses* learns those virtues which enable man to survive with dignity and nobility — "honor and pride and pity and justice and courage and love." It is significant that Faulkner chose to identify these ideals with the "moment of truth and beauty" embodied by Keats's "Ode on the Grecian Urn," the image with which he associates the idealized qualities of woman. The subsequent actions of Ike's life are determined by his commitment to the idealization of the land and the virtues he has learned through it.

However, the meaning of the short story is significantly qualified by the novel, for Faulkner demonstrates in *Go Down, Moses* that Ike's commitment to idealism results in an isolated and sterile existence. Like woman, the land does suggest to man the ideals by which he must live, but the land also embodies man's inescapable human limitations. By relinquishing the land to escape the curse of evil which his ancestors have bestowed upon him, Ike relinquishes life. Man cannot escape the evil of life without sacrificing life itself:

"There are things, circumstances, conditions in the world which should not be there but are, and you cant escape them and indeed, you would not escape them even if you had the choice, since they too are a part of Motion, of participating in life, being alive." (*R*, p. 155)

In Faulkner's fiction the earth and woman are symbolic of the nature of the human condition, and they embody both its limitations and its potentialities. Man cannot escape the hold of woman and the land over him because he cannot escape the limitations of human existence. He is required to cope with the evil, the chaos, and the minor imperfections of human life if he is to avoid self-destruction. The effort to deny his human limitations results inevitably in the final triumph of the human condition over him, for he must either withdraw from life and live a death-in-life existence or he must submit himself to death. Ultimately, it is impossible for man to escape his finitude, for he is mortal and he must inevitably return to the earth which bore him. However, when man accepts the limitations of the human situation and submits himself to the natural processes of life, he can survive meaningfully. Nature's beauty, its eternalness, and its never-ending cycle of renewal and woman's capacities for fecundity, sustenance, and endurance are the signs that human life will "prevail."

Faulkner's belief in the capacity of human life not only to endure but also to prevail is the result of his fascination with all types of human character, a fascination which resulted in the creation of a vast fictional world which abounds with an endless variety of individualized and vividly realized characters. Faulkner's women characters are no exception; though they perform the function of embodying the polar extremes of the human situation, they also display the "furious motion of being alive."

Selected Bibliography

I. The Works of William Faulkner
(Original publication date
followed by edition used
in this study.)

1924: *The Marble Faun.* Boston, 1924.
1926: *Soldier's Pay.* New York, 1926.
1927: *Mosquitoes.* New York, 1927.
1929: *Sartoris.* New York, 1929.
1929: *The Sound and the Fury.* New York, 1929.
1930: *As I Lay Dying.* New York, 1930.
1931: *Sanctuary.* New York, 1931.
1931: *These Thirteen.* New York, 1931.
1931: *Idyll in the Desert.* New York, 1931.
1932: *Miss Zilphia Gant.* Dallas, Texas, 1932.
1932: *Light in August.* New York, 1932.
1932: *Salmagundi.* Ed. Paul Romaine. Milwaukee, Wis., 1932.
1933: *A Green Bough.* New York, 1933.
1934: *Doctor Martino and Other Stories.* New York, 1934.
1935: *Pylon.* New York, 1935.
1936: *Absalom, Absalom!* New York, 1936.
1938: *The Unvanquished.* New York, 1959.

1939: *The Wild Palms.* New York, 1939.
1940: *The Hamlet.* New York, 1940.
1942: *Go Down, Moses.* New York, 1942.
1948: *Intruder in the Dust.* New York, 1948.
1949: *Knight's Gambit.* New York, 1949.
1950: *Collected Stories of William Faulkner.* New York, 1950.
1951: *Requiem for a Nun.* New York, 1954. (Reprinted with *Sanctuary,* The New American Library).
1953: *Mirrors of Chartres Street.* Minneapolis, Minn., 1953.
1954: *A Fable.* New York, 1954.
1955: *Big Woods.* New York, 1955.
1957: *The Town.* New York, 1957.
1958: *New Orleans Sketches.* Ed. Carvel Collins. New Brunswick, N. J., 1958.
1959: *The Mansion.* New York, 1959.
1962: *The Reivers: A Reminiscence.* New York, 1962.
1962: *Early Prose and Poetry.* Ed. Carvel Collins. Boston, 1962.
1964: *The Wishing Tree.* New York, 1964.
1966: *Essays, Speeches, and Public Letters.* Ed. James B. Meriwether. New York, 1966.

II. Secondary Works

Abel, Darrel. "Frozen Movement in *Light in August*." *Boston University Studies in English*, III (Spring 1957), 32-44.

Adams, J. Donald. *The Shape of Books to Come.* New York, 1944.

Adams, Percy G. "Humor as Structure and Theme in Faulkner's Trilogy," *Wisconsin Studies in Contemporary Literature*, V (Autumn 1964), 205-212.

Adams, Richard P. "Faulkner and the Myth of the South," *Mississippi Quarterly*, XIV (Summer 1961), 131-137.

Faulkner: Myth and Motion. Princeton, N. J., 1968.

Adams, Robert M. "Poetry in the Novel: Or, Faulkner Esemplastic," *Virginia Quarterly Review*, XXIX (Summer 1953), 419-434.

Aiken, Conrad. "William Faulkner: The Novel as Form." In *William Faulkner: Three Decades of Criticism*, Hoffman and Vickery, eds., pp. 135-142.

Allen, Charles. "William Faulkner: Comedy and the Purpose of Humor," *Arizona Quarterly*, XVI (Spring 1960), 59-69.

Anderson, Charles. "Faulkner's Moral Center," *Etudes Anglaises*, VII (January 1954), 48-58.

Applewhite, Davis. "The South of *Light in August*," *Mississippi Quarterly*, XI (Fall 1958), 167-172.

Arthos, John. "Ritual and Humor in the Writing of William Faulkner." In *William Faulkner: Two Decades of Criticism*, Hoffman and Vickery, eds., pp. 101-118.

Bache, William B. "Moral Awareness in 'Dry September,' " *Faulkner Studies*, III (Winter 1954), 53-57.

Backman, Melvin. "Faulkner's *The Wild Palms*: Civilization against Nature," *University of Kansas City Review*, XXVIII (Spring 1962), 199-204.

"Sickness and Primitivism: A Dominant Pattern in William Faulkner's Work," *Accent*, XIV (Winter 1954), 61-73.

Faulkner: The Major Years. A Critical Study. Bloomington, Ind., 1966.

Backus, Joseph M. "Names of Characters in Faulkner's *The Sound and the Fury*," *Names*, VI (December, 1958), 226-233.

Baker, James R. "The Symbolic Extension of Yoknapatawpha County," *Arizona Quarterly*, VIII (Autumn 1952), 223-228.

Baldanza, Frank. "The Structure of *Light in August*," *Modern Fiction Studies*, XIII (Spring 1967), 67-78.

Bass, Eben. "Meaningful Images in *The Sound and the Fury*," *Modern Language Notes*, LXXVI (December 1961), 728-731.

Bassan, Maurice. "Benjy at the Monument," *English Language Notes*, II (September 1964), 46-50.

Baum, Catherine B. " 'The Beautiful One': Caddy Compson as Heroine of *The Sound and the Fury*," *Modern Fiction Studies*, XIII (Spring 1967), 33-44.

Beach, Joseph Warren. *American Fiction: 1920-1940*. New York, 1941. Pp. 123-169.

Beck, Warren. "Faulkner: A Preface and a Letter," *Yale Review*, LII (1962), 157-160.

"Faulkner and the South," *Antioch Review*, I (Spring 1941), 82-94.

"Faulkner's Point of View," *College English*, II (May 1941), 736-749.

William Faulkner's Style." In *William Faulkner: Three Decades of Criticism*, Hoffman and Vickery, eds., pp. 142-156.

Man in Motion: Faulkner's Trilogy. Madison, Wis., 1961.

Beebe, Maurice. "Criticism of William Faulkner: A Selected Checklist," *Modern Fiction Studies*, XIII (Spring 1967), 115-161.

Benson, Carl. "Thematic Design in *Light in August*," *South Atlantic Quarterly*, LIII (October 1954), 540-555.

Bergel, Lienhard. "Faulkner's *Sanctuary*," *Explicator*, VI (December 1947), item 20.

Bernberg, Raymond E. *"Light in August:* A Psychological View," *Mississippi Quarterly,* XI (Fall 1958), 173-176.

Bjork, Lennart. "Ancient Myths and the Moral Framework of Faulkner's *Absalom, Absalom!" American Literature,* XXXV (May 1963), 196-204.

Blackwell, Louise. "Faulkner and the Womenfolk, " *Kansas Magazine,* LXXIII (1967), 77. *N.V.*

Blotner, Joseph. *"As I Lay Dying:* Christian Lore and Irony," *Twentieth Century Literature,* III (April 1957), 14-19.

William Faulkner's Library: A Catalogue. Charlottesville, Va., 1964.

Bouvard, Loic. "Conversation with William Faulkner," *Modern Fiction Studies,* V (Winter 1959-1960), 361-364.

Bowling, Lawrence E. "Faulkner and the Theme of Innocence," *Kenyon Review,* XX (Summer 1958), 466-478.

"Faulkner and the Theme of Isolation," *Georgia Review,* XVIII (Spring 1964), 50-66.

"Faulkner: The Theme of Pride in *The Sound and the Fury," Modern Fiction Studies,* XI (Summer 1965), 129-239.

"The Technique of *The Sound and the Fury," Kenyon Review,* X (Autumn 1948), 552-566.

"William Faulkner: The Importance of Love," *Dalhousie Review,* XLIII (Winter 1963), 474-482.

Boyle, Kay, "Tattered Banners," *The New Republic,* XCIV (March 9, 1938), 136-137.

Boynton, Percy. *America in Contemporary Fiction*. Chicago, 1940. Pp. 103-112.

Bradbury, John M. *Renaissance in the South: A Critical History of the Literature, 1920-1960*. Chapel Hill, N. C., 1963. Pp. 50-57.

Bradford, Melvin E. "Faulkner's 'Elly': An Expose," *Mississippi Quarterly*, XXI, 179-187.

Breaden, Dale G. "William Faulkner and the Land," *American Quarterly*, X (Fall 1958), 344-57.

Breit, Harvey. "A Sense of Faulkner," *Partisan Review*, XVIII (January-February 1951), 88-94.

Brennan, Dan. "Journey South," *University of Kansas City Review*, XX (Autumn 1955), 11-16.

Brennan, Joseph, and Seymour L. Gross. "The Problem of Moral Values in Conrad and Faulkner," *Personalist*, XLI (Winter 1960), 60-70.

Bridgman, Richard. "As Hester Prynne Lay Dying," *English Language Notes*, II (June 1965), 294-296.

Brien, Delores E. "William Faulkner and the Myth of Woman," *Research Studies*, XXXV (1967), 132-140. *N. V.*

Brooks, Cleanth. "Notes on Faulkner's *Light in August*," *Harvard Advocate*, CXXXV (November 1951), 10-11, 27.

"The Poetry of Miss Rosa Coldfield," *Shenandoah*, XXI (Spring 1970), 199-206.

"Primitivism in *The Sound and the Fury*." In *English Institute Essays 1952*. New York, 1954. Pp. 5-28.

"William Faulkner: Vision of Good and Evil." In *The Hidden God: Studies in Hemingway, Faulkner, Yeats, Eliot, and Warren.* New Haven, Conn., 1963. Pp. 22-43.

William Faulkner: The Yoknapatawpha Country. New Haven, Conn., 1963.

Bross, Addison C. "*Soldier's Pay* and the Art of Aubrey Beardsley," *American Quarterly,* XIX (Spring 1967), 3-23.

Brown, James. "Shaping the World of *Sanctuary,*" *University of Kansas City Review,* XXV (Winter 1958), 137-142.

Brumm, Ursula. "Wilderness and Civilization: A Note on William Faulkner." In *William Faulkner: Three Decades of Criticism,* Hoffman and Vickery, eds., pp. 125-134.

Brylowski, Walter. *Faulkner's Olympian Laugh: Myth in the Novels.* Detroit, Mich., 1968.

Buttitta, Anthony. "William Faulkner: That Writin' Man of Oxford," *Saturday Review,* XVIII (May 21, 1938), 6-8.

Canby, H. S. *Seven Years Harvest.* New York, 1936.

Campbell, Harry M. "Experiment and Achievement: *As I Lay Dying* and *The Sound and the Fury,*" *Sewanee Review,* LI (April 1943), 305-320.

and Ruel E. Foster. *William Faulkner: A Critical Appraisal.* Norman, Okla., 1951.

and James P. Pilkington. "Faulkner's *Sanctuary,*" *Explicator,* IV (June 1946), item 61.

Cantwell, Robert. "Faulkner's 'Popeye,' " *Nation,* CLXXXVI (February 15, 1958), 140-141, 148.

"The Faulkners: Recollections of a Gifted Family." In *William Faulkner: Three Decades of Criticism*, Hoffman and Vickery, eds., pp. 51-66.

Carey, Glenn O. "Social Criticism in Faulkner's 'Dry September,' "*English Record*, XV (December 1964), 27-30.

Carter, Hodding. "Faulkner and His Folk," *Princeton University Library Chronicle*, XVIII (Spring 1957), 95-107.

Chase, Richard. "Faulkner – The Great Years." In *The American Novel and Its Tradition*. Garden City, 1957. Pp. 205-236.

"The Stone and the Crucifixion: Faulkner's *Light in August*," *Kenyon Review*, X (Autumn 1948), 539-551.

Coffee, Jessie A. "Empty Steeples: Theme, Symbol and Irony in Faulkner's Novels," *Arizona Quarterly*, XXIII (Autumn 1967), 197-206.

Coindreau, Maurice. "Preface to *The Sound and the Fury*," trans. by George Reeves, *Mississippi Quarterly*, XIX (Summer 1966), 107-115.

"William Faulkner in France," *Yale French Studies*, No. 10 (Fall 1952), 85-91.

Cole, Douglas. "Faulkner's *Sanctuary*: Retreat from Responsibility," *Western Humanities Review*, XIV (Summer 1960), 291-298.

Collins, Carvel. "A Note on *Sanctuary*," *Harvard Advocate*, CXXXV (November 1951), 16.

"Faulkner and Certain Earlier Southern Fiction," *College English*, XVI (November 1954), 92-97.

"The Interior Monologues of *The Sound and the Fury.*" In *English Institute Essays 1952.* New York, 1954. Pp. 29-55.

"Miss Quentin's Paternity Again," *Texas Studies in Literature and Language,* II (Autumn 1960), 253-260.

"Nathaniel West's *Day of the Locust* and *Sanctuary,*" *Faulkner Studies,* II (Summer 1953), 23-24.

"The Pairing of *The Sound and the Fury* and *As I Lay Dying,*" *Princeton University Library Chronicle,* XVIII (Spring 1957), 114-123.

Cottrell, Beekman. "Christian Symbols in *Light in August,*" *Modern Fiction Studies,* II (Winter 1956), 207-213.

Coughlan, Robert. *The Private World of William Faulkner: The Man, The Legend, The Writer.* New York, 1953.

Cowley, Malcolm. *The Faulkner-Cowley File: Letters and Memories, 1944-1962.* New York, 1966.

ed. *The Portable Faulkner.* New York, 1946.

Cross, Barbara M. "Apocalypse and Comedy in *As I Lay Dying,*" *Texas Studies in Literature and Language,* III (Summer 1961), 251-258.

"*The Sound and the Fury:* The Pattern of Sacrifice," *Arizona Quarterly,* XVI (Spring 1960), 5-16.

Cross, Richard K. "The Humor of *The Hamlet,*" *Twentieth Century Literature,* XII (January 1967), 203-215.

Cullen, John B. with Floyd C. Watkins. *Old Times in the Faulkner Country.* Chapel Hill, N. C., 1961.

Cypher, James R. "The Tangled Sexuality of Temple Drake," *American Imago,* XIX (Fall 1962), 243-252.

Dauner, Louise. "Quentin and the Walking Shadow: The Dilemma of Nature and Culture," *Arizona Quarterly,* XXI (Summer 1965), 159-170.

DeVoto, Bernard. *Minority Report.* Boston, 1940. Pp. 209-218.

Dickerson, Mary Jane. "*As I Lay Dying* and *The Waste Land* — Some Relationships," *Mississippi Quarterly,* XVII (Summer 1964), 129-135.

_____ "Some Sources of Faulkner's Myth in *As I Lay Dying,*" *Mississippi Quarterly,* XIX (Summer 1966), 132-142.

Dominicis, A. M. "An Interview with Faulkner," *Faulkner Studies,* III (Summer-Autumn 1954), 33-37.

Doran, Leonard. "Form and the Story Teller," *Harvard Advocate,* CXXXV (November 1951), 12, 38-41.

Douglas, Harold J., and Robert Daniel. "Faulkner and the Puritanism of the South," *Tennessee Studies in Literature,* II (1957), 1-13.

Dussinger, Gloria R. "Faulkner's Isaac McCaslin as Romantic Hero Manque," *South Atlantic Quarterly,* LXVIII (Summer 1969), 377-385.

Eby, Cecil D. "Faulkner and the Southwestern Humorists," *Shenandoah,* XI (Autumn 1959), 13-21.

Edmonds, Irene C. "Faulkner and the Black Shadow." In *Southern Renascence: The Literature of the Modern South,* Louis D. Rubin, Jr., and Robert D. Jacobs, eds. Baltimore, Md., 1953. Pp. 192-206.

Elias, Robert H. "Gavin Stevens: Intruder?" *Faulkner Studies,* III (Spring 1954), 1-4.

Emmanuel, Pierre. "Faulkner and the Sense of Sin," *Harvard Advocate,* CXXXV (November 1951), 20.

England, Martha W. "Quentin's Story: Chronology and Explication," *College English,* XXII (January 1961), 228-235.

Falkner, Murry C. *The Falkner's of Mississippi.* Baton Rouge, La., 1967.

Fant, Joseph L., and Lt. Col. Robert P. Ashley. *Faulkner at West Point.* New York, 1964.

Farmer, Norman, Jr. "The Love Theme: A Principal Source of Thematic Unity in Faulkner's Snopes Trilogy," *Twentieth Century Literature,* VIII (January 1963), 111-123.

Farnham, James F. "Faulkner's Unsung Hero: Gavin Stevens," *Arizona Quarterly,* XXI (Summer 1965), 115-132.

Faulkner, John. *My Brother Bill: An Affectionate Reminiscence.* New York, 1963.

Feaster, John. "Faulkner's Old Man: A Psychoanalytic Approach," *Modern Fiction Studies,* XIII (Spring 1967), 89-93.

Fiedler, Leslie A. "William Faulkner: An American Dickens," *Commentary,* X (October 1950), 384-387.

————. *Love and Death in the American Novel.* New York, 1960.

Fisher, Richard E. "The Wilderness, the Commissary, and the Bedroom: Faulkner's Ike McCaslin as Hero in a Vacuum," *English Studies,* XLIV (February 1963), 19-28.

Flint, R. W. "Faulkner as Elegist," *Hudson Review*, VII (Summer 1954), 246-257.

Flynn, Robert. "The Dialectic of *Sanctuary*," *Modern Fiction Studies*, II (Autumn 1956), 109-113.

Ford, Arthur L. "Dust and Dreams: A Study of Faulkner's 'Dry September,' " *College English*, XXIV (December 1962), 219-220.

Foster, Ruel E. "Dream as Symbolic Act in Faulkner," *Perspective*, II (Summer 1949), 179-194.

Franklin, Rosemary. "Animal Magnetism in *As I Lay Dying*," *American Quarterly*, XVIII (Spring 1966), 24-34.

Franklin, R. W. "Narrative Management in *As I Lay Dying*," *Modern Fiction Studies*, XIII (Spring 1967), 57-65. √

Frazier, David L. "Gothicism in *Sanctuary*: The Black Pall and the Crap Table," *Modern Fiction Studies*, II (Autumn 1956), 114-124.

"Lucas Burch and the Polarity of *Light in August*," *Modern Language Notes*, LXXIII (June 1958), 417-419.

Frederick, John T. "Anticipation and Achievement in Faulkner's *Soldier's Pay*," *Arizona Quarterly*, XXIII (Autumn 1967), 243-249.

Freedman, William A. "The Technique of Isolation in *The Sound and the Fury*," *Mississippi Quarterly*, XV (Winter 1962), 21-26.

Frey, Leonard. "Irony and Point of View in 'That Evening Sun,' " *Faulkner Studies*, II (Autumn 1953), 33-40.

Frohock, W. M. "William Faulkner: The Private Vision." In *The Novel of Violence in America*. Second edition. Dallas, Texas, 1957. Pp. 144-165.

Galharn, Carl. "Faulkner's Faith: Roots from *The Wild Palms*," *Twentieth Century Literature*, I (October 1955), 139-160.

Garrett, George P., Jr. "An Examination of the Poetry of William Faulkner," *Princeton University Library Chronicle*, XVIII (Spring 1957), 124-135.

Gavin, Jerome. "*Light in August:* The Act of Involvement," *Harvard Advocate*, CXXXV (November 1951), 14-15, 34-37.

Gibbons, Kathryn G. "Quentin's Shadow," *Literature and Psychology*, XII (Winter 1962), 16-24.

Geismar, Maxwell. "William Faulkner: The Negro and the Female." In *Writers in Crisis: The American Novel Between Two Wars*. Boston, 1942. Pp. 143-183.

"William Faulkner: Before and After the Nobel Prize." In *American Moderns: From Rebellion to Conformity*. New York, 1958. Pp. 91-106.

Gerard, Albert. "Justice in Yoknapatawpha County: Some Symbolic Motifs in Faulkner's Later Writings," *Faulkner Studies*, II (Winter 1954), 47-57.

Glicksberg, Charles I. "William Faulkner and the Negro Problem," *Phylon*, X (June 1949), 153-160.

"The World of William Faulkner," *Arizona Quarterly*, V (Spring 1949), 46-58.

Goellner, Jack G. "A Closer Look at *As I Lay Dying*," *Perspective*, VII (Spring 1954), 42-54.

Going, William T. "Faulkner's 'A Rose for Emily'," *Explicator,* XVI (February 1958), item 27.

Gold, Joseph. "No Refuge: Faulkner's *Sanctuary*," *University Review,* XXXIII (Winter 1966), 129-135.

"The 'Normality' of Snopesism: Universal Themes in Faulkner's *The Hamlet*," *Wisconsin Studies in Contemporary Literature,* III (Winter 1962), 25-34.

"The Two Worlds of *Light in August*," *Mississippi Quarterly,* XVI (Summer 1963), 160-167.

"William Faulkner's 'One Compact Thing,' " *Twentieth Century Literature,* VIII (April 1962), 3-9.

William Faulkner: A Study in Humanism from Metaphor to Discourse. Norman, Okla., 1966.

Green, A. Wigfall. "William Faulkner at Home," *Sewanee Review,* XL (Summer 1932), 294-306.

Greene, Theodore M. "The Philosophy of Life Implicit in Faulkner's *The Mansion*," *Texas Studies in Literature and Language,* II (Winter 1961), 401-418.

Greer, Dorothy. "Dilsey and Lucas: Faulkner's Use of the Negro as a Gauge of Moral Character," *Emporia State Research Studies,* XI (September 1962), 43-61.

Greer, Scott. "Joe Christmas and the 'Social Self,' " *Mississippi Quarterly,* XI (Fall 1958), 160-166.

Greet, T. Y. "The Theme and Structure of Faulkner's *The Hamlet*." In *William Faulkner: Three Decades of Criticism,* Hoffman and Vickery, eds., pp. 330-347.

"Toward the Light: The Thematic Unity of Faulkner's 'Cycle'," *Carolina Quarterly*, III (Fall 1950), 38-44.

Grenier, Cynthia. "The Art of Fiction: An Interview with William Faulkner — September, 1955," *Accent*, XVI (Summer 1956), 167-177.

Gresset, Michel. "Psychological Aspects of Evil in *The Sound and the Fury*," *Mississippi Quarterly*, XIX (Summer 1966), 143-153.

Guerard, Albert, Jr. "*Requiem for a Nun*: An Examination," *Harvard Advocate*, CXXXV (November 1951), 19, 41-42.

Guttmann, Allen. "Collisions and Confrontations," *Arizona Quarterly*, XVI (Spring 1960), 46-52.

Gwynn, Frederick L. "Faulkner's Purfrock — and Other Observations," *JEGP*, LII (January 1953), 63-70.

"Faulkner's Raskolnikov," *Modern Fiction Studies*, IV (Summer 1958), 169-172.

and Joseph L. Blotner, eds. *Faulkner in the University: Class Conferences at the University of Virginia, 1957-1958*. Charlottesville, Va., 1959.

Hogopian, John V. "Nihilism in Faulkner's *The Sound and the Fury*," *Modern Fiction Studies*, XIII (Spring 1967), 45-55.

Hamblen, Abigail Ann. "Faulkner's Pillar of Endurance: *Sanctuary* and *Requiem for a Nun*," *Midwest Quarterly*, VI (July 1965), 369-375.

Hamilton, Edith. "Faulkner: Sorcerer or Slave." In *Saturday Review Gallery*, Jerome Beatty, Jr., ed. New York, 1959. Pp. 419-429.

Handy, William J. "*As I Lay Dying:* Faulkner's Inner Reporter," *Kenyon Review,* XXI (Summer 1959), 437-451.

Harder, Kelsie B. "Charactonyms in Faulkner's Novels," *Bucknell Review,* VIII (May 1959), 189-201.

Hardwick, Elizabeth. "Two Contrasting Views of *Intruder in the Dust.*" In *William Faulkner: Two Decades of Criticism,* Hoffman and Vickery, eds., pp. 244-250.

Harrington, Evans B. "Technical Aspects of William Faulkner's 'That Evening Sun,' " *Faulkner Studies* (Winter 1952), 54-59.

Hartwick, Harry. *The Foreground of American Fiction.* New York, 1934.

Harvey, W. J. *Character and the Novel.* Ithaca, N.Y., 1965.

Hatcher, Harlan. *Creating the Modern American Novel.* New York, 1935.

Haugh, R. F. "Faulkner's Corrupt Temple," *English Studies in Africa,* IV (March 1961), 7-16.

Heald, William F. "Morality in 'Spotted Horses,' " *Mississippi Quarterly,* XV (Spring 1962), 85-91.

Hicks, Granville. "The Past and Future of William Faulkner," *Bookman,* LXXIV (September 1931), 17-24.

The Great Tradition: An Interpretation of American Literature Since the War. New York, 1933.

Hirshleifer, Phyllis. "As Whirlwinds in the South: Analysis of *Light in August,*" *Perspective,* II (Summer 1949), 225-238.

Hoffman, Frederick J. *The Modern Novel in America.* Chicago, 1951. Pp. 168-180.

William Faulkner. New York, 1961.

and Olga Vickery, eds. *William Faulkner: Three Decades of Criticism.* East Lansing, Mich., 1960.

and Olga Vickery, eds. *William Faulkner: Two Decades of Criticism.* East Lansing, Mich., 1951.

Hogan, Patrick G., Jr. "Critical Misconceptions of Southern Thought: Faulkner's Optimism," *Mississippi Quarterly,* X (January 1957), 19-28.

Holman, C. Hugh. "The Unity of Faulkner's *Light in August,*" *PMLA,* LXXIII (March 1958), 155-166.

"William Faulkner: The Anguished Dream of Time." In *Three Modes of Southern Fiction.* Athens, Ga., 1966. Pp. 27-47.

Hopkins, Viola. "William Faulkner's *The Hamlet:* A Study in Meaning and Form," *Accent,* XV (Spring 1955), 125-144.

Howe, Irving. "The Southern Myth and William Faulkner," *American Quarterly,* III (Winter 1951), 357-362.

William Faulkner: A Critical Study. New York, 1952. Second edition, New York, 1962.

Howe, Russell Warren. "A Talk with William Faulkner," *The Reporter,* XIV (March 22, 1956), 18-20.

Howell, Elmo. "A Note on Faulkner's Negro Characters," *Mississippi Quarterly,* II (Fall 1958), 201-203.

"Faulkner's 'A Rose for Emily,' " *Explicator,* XIX (January 1961), item 26.

"Faulkner's Jumblies: The Nonsense World of *As I Lay Dying*," *Arizona Quarterly*, XVI (Spring 1960), 70-78.

"Faulkner's *Sartoris* and the Mississippi Country People," *Southern Folklore Quarterly*, XXV (June 1961), 136-146.

"The Quality of Evil in Faulkner's *Sanctuary*," *Tennessee Studies in Literature*, IV (1959), 99-107.

Hughes, Richard. "Faulkner and Bennett," *Encounter*, XXI (September 1963), 59-61.

Humphrey, Robert. "Form and Function in William Faulkner's *The Sound and the Fury*," *University of Kansas City Review*, XIX (Autumn 1952), 34-40.

Hunt, John W. *William Faulkner: Art in Theological Tension.* Syracuse, N. Y., 1965.

Hurt, Lester E. "Mysticism in *Go Down, Moses*," *English Record*, XV (December 1964), 17-22.

Inge, M. Thomas. "William Faulkner and George Washington Harris: In the Tradition of Southwestern Humor," *Tennessee Studies in Literature*, VII (1962), 47-59.

Jackson, James Turner. "Delta Cycle: A Study of William Faulkner," *Chimera*, V (Autumn 1946), 3-14.

Jackson, Naomi. "Faulkner's Woman: 'Demon-Nun and Angel-Witch,' " *Ball State University Forum*, VIII (Winter 1967), 12-20.

Jacobs, Robert D. "Faulkner's Tragedy of Isolation." In *Southern Renascense: The Literature of the Modern South*, Louis D. Rubin, Jr., and Robert D. Jacobs, eds. Baltimore, Md., 1953. Pp. 170-191.

"William Faulkner: The Passion and the Penance." In *South: Modern Southern Literature in Its Cultural Setting*, Louis D. Rubin, Jr., and Robert D. Jacobs, eds. New York, 1961. Pp. 142-176.

Jelliffe, Robert A., ed. *Faulkner at Nagano*. Tokyo, 1962.

Jewkes, W. T. "Counterpoint in Faulkner's *The Wild Palms*," *Wisconsin Studies in Contemporary Literature*, II (Winter 1961), 39-53.

Johnson, C. W. M. "Faulkner's 'A Rose For Emily'," *Explicator*, VI (May 1948), item 45.

Kaplan, Harold. "The Inert and the Violent: Faulkner's *Light in August*." In *The Passive Voice: An Approach to Modern Fiction*. Athens, Ohio, 1966. Pp. 111-130.

Kazin, Alfred. "Faulkner in his Fury." In *The Inmost Leaf*. New York, 1955. Pp. 257-273.

"The Rhetoric and the Agony." In *On Native Grounds*. New York, 1942. Pp. 453-465.

"The Stillness of *Light in August*." In *William Faulkner: Three Decades of Criticism*, Hoffman and Vickery, eds., pp. 247-265.

Kerr, Elizabeth M. "*As I Lay Dying* as Ironic Quest," *Wisconsin Studies in Contemporary Literature*, III (Winter 1962), 5-19.

"*The Reivers*: The Golden Book of Yoknapatawpha County," *Modern Fiction Studies*, XIII (Spring 1967), 95-113.

"Snopes," *Wisconsin Studies in Contemporary Literature*, I (Spring-Summer 1960), 66-83.

"William Faulkner and the Southern Concept of Woman," *Mississippi Quarterly,* XV (Winter 1961-1962), 1-16.

Kimmey, John L. "The Good Earth in *Light In August,*" *Mississippi Quarterly,* XVII (Winter 1963-1964), 1-8.

King, Roma, Jr. "The Janus Symbol in *As I Lay Dying,*" *University of Kansas City Review,* XXI (Summer 1955), 287-290.

Kinney, Arthur F. " 'Delta Autumn': William Faulkner's Answer for David H. Stewart," *Papers of the Michigan Academy of Science, Arts and Letters,* XLIX (1963), 541-549.

Kirk, Robert W. "Faulkner's Anse Bundren," *Georgia Review,* XIX (Winter 1965), 446-452.

"Faulkner's Lena Grove," *Georgia Review,* XXI (Spring 1967), 57-64.

with Marvin Klotz. *Faulkner's People: A Complete Guide and Index to the Characters in the Fiction of William Faulkner.* Berkeley, Calif., 1963.

Kubie, Lawrence S. "William Faulkner's *Sanctuary:* An Analysis," *Saturday Review of Literature,* II (October 20, 1934), 218, 224-226.

Langston, Beach. "The Meaning of Lena Grove and Gail Hightower in *Light in August,*" *Boston University Studies in English,* V (Spring 1961), 46-63.

Larsen, Eric E. "The Barrier of Language: The Irony of Language in Faulkner," *Modern Fiction Studies,* XIII (Spring 1967), 19-31.

Lawson, Lewis A. "The Grotesque-Comic in the Snopes Trilogy," *Literature and Psychology*, XV (Spring 1965), 107-119.

Leaver, Florence. "Faulkner: The Word as Principle and Power." In *William Faulkner: Three Decades of Criticism*, Hoffman and Vickery, eds., pp. 199-209.

"The Structure of *The Hamlet*," *Twentieth Century Literature*, I (July 1955), 77-84.

Leavis, F. R. "Dostoevsky or Dickens?" *Scrutiny*, II (June 1933), 91-93.

Leibowitz, Herbert A. "The Snopes Dilemma and the South," *University of Kansas City Review*, XXVIII (Summer 1962), 273-284.

Levine, Paul. "Love and Money in the Snopes Trilogy," *College English*, XXIII (December 1961), 196-203.

Lewis, R. W. B. "The Hero in the New World: William Faulkner's 'The Bear,'" *Kenyon Reveiw*, XIII (Autumn 1951), 641-660.

Lewis, Wyndham. *Men Without art*. London, 1934. Pp. 42-64.

Lind, Ilse Dusoir. "The Calvinistic Burden of *Light in August*," *New England Quarterly* XXX (September 1957), 307-329.

"The Design and Meaning of *Absalom, Absalom!*" In *William Faulkner: Three Decades of Criticism*, Hoffman and Vickery, eds., pp. 278-304.

Linn, Robert. "Robinson Jeffers and William Faulkner." In *The American Spectator Yearbook*, George Jean Nathan, et al., eds. New York, 1934. Pp. 304-307.

Lisca, Peter. *"The Hamlet:* Genesis and Revisions," *Faulkner Studies,* III (Spring 1954), 5-13.

"Some New Light on Faulkner's *Sanctuary,"* *Faulkner Studies,* II (Spring 1953), 5-9.

Litz, Walton. "William Faulkner's Moral Vision," *Southwest Review,* XXXVII (Summer 1952), 200-209.

Longley, John L., Jr. "Joe Christmas: The Hero in the Modern World." In *William Faulkner: Three Decades of Criticism,* Hoffman and Vickery, eds., pp. 265-278.

The Tragic Mask: A Study of Faulkner's Heroes. Chapel Hill, N. C., 1963.

and Robert Daniel. "Faulkner's Critics: A Selective Bibliography," *Perspective,* III (Autumn 1950), 202-208.

Lorch, Thomas M. "Thomas Sutpen and the Female Principle," *Mississippi Quarterly,* XX (Winter 1966-1967), 38-42.

Lowery, Perrin. "Concepts of Time in *The Sound and the Fury."* In *English Institute Essays 1952.* New York, 1954. Pp. 57-82.

Lydenberg, John. "Nature Myth in Faulkner's 'The Bear,' " *American Literature,* XXIV (March 1952), 62-72.

Lytle, Andrew. "Regeneration for the Man." In *William Faulkner: Two Decades of Criticism,* Hoffman and Vickery, eds., pp. 251-259.

The Hero with the Private Parts. Baton Rouge, La., 1966. Pp. 103-147.

McCole, C. J. "William Faulkner: Cretins, Coffin-worms, and Cruelty." In *Lucifer at Large.* London, 1937. Pp. 203-228.

McElderry, B. R., Jr. "The Narrative Structure of *Light in August*," *College English*, XIX (February 1958), 200-207.

McFadden, Nancy. "Faulkner's Women in the Structure of the Yoknapatawpha World." Unpublished MA Thesis, University of North Carolina, 1959.

MacLeish, Archibald. "Faulkner and the Responsibility of the Artist," *Harvard Advocate*, CXXXV (November 1951), 18, 43.

Machlachlan, John M. "William Faulkner and the Southern Folk," *Southern Folklore Quarterly*, IX (June 1945), 153-167.

Malin, Irving. *William Faulkner: An Interpretation*. Stanford, Calif., 1957.

Malroux, André. "A Preface for Faulkner's *Sanctuary*," *Yale French Studies*, No. 10 (Fall 1952), 92-94.

Marcus, Steven. "Snopes Revisited." In *William Faulkner: Three Decades of Criticism*, Hoffman and Vickery, eds., pp. 382-391.

Marvin, John R. "*Pylon:* The Definition of Sacrifice," *Faulkner Studies*, I (Winter 1952), 20-23.

Mason, Robert L. "A Defense of Faulkner's *Sanctuary*," *Georgia Review*, XXI (Winter 1967), 430-438.

Massey, Linton. "Notes on Unrevised Galleys of Faulkner's *Sanctuary*," *Studies in Bibliography*, VIII (1956), 195-208.

Materassi, Mario. "Le Immagini in *Soldier's Pay*," *Studi Americani*, IX (1963), 353-378.

Mayoux, Jean-Jacques. "The Creation of the Real in William Faulkner." In *William Faulkner: Three Decades of Criticism*, Hoffman and Vickery, eds., pp. 156-173.

Meriwether, James B. "Early Notices of Faulkner by Phil Stone and Louis Cochran," *Mississippi Quarterly*, XVII (Summer 1964), 136-164.

"Faulkner and the South." In *The Dilemma of the Southern Writer*, Richard K. Meeker, ed. Farmville, Va., 1961. Pp. 143-163.

"The Literary Career of William Faulkner: Catalogue of an Exhibition in the Princeton University Library," *Princeton University Library Chronicle*, XXI (Spring 1960), 111-164.

"Notes on the Textual History of *The Sound and the Fury*," *Papers of the Bibliographical Society of America*, LVI (1962), 285-316.

"Some Notes on the Text of Faulkner's *Sanctuary*," *Papers of the Bibliographical Society of America*, LV (1961), 192-206.

"The Text of Faulkner's Books: An Introduction and Some Notes," *Modern Fiction Studies*, IX (Summer 1963), 159-170.

"William Faulkner: A Check List," *Princeton University Library Chronicle*, XVIII (Spring 1957), 136-158.

The Literary Career of William Faulkner: A Bibliographical Study. Princeton, 1961.

Miller, David M. "Faulkner's Women," *Modern Fiction Studies*, XIII (Spring 1967), 3-17.

Millgate, Michael. *The Achievement of William Faulkner*. New York, 1965.

Miner, Ward L. *The World of William Faulkner.* Durham, N. C., 1952.

Mizener, Arthur. "The American Hero as Gentleman: Gavin Stevens." In *The Sense of Life in the Modern Novel.* Boston, 1964. Pp. 161-181.

Moldenhauer, Joseph F. "Unity of Theme and Structure in *The Wild Palms.*" In *William Faulkner: Three Decades of Criticism,* Hoffman and Vickery, eds., pp. 305-322.

Monteiro, George. "Initiation and the Moral Sense in Faulkner's *Sanctuary,*" *Modern Language Notes,* LXXIII (November 1958), 500-504.

Mooney, Stephen L. "Faulkner's *The Town:* A Question of Voices," *Mississippi Quarterly,* XIII (Summer 1960), 117-122.

Morris, Wright. "The Function of Rage." In *The Territory Ahead.* New York, 1958. Pp. 171-184.

Morrison, Sister Kristin. "Faulkner's Joe Christmas: Character through Voice," *Texas Studies in Literature and Language,* II (Winter 1961), 419-443.

Moses, W. R. "The Unity of *The Wild Palms,*" *Modern Fiction Studies,* II (Autumn 1956), 125-131.

Muste, John M. "The Failure of Love in *Go Down, Moses,*" *Modern Fiction Studies* X (Winter 1964-1965), 366-378.

Nemerov, Howard. "Calculation Raised to Mystery: The Dialectics of *Light in August.*" In *Poetry and Fiction: Essays.* New Brunswick, N. J., 1963. Pp. 246-259.

O'Brien, Frances Blazer. "Faulkner and Wright, Alias S. S. Van Dine," *Mississippi Quarterly,* XIV (Spring 1961), 101-107.

O'Conner, William Van. "Hawthorne and Faulkner: Some Common Ground," *Virginia Quarterly Review*, XXXIII (Winter 1957), 105-123.

———. "Rhetoric in Southern Writing: 3. Faulkner," *Georgia Review*, XII (Spring 1958), 83-86. ✓

———. *The Tangled Fire of William Faulkner*. Minneapolis, Minn., 1954.

O'Donnell, George M. "Faulkner's Mythology." In *William Faulkner: Three Decades of Criticism*, Hoffman and Vickery, eds., pp. 82-93.

O'Faolain, Sean. "William Faulkner: More Genius than Talent." In *The Vanishing Hero: Studies in Novelists of the Twenties*. Boston, 1956. Pp. 73-111.

Page, Ralph. "John Sartoris: Friend or Foe," *Arizona Quarterly*, XXIII (Spring 1967), 27-33.

Palmer, William J. "The Mechanistic World of Snopes," *Mississippi Quarterly*, XX (Fall 1967), 185-194.

Penick, Edward. "The Testimony of William Faulkner," *The Christian Scholar*, XXXVIII (June 1955), 121-133.

Pearson, Norman Holmes. "Lena Grove," *Shenandoah*, III (Spring 1952), 3-7.

Perluck, Herbert A. " 'The Heart's Driving Complexity': An Unromantic Reading of Faulkner's 'The Bear,' " *Accent*, XX (Winter 1960), 23-46.

Poirier, William R. " 'Strange Gods' in Jefferson, Mississippi: Analysis of *Absalom, Absalom!*" In *William Faulkner: Two Decades of Criticism*, Hoffman and Vickery, eds., pp. 217-243.

Pommer, Henry F. *"Light in August:* A Letter by Faulkner," *English Language Notes,* IV (September 1966), 47-48.

Powell, Sumner C. "William Faulkner Celebrates Easter," *Perspective,* II (Summer 1949), 195-218.

Price-Stephens, Gordon. "Faulkner and the Royal Air Force," *Mississippi Quarterly,* XVII (Summer 1964), 123-128.

Rabi. "Faulkner and the Exiled Generation." In *William Faulkner: Two Decades of Faulkner Criticism,* Hoffman and Vickery, eds., pp. 118-138.

Randall, Julia. "Some Notes on *As I Lay Dying,*" *Hopkins Review,* IV (Summer 1951), 47-51.

Ransom, John Crowe. "William Faulkner: An Impression," *Harvard Advocate,* CXXXV (November 1951), 17.

Rasco, Kay Frances. "The Yoknapatawpha Woman." Unpublished MA Thesis, University of Mississippi, 1953.

Rascoe, Lavon. "An Interview with William Faulkner," *Western Review,* XV (Summer 1951), 300-304.

Reeves, Carolyn H. *"The Wild Palms:* Faulkner's Chaotic Cosmos," *Mississippi Quarterly,* XX (Summer 1967), 148-157.

Rice, Philip Blair. "Faulkner's Crucifixion." In *William Faulkner: Three Decades of Criticism,* Hoffman and Vickery, eds., pp. 373-381.

Richardson, H. Edward. "Anderson and Faulkner," *American Literature,* XXVI (November 1964), 289-314.

Richardson, Edward. *William Faulkner: The Journey to Self Discovery.* Columbia, Mo., 1969.

Richardson, Kenneth. *Force and Faith in the Novels of William Faulkner*. Paris, 1967.

Riedal, F. C. "Faulkner as Stylist," *South Atlantic Quarterly*, LVI (Autumn 1957), 462-479.

Rinaldi, N. M. "Game Imagery and Game-Consciousness in Faulkner's Fiction," *Twentieth Century Literature*, X (October 1964), 108-118.

Robb, Mary Cooper. *William Faulkner: An Estimate of His Contribution to the American Novel*. Pittsburgh, Pa., 1957.

Roberts, James L. "Experimental Exercises — Faulkner's Early Writings," *Discourse*, VI (Summer 1963), 183-197.

"The Individual and the Family: Faulkner's *As I Lay Dying*," *Arizona Quarterly*, XVI (Spring 1960), 26-38.

"Snopeslore: *The Hamlet, The Town, The Mansion*," *University of Kansas City Review*, XXVIII (October 1961), 65-71.

Rogers, Katharine M. *The Troublesome Helpmate: A History of Misogyny in Literature*. Seattle, Wash., 1966. Pp. 252-257.

Rossky, William. "*As I Lay Dying*: The Insane World," *Texas Studies in Literature and Language*, IV (Spring 1962), 87-95.

"Faulkner: The Image of the Child in *The Mansion*," *Mississippi Quarterly*, XV (1962), 17-20.

Roth, Russell. "The Brennan Papers: Faulkner in Manuscript," *Perspective*, II (Summer 1949), 219-224.

"The Centaur and the Pear Tree," *Western Review*, XVI (Spring 1952), 199-205.

"William Faulkner: The Pattern of Pilgrimage," *Perspective*, II (Summer 1949), 246-254.

Rovere, Richard. "Introduction." *Light in August*. New York, 1950.

Runyan, Harry. "Faulkner's Poetry," *Faulkner Studies*, III (Summer-Autumn 1954), 23-29.

A Faulkner Glossary. New York, 1964.

Ryan, Marjorie. "The Shakespearean Symbolism in *The Sound and the Fury*," *Faulkner Studies*, II (Autumn 1953), 40-44.

Sadler, David F. "The Second Mrs. Bundren: Another Look at the Ending of *As I Lay Dying*," *American Literature*, XXXVII (March 1965), 65-69.

Sartre, Jean-Paul. "*Sartoris*." In *Literary and Philosophical Essays*, trans. Annette Michelson. London, 1955. Pp. 72-78.

"Time in Faulkner: *The Sound and the Fury*." In *William Faulkner: Three Decades of Criticism*, Hoffman and Vickery, eds., pp. 225-232.

Sawyer, Kenneth B. "Hero in *As I Lay Dying*," *Faulkner Studies*, III (Summer-Autumn 1954), 30-33.

Schappes, Morris. "Faulkner as a Poet," *Poetry*, XLIII (October 1933), 48-52.

Scholes, Robert E. "Myth and Manners in *Sartoris*," *Georgia Review*, XVI (Summer 1962), 195-201.

and Robert Kellogg. *The Nature of Narrative*. New York, 1966.

Schwartz, Delmore. "The Fiction of William Faulkner," *Southern Review*, VII (Summer 1941), 145-160.

Scott, Evelyn. "On William Faulkner's *The Sound and the Fury*." In *Twentieth Century Interpretations of* The Sound and the Fury, Michael H. Cowan, ed. Englewood Cliffs, N. J., 1968.

Sherwood, John C. "The Traditional Element in Faulkner," *Faulkner Studies*, III (Summer-Autumn 1954), 17-23.

Sidney, George R. "William Faulkner and Hollywood," *Colorado Quarterly*, IX (Spring 1961), 367-377.

Simon, John K. "Faulkner and Sartre: Metamorphosis and the Obscene," *Comparative Literature*, XV (Summer 1963), 216-225.

"The Scene and the Imagery of Metamorphosis in *As I Lay Dying*," *Criticism*, VII (Winter 1965), 1-22.

"What Are You Laughing at Darl?" *College English*, XXV (November 1963), 104-110.

Simpson, Lewis P. "Ike McCaslin and Temple Drake: The Fall of the New World Man." In *Nine Essays in Modern Literature*, Donald E. Stanford, ed. Baton Rouge, La., 1965. Pp. 88-106.

Slabey, Robert M. "*As I Lay Dying* as an Existential Novel," *Bucknell Review*, XI (December 1963), 12-23.

"Faulkner's *Sanctuary*," *Explicator*, XXI (January 1963), item 45.

"Faulkner's 'Waste Land' Vision in *Absalom, Absalom!*" *Mississippi Quarterly*, XIV (Summer 1961), 153-161.

"Joe Christmas, Faulkner's Marginal Man," *Pylon,* XXI (Fall 1960), 266-277.

"Myth and Ritual in *Light in August*," *Texas Studies in Literature and Language,* II (Autumn 1960), 328-349.

"The Romanticism of *The Sound and the Fury*," *Mississippi Quarterly,* XVI (Summer 1963), 146-159.

Slatoff, Walter J. "The Edge of Order: The Pattern of Faulkner's Rhetoric." In *William Faulkner: Three Decades of Criticism,* Hoffman and Vickery, eds., pp. 173-198.

Quest for Failure: A Study of William Faulkner. Ithaca, N. Y., 1960.

Sleeth, Irene Lynn. *William Faulkner: A Bibliography of Criticism.* Denver, Col., 1962.

Smart, George K. *Religious Elements in Faulkner's Early Novels: A Selective Concordance.* Coral Gables, Fla., 1965.

Smith, Henry Nash. "William Faulkner and Reality," *Faulkner Studies* (Summer 1953), 17-19.

Smith, Marshall J. "Faulkner of Mississippi," *Bookman,* LXXIV (December 1931), 411-417.

Snell, George. *Shapers of American Fiction: 1798-1947.* New York, 1947. Pp. 87-104.

Sorenson, Dale A. "Structure in William Faulkner's *Sartoris:* The Contrast Between Psychological and Natural Time," *Arizona Quarterly,* XXV (Autumn 1969), 262-270.

Stein, Jean. "William Faulkner." In *William Faulkner: Three Decades of Criticism,* Hoffman and Vickery, eds., pp. 67-82.

Stevick, Philip. *The Theory of the Novel.* New York, 1967.

Stewart, David H. "The Purpose of Faulkner's Ike," *Criticism,* III (Fall 1961), 333-342.

Stewart, George R., and Joseph M. Backus. "Each in Its Ordered Place: Structure and Narrative in 'Benjy's Section' of *The Sound and the Fury,*" *American Literature,* XXIX (January 1958), 440-456.

Stewart, Randall. *American Literature and Christian Doctrine.* Baton Rouge, La., 1958. Pp. 136-142.

Stonesifer, Richard J. "In Defense of Dewey Dell," *Educational Leader,* XXII (July 1, 1959), 27-33.

Strandberg, Victor. "Faulkner's Poor Parson and the Technique of Inversion," *Sewanee Review,* LXXIII (April-June 1965), 181-190.

Straumann, Henrich. "An American Interpretation of Existence: Faulkner's *A Fable.*" In *William Faulkner: Three Decades of Criticism,* Hoffman and Vickery, eds., pp. 349-372.

Sutherland, Ronald. "*As I Lay Dying:* A Faulkner Microscosm," *Queen's Quarterly,* LXXIII (Winter 1966), 541-549.

Swiggart, Peter. "Moral and Temporal Order in *The Sound and the Fury,*" *Sewanee Review,* LXI (Spring 1953), 221-237.

The Art of Faulkner's Novels. Austin, Texas, 1962.

Taylor, Nancy Dew. "The River of Faulkner and Twain," *Mississippi Quarterly,* XVI (Fall 1963), 191-199.

Taylor, Walter F., Jr. "Let My People Go: The White Man's Heritage in *Go Down, Moses*," *South Atlantic Quarterly*, LVIII (Winter 1959), 20-32.

Thompson, Alan R. "The Cult of Cruelty," *Bookman*, LXXIV (January-February 1932), 477-487.

Thompson, Lawrance. "Mirror Analogues in *The Sound and the Fury*." In *English Institute Essays 1952*. New York, 1954. Pp. 83-106.

William Faulkner: An Introduction and Interpretation. New York, 1963.

Turner, Arlin. "William Faulkner, Southern Novelist," *Mississippi Quarterly*, XIV (Summer 1961), 117-130.

Vickery, John B. "Ritual and Theme in Faulkner's 'Dry September,' " *Arizona Quarterly*, XVIII (Spring 1962), 5-14.

Vickery, Olga W. "Faulkner's First Novel," *Western Humanities Review*, II (Summer 1957), 251-256.

"Faulkner's *Mosquitoes*," *University of Kansas City Review*, XXIV (Spring 1958), 219-224.

"William Faulkner and the Figure in the Carpet," *South Atlantic Quarterly*, LXIII (Summer 1964), 318-335.

The Novels of William Faulkner: A Critical Interpretation. Baton Rouge, La., 1959.

Waggoner, Hyatt H. *William Faulkner: From Jefferson to the World*. Lexington, Ky., 1959.

Walcutt, Charles Child. *Man's Changing Mask: Modes and Methods of Characterization in Fiction*. Minneapolis, 1966.

Waldman, Milton. "Tendencies of the Modern Novel in America," *Fortnightly Review,* CXL (December 1933), 717-725.

Warren, Joyce W. "Faulkner's 'Portrait of the Artist,' " *Mississippi Quarterly,* XIX (Summer 1966), 121-131.

Warren, Robert Penn. "Cowley's Faulkner." In *William Faulkner: Three Decades of Criticism,* Hoffman and Vickery, eds., pp. 109-124.

——— ed. *Faulkner: A Collection of Critical Essays.* Englewood Cliffs, N. J., 1966.

Wasiolek, Edward. "*As I Lay Dying:* Distortion in the Slow Eddy of Current Opinion," *Critique,* III (Spring-Fall 1959), 15-23.

——— "Dostoevsky and *Sanctuary,*" *Modern Language Notes,* LXXIV (February 1959), 114-117.

Watkins, Floyd C. "The Gentle Reader and Mr. Faulkner's Morals," *Georgia Review,* XIII (Spring 1959), 68-75.

——— "What Happens in *Absalom, Absalom!*" *Modern Fiction Studies,* XIII (Spring 1967), 79-87.

——— and Willaim B. Dillingham. "The Mind of Vardaman Bundren," *Philological Quarterly,* XXXIX (April 1960), 247-251.

Way, Brian. "William Faulkner," *Critical Quarterly,* III (Spring 1961), 42-53.

Webb, James W., and A. Wigfall Green. *William Faulkner of Oxford.* Baton Rouge, La., 1965.

Wellek, Rene and Austin Warren. *Theory of Literature.* New York, 1956.

West, Ray B., Jr. "Atmosphere and Theme in Faulkner's 'A Rose for Emily.' " In *William Faulkner: Two Decades of Criticism*, Hoffman and Vickery, eds., pp. 259-267.

———. "Faulkner's 'A Rose for Emily,' " *Explicator*, VII (October 1948), item 8.

———. "Faulkner's *Light in August:* A View of Tragedy," *Wisconsin Studies in Contemporary Literature*, I (Winter 1960), 5-12.

———. "Hemingway and Faulkner." In *The Short Story in America*. Chicago, 1951. Pp. 85-106.

——— and R. W. Stallman. *The Art of Modern Fiction*. New York, 1949. Pp. 270-275.

Wheeler, Otis B. "Some Uses of Folk Humor by Faulkner," *Mississippi Quarterly*, XVII (Spring 1964), 107-122.

Whicher, Stephen E. "The Compsons' Nancies — A Note on *The Sound and the Fury* and 'That Evening Sun,' " *American Literature*, XXVI (May 1954), 253-255.

Williams, Aubrey. "William Faulkner's 'Temple' of Innocence," *Rice Institute Pamphlet*, XLVII (October 1960), 51-67.

Wilson, Colin. *The Strength to Dream: Literature and the Imagination*. London, 1962.

Wolfe, Ralph H., and Edgar F. Daniels. "Beneath the Dust of 'Dry September,' " *Studies in Short Fiction*, I (Winter 1964), 158-159.

Yorks, Samuel A. "Faulkner's Woman: The Peril of Mankind," *Arizona Quarterly*, XVII (Summer 1961), 119-129.

Young, T. D., and Floyd C. Watkins. "Faulkner's Snopeses," *Mississippi Quarterly*, II (Fall 1958), 196-200.

Zink, Karl E. "Faulkner's Garden: Woman and the Immemorial Earth," *Modern Fiction Studies*, II (Autumn 1956), 139-149.

"Flux and the Frozen Moment: The Imagery of Motion and Stasis in Faulkner's Prose," *PMLA*, LXXI (June 1956), 285-301.

"William Faulkner: Form as Experience," *South Atlantic Quarterly*, LIII (July 1954), 384-403.

Index

Absalom, Absalom!, 94, 102-109, 134, 185
  Charles Bon, 105-107
  Clytie, 107
  Rosa Coldfield, 94, 102-109, 134, 178-179
  Quentin Compson, 105
  Milly Jones, 108, 185
  Ellen Coldfield Sutpen, 108, 185
  Henry Sutpen, 106
  Judith Sutpen, 106-108, 178-179, 184
  Thomas Sutpen, 103-104, 107-108, 179
Adolesence, 6, 56, 64, 80, 82-83, 101, 105. *See also* Women, girls.
Alienation, 1, 17, 24, 28, 108-109, 144, 146, 148-150, 171-172, 178. *See also* Isolation.
Anderson, Sherwood, 27.
Appearance (garments, physical appearance), 16-17, 20, 30, 42, 52, 61, 76, 94, 102-103, 109, 122, 148, 159, 161, 176
  of specific characters
    Joanna Burden, 149
    Rosa Coldfield, 104-105
    Caddy Compson, 49
    Minnie Cooper, 100-101
    Dilsey, 66-69, 181
    Temple Drake, 77-80
    Emmy, 24
    Ruby Goodwin, 73-76, 87-88
    Emily Grierson, 101-102
    Lena Grove, 141-142
    Dorothy Jameson, 8-9
    Popeye, 86-87
    Charlotte Rittenmeyer, 123-124, 130, 133-134
    Pat Robyn, 29
    Narcissa Sartoris, 37, 76
    Cecily Saunders, 17-21
    Eula Varner Snopes, 161-162, 164, 167, 169-170
    Linda Snopes, 171-172
  gestures, 19, 20, 42, 49, 66, 68, 74, 88, 125. *See also* Beauty, of woman.
Art (artists), 27-31, 33, 35, 38 40, 56, 123, 128.

As I Lay Dying, 94, 111-122, 134, 164
  Lula Armstid, 183
  Addie Bundren, 94, 111-112, 133-134, 143, 178
  Anse Bundren, 112-118, 122
  Cash Bundren, 116, 120
  Darl Bundren, 116, 120-121
  Dewey Dell Bundren, 118-120
  Jewel Bundren, 118, 120-122
  Vardaman Bundren, 118
  Rachel Samson, 183
  Cora Tull, 114, 184-185
  Reverend Whitfield, 112, 117-118, 121-122.

"The Bear," 186-187.
Beardsley, Aubrey, 21.
Beatrice, 2, 29.
Beauty
  of nature, 11-17, 23, 32-35, 114-115, 150, 164, 170, 186-187
  of woman, 1-5, 15-21, 24-25, 28, 32-33, 41-48, 52, 72, 85, 141, 166, 169-171, 176, 182, 186.
Birth, 12, 15, 36, 46, 58-59, 116, 118-119, 132, 142-143, 149, 186
  re-birth, 14, 23, 58, 63, 115, 129. *See also* Renewal.
Brooks, Cleanth, 166, 183-184.

"Carcassone," 40, 145.
Children (childhood), 3, 6, 47, 49, 53, 62, 71-72, 75, 80, 82, 89, 97-99, 103-104, 113-121, 127-129, 131, 142-143, 148-150, 157-158, 169, 178, 181, 186
  childishness, 6, 15, 18, 47, 53, 56, 58, 60-65, 68, 71, 80-89, 105-109, 168.
Comedy, 3, 5, 9, 36, 67-69, 106, 113, 119, 122, 140-141, 151, 161-166, 181, 185-186.
Community, 97, 99-100, 109, 113-114, 120, 142, 145, 150, 159, 182-185. *See also* Jefferson.

Death, 6, 12-16, 23-27, 30, 33-35, 40-41, 55-56, 59-61, 63, 71, 85, 93-95, 101-102, 104-109, 112-115,

122, 124, 129-135, 139, 141, 143, 145-151, 166, 169-172, 177-180, 187
  death in life, 101-102, 108, 133, 145, 187
  suicide, 36, 55, 57, 61, 145, 169-171. *See also* Mortality.
Decadence, See Morality, moral decay.
"Desire of the heart," 6, 20, 29-34, 41, 48-49, 105-107, 177. *See also* Idealism; Sex, sexual desire.
Despair, 6-9, 24-25, 34-38, 42, 54-55, 65, 69, 97, 101, 118, 120-121, 140-141, 150. *See also* Futility.
Destructiveness, 4, 25, 39, 41, 46, 48, 53, 55 57-60, 65-67, 72, 90-95, 107-109, 125, 129, 130-133, 143-149, 155-160, 163, 165, 167-168, 170-172, 175-181, 187.
Domestic labor, 16, 36, 68-69, 73-76, 89, 112-114, 118-120, 148, 154-156, 159, 181-185
  Cooking, serving food, 10, 16, 51, 69, 73-74, 147-148, 159, 183, 185. *See also* Servanthood.
Dream, See Fantasy, Idealism.
"Dry September," 94, 97, 99-103, 134
  Minnie Cooper, 94, 97, 99-103, 108-109, 134.

Earth, 12, 15, 40-41, 70, 114, 119, 142-143, 145, 172-173, 186-187
  Land, 117, 159, 160-161, 170, 187. *See also* Motherhood, "earth-mother," and Nature.
"Elly," 94-96, 108-109, 134, 178.
Escape (from reality, from limitations of human condition), 17, 28, 35, 40, 63, 85, 104, 109, 129, 134, 146-148, 156-157, 161, 167-168, 171-172, 176, 185, 187.
Evil, See Morality.

A Fable, 185
  Marthe and Marya, 185.
Family, 46-49, 65-66, 70-71, 93-94, 103-104, 111-114, 120, 143, 153-155, 158, 180, 182. *See also* Children, Motherhood.
Fantasy, 63, 84, 87, 101, 104, 106-109.
Female principle (femininity), 11-12, 15-17, 28-29, 35-38, 41-42, 46, 49, 89, 103, 108-109, 112-114, 123-124, 130, 139-140, 146-149, 153-168,

171-173, 175-188. *See also* Women, nature of
Fertility, 15, 101, 139, 146, 160, 163-164, 170, 173, 186, 188. *See also* Force of life; Process of life; Sex, reproduction; Women, creativity.
"The Fire and the Hearth," 185.
Flowers, See Imagery.
Force of death, 70, 72, 86, 88, 108, 130, 134, 146, 151, 158, 161, 164-165, 171-176, 178-180
  Force of life, 3, 31-32, 36, 70, 108, 117, 140, 146, 148-151, 161-168, 171-176, 181-183, 186-188.
Frustration, 4-6, 9, 16-17, 33-35, 41-42, 47, 52, 54, 62, 66, 102-109, 162-163. 168.
Freedom, 4, 6, 11-12, 15, 17, 65, 109, 114, 139, 143, 154, 156, 158, 168, 172. *See also,* Idealism.
Futility, 5, 7, 9, 17, 20, 27, 35, 38-39, 62. *See also,* Despair.

Go Down, Moses, 185-187
  Molly Beauchamp, 185-187
  Ike McCaslin, 186-187
  Miss Sophonsiba, 185
  Roth's mistress, 185
Golden Age, 2, 10-16, 32, 140. *See also* Idealism, Romanticism.

"Hair," 176-177
  Ratliff, 176-177
  Susan Reed, 176
The Hamlet, 139, 153-165, 167, 183, 185
  Henry Armstid, 154, 156, 158, 164
  Mrs. Armstid, 158-160, 185
  Jack Houston, 156-157, 164
  Labove, 162-163
  Mrs. Littlejohn, 158-159, 183
  Lucy Pate, 156-157
  Flem Snopes, 161-165. *See also The Mansion, The Town*
  Mink Snopes, 154, 156-157, 164. *See also The Mansion*
  Mrs. Mink Snopes, 157-158
  Mrs. Tull, 160, 183
  Eula Varner, 139-142, 161-165, 186. *See also the Town*
  Mrs. Varner, 155, 185
  Will Varner, 160.
Helen, 2, 157, 164, 166, 168.
"The Hill," 32.
Horses, See Imagery.

Human condition (nature of man, reality), 25, 41-42, 46, 56, 73, 89-90, 101-102, 112-113, 120-121, 129-130, 133-135, 139-140, 146-147, 160-161, 168, 172-173, 186-188. *See also* Limitations of human condition.

Idealism, 5, 16-17, 25-36, 38-42, 45-46, 48, 53-57, 61-62, 68-70, 85-86, 89-94, 112-113, 115-116, 118, 121-122, 130-135, 141, 143-146, 166, 168, 172, 176-178, 187
Idealization of
beauty, 4, 27-28, 30-33, 41-42, 176, 187
love, 10-11, 20, 24, 25, 27, 29-32, 35, 41, 57, 127-129, 140-141, 168, 172, 186
woman, 28-38, 41-42, 45-46, 48, 53-57, 69, 70, 74, 85, 89, 139-144, 164-166, 168, 186-187. *See also* Motherhood.
See also Art, Escape, Freedom, Golden Age, Immortality, Romanticism, Unity, Virginity.
Idyll in the Desert, 94, 130-132, 134.
Imagery, 1-5, 11, 15, 17-20, 29-30, 42, 48, 52-63, 66, 73, 84-85, 104-107, 130, 154-155, 160, 175, 186-187
Imagery of
birds, 13, 20, 23, 25, 29, 32, 54, 61-62, 114, 160, 170
coldness, 12-16, 30, 36, 41, 131, 147
cows, 10, 68, 154-155, 164-165
darkness, 13-14, 24-25, 37, 40-41, 49, 59-63, 79, 98-102, 104, 107, 114, 117, 119, 145, 147-150, 170-171
dust, 101-102, 104
eyes, 1-2, 8, 11, 37, 40, 130, 142, 167, 170-171
fauns, 2, 11, 24, 32, 35, 140. *See also The Marble Faun*
fire (flame), 3, 13, 30, 40-41, 51, 53-55, 120, 122, 134
fish, 54, 63
flowers, 11-13, 19, 23-24, 35-39, 57, 62, 76, 84-86, 104, 160, 164, 170-171
gardens, 11-13, 15, 23, 36, 76
glass, 19, 20, 38
glass vases, 38-39, 48, 53, 141
hills, 8, 30, 32, 40, 170. *See also* "The Hill."

horses, 3, 9, 39-41, 121-122, 145, 148, 150, 153-162, 164-165, 179
marble statuary, 11, 13-15, 21, 29-34, 37, 39, 41, 53, 56, 141, 155, 159, 164. *See also The Marble Faun.*
mirrors, 9, 15, 73, 80, 85-86
moon, 10, 15, 24, 25, 101, 160, 164
odors (scents), 3, 30, 52, 57, 61, 122, 148
pipes of Pan (piping), 12, 30-32, 38, 115
shadows, 30, 59, 62-63, 79, 102, 149
sky (horizon), 13, 15, 25, 32, 40, 49, 58, 170
stars, 2, 3, 14, 32, 40-41, 101, 170
sun, 1, 12, 19, 30, 32, 58-59, 62, 104, 114, 161, 164
trees, 2, 13, 18-19, 21, 24, 28-30, 50, 52, 59, 62, 114, 159, 162
palms, 130
pear trees, 23, 48-49, 67, 160
poplars, 1, 15, 18-20, 29, 34, 141, 176
leaves, 2, 18, 23, 50, 106, 114. *See also,* flowers.
water, 1-2, 10, 15, 19, 30-31, 34, 49, 54, 59-63, 102, 114
ocean, 128, 160, 167
rain, 8, 23, 49, 68-69
flood, 117, 122, 125, 130, 134, 159. *See also* Earth, Immobility, Motion, "Ode on a Grecian Urn," Seasons.
Immobility (motionlessness, stillness), 1-2, 10, 12-17, 30-32, 35, 39, 61-62, 74, 76, 79, 89, 121, 133, 141, 154-155, 159-162. *See also* Motion.
Immortality, 3, 24, 28, 31-33, 41-42, 46, 58, 122, 186-188.
Impotence, 6, 12, 14-16, 33, 41, 87, 108, 160, 162-164, 167-168, 170.
Innocence, 16, 49, 52-53, 81, 83-86. *See also* Woman, innocence.
Intruder in the Dust, 182-184
Miss Habersham, 182, 184
Charles Mallison, 183-184
Margaret Mallison, 183
Irony, 17, 33-34, 41, 70, 76, 83, 112-113, 126, 128, 134, 144-145, 147, 164, 170, 181.
Isolation, 34, 39-41, 46, 53, 55-57, 63, 95-103, 112, 115, 121-122, 126, 129-130, 144-146, 148, 151, 156-157, 163, 177, 187. *See also* Alienation.

Jefferson, 87, 97, 100-101, 113, 117, 145, 147, 166-170, 172, 182-183.
Joyce, James, 10, 31.
Jung, Carl, 57-60.

Keats, John, 31, 140, 187.
Knight's Gambit, 176.

Land, See Earth.
Light in August, 139-153, 164, 183-185
Bobbie Allen, 148, 178
Martha Armstid, 184
Miss Atkins (dietician), 178
Mrs. Beard, 183
Byron Bunch, 143, 145, 151
Lucas Burch, 142-143
Joanna Burden, 143-144, 148-149, 151, 178
Joe Christmas, 139, 143-144, 146-151, 178
Lena Grove, 139-144, 147, 150, 173, 184
Gail Hightower, 143-146, 150, 151
Mrs. Hines, 185
Mrs. McEachern, 185.
Lilith, 167
Limitations (of human condition), 6, 11, 16-17, 28, 33-34, 39-42, 46, 49, 69-73, 89, 113-117, 120, 122, 127, 129-134, 141, 144, 168, 172-173, 176, 181, 184, 187.
Love
mating relationship (romantic love), 1-10, 17, 19-20, 22-23, 37-38, 62, 65, 97, 101-102, 105-107, 116-117, 131-132, 140, 149, 156-157, 164, 169, 179, 186. *See also* Sex sexual desire.
mother-child relationship, 36, 45-48, 49-53, 64, 66, 70-73, 87-90, 93-94, 168-169, 175, 181-184. *See also* Motherhood.
See also, Idealism, idealization of love.

Male principle (masculinity), 11, 16, 39-42, 66, 103, 108-109, 112-113, 123-124, 130, 139-140, 148-149, 154-168, 171-173, 175-183. *See also* Sex, virility.
Man's need of woman, 6, 16, 38, 46-47, 49, 53, 57, 63, 177, 187-188.
The Marble Faun, 11-16, 18, 23, 29, 32, 34-37, 41-42, 52, 70, 140-141, 160, 176

the marble faun, 11-17, 22, 24, 34, 36, 85, 101, 115
The Mansion, 165-166, 171-173, 176, 182
Melisandre Harriss, 176
Eula Varner Snopes, 171-173. *See also* *The Hamlet, The Town*
Flem Snopes, 166, 171-173. *See also* *The Hamlet, The Town*
Linda Snopes, 166, 171-173, 178-179. *See also The Town*
Mink Snopes, 172-173
Gavin Stevens, 166, 171-173.
Marriage, 7, 9, 22-23, 40, 55, 65-66, 85, 96, 98-100, 102, 105-107, 113-115, 118, 123, 125-127, 132, 142, 156-157, 163, 165-166, 169-170, 176-177.
Miss Zilphia Gant, 94-96, 134, 178
Zilphia Gant, 94-96, 108-109.
"Mistral," 176
Morality, 17-18, 22, 49, 56, 73-76, 88-90, 104, 142, 150-151, 172-173, 180-187
evil, 16, 24, 46, 54, 69, 71-73, 79, 81, 93, 145-147, 150, 158, 160, 169-172, 180-182, 186-187. *See also* Destructiveness.
moral chaos, 22, 70-71, 79-80, 89, 104, 107, 158, 187
moral decay, 17, 38-39, 47, 53, 55, 61, 71, 73-76, 80-88, 94-102, 109, 122, 130-135, 178, 181
moral order, 45-49, 53, 70-74, 93, 114, 134, 142-143, 175, 181, 186.
Mortality, 6, 11, 23-24, 28, 34-35, 39, 102, 115, 134, 168, 172, 177, 187. *See also* Death.
Mosquitoes, 4-10, 16-17, 27-34, 36, 42, 56, 94, 140-141, 161
Dawson Fairchild, 4-5, 9-10, 27-31, 34
Mark Frost, 4-5, 8-9
Gordon, 4, 27-35, 56, 141-142, 177
Dorothy Jameson, 4-5, 8-9
Mrs. Maurier, 4-5, 8, 94
Patricia Robyn, 4-5, 8, 17, 29, 37, 42, 142, 176
Jenny Steinbauer, 4-5, 10, 161
Mr. Talliaferro, 4-5, 9-10.
Motherhood, 20-23, 36, 39-42, 45-48, 50-53, 55, 57-65, 70-73, 87-90, 93-94, 97-99, 102, 112-122, 142-143, 157, 169-172, 175, 177, 180-186

"earthmother," 15, 36, 70, 140
"terrible mother," 57-61, 63
  See also Fertility; Force of life; Process of life; Sex, reproduction; Woman, creativity.
Motifs, 3, 6-7, 28, 81-84, 108, 153-154, 175-186. *See also* Imagery, Search motif.
Motion, 21, 25, 30-31, 37, 40, 59, 62, 74, 76-77, 79, 82, 128, 133, 141, 144-145, 147, 155, 158-165, 172, 187-188.
Motionlessness, See Immobility.
"Mule in the Yard," 165.

Naïveté, 18, 71-72, 81-87, 89, 169.
Nature, 2-3, 12, 14-16, 20, 23, 32-36, 46, 55, 84-86, 114, 119, 129-130, 132, 134, 147, 150, 159-160, 163, 168, 177, 186. *See also* Beauty of nature, Earth, Process of life, Seasons.
Negro, 25, 69-70, 95, 101, 108, 146-150, 150, 179, 181, 183-184.

O'Conner, William Van, 40.
"Ode on a Grecian Urn," 31, 140-141, 187
"unravished bride of quietness," 31, 39, 84, 141.

Past, 11-12, 100, 104, 125-126.
Peacefulness, 2, 10, 12-14, 36, 39, 60, 63, 89, 150.
Personification, 2, 12, 15, 73.
Poet, 38, 41, 106-107.
Poetry, Faulkner's, 1-4, 16, 18
  "A Poplar," 18
  "Faun," 2
  "L'Apres-Midi d'un Faun," 2, 3, 12
  "Study," 1, 3, 4, 33.
  See also The Marble Faun.
Polarity, 11, 14, 33, 35, 41-42, 70, 72, 112, 150, 161, 163-165, 175, 188.
  See also Female principle, Force of death, of life; Male principle; Tension.
A Portrait of the Artist as a Young Man, 10, 31.
Process of life
  natural process of life, 16-17, 52, 61-63, 65, 93, 102, 108-109, 129-130, 134, 139, 141-143, 149, 163, 172-173, 177-178, 186, 187
  reproductive process of life, 15, 23, 28, 35-36, 41-42, 45-46, 58-66, 71-72, 142-143, 147, 181, 186.

Psychology of the Unconscious, 57-60.
Pylon, 178
  Laverne Shumann, 178.

The Reivers: A Reminiscence, 183-184, 186
  Aunt Callie, 183
  Everbe Corinthia, 186
  Minnie, 184
  Lucius Priest, 186
  Miss Reba, 184, 186.
Renewal, 13, 17, 23, 36, 58-60, 150, 164, 170, 187.
Requiem for a Nun, 176, 181-182
  Cecilia Farmer, 176
  Nancy Mannigoe, 181-182, 184
  Temple Drake Stevens, 181.
Responsibility, 61, 71-72, 87-90, 146, 154, 163, 181.
Romanticism, 31-35, 40-46, 53, 115, 141, 145, 176-177.
  See also Idealism.
"A Rose for Emily," 94, 97, 99-103, 134
  Emily Grierson, 94, 97, 99-103, 108-109, 134, 178.

Sacrifice, 63, 65, 73, 87-90, 129-131, 134, 149, 151, 158, 164, 166, 168, 172, 175, 177, 181-182, 187.
Sanctuary, 38-39, 45-47, 71-90, 93, 160, 183-184, 186.
  Horace Benbow, 46, 73-76, 82-90, 112, 140-141, 143, 166, 177. *See also Sartoris*
  Temple Drake, 46, 76-90, 93-94, 177
  Virginia Du Pre, 76, *See also Sartoris*
  Ruby Goodwin, 46, 72-76, 80, 83-84, 184
  Popeye, 73, 81, 86, 89
  Belle Mitchell, 178. *See also Sartoris*
  "Little Belle," 73-77, 84-86, 177
  Miss Reba, 186. *See also The Reivers*
  Narcissa Benbow Sartoris, 46, 72-73, 76-77, 83-84, 86-87, 89. *See also Sartoris*
  Gowan Stevens, 76, 87
  Mrs. Walker, 183.
Sartoris, 32, 34-42, 45, 112 121
  Horace Benbow, 38-39, 56. *See also Sanctuary*
  Narcissa Benbow (Sartoris), 37-42, 45. *See also Sanctuary*
  Virginia Du Pre, 36-37, 42, 182, 185. *See also Sanctuary*

Elnora, 183
Belle Mitchell, 38-39, 178
Bayard Sartoris, 34-41, 55, 112, 121, 140, 145, 177
Caroline White Sartoris, 176
John Sartoris, 35, 40.
Satire, 9, 17, 24, 33-34, 141.
Search motif, 21, 27-28, 34-35, 53, 57-61, 112, 142-143, 170.
Seasons, 11-23, 33-36, 129
Autumn, 2, 13, 16, 24
Spring, 1-3, 11-17, 23-24, 30, 32-36, 57, 84-86, 114-115, 129, 140, 162, 164, 170
Summer, 12, 23, 34, 36, 57, 105-107, 114, 122, 129, 164
Winter, 13, 14, 16, 34, 36, 129, 164.
Selfishness, 18, 20-21, 29, 54, 58, 61, 70, 72, 81, 85, 89, 93, 108-109.
Serene, 39.
Servanthood, 24, 68-71, 73-75, 89-90, 181, 183-184. *See also* Domestic labor.
Sex, 1, 8-10, 18-19, 21, 23-29, 31, 33-34, 38, 41-42, 52, 65, 72, 77-83, 93-98, 103, 105-109, 117, 123, 134-135, 145, 147-149, 160-163, 167-168, 175-178, 186
incest, 47, 57-58, 60, 62, 72
intercourse, 10, 19, 21, 57, 128, 178
lust, 4, 6, 8, 10, 17, 20, 21, 24, 33, 39, 41, 72, 81, 85, 118, 149, 162-163, 165
pregnancy, 15, 37, 116, 119, 129, 132, 141-143, 178, 184
promiscuity, 33, 56, 65-66, 72-73, 76-80, 87, 148, 156-158, 171, 178, 181
rape, 4, 78-79, 81, 101, 163
reproduction, 28, 41-42, 112, 130, 134-135, 143, 150, 163. *See also* Birth, Fertility, Process of life
sexual desire, 1-10, 15, 17, 20, 22-24, 32-34, 38, 53, 56-57, 62, 86, 93-98, 101-102, 112, 115, 125, 162, 179
sexual perversity, 42, 61, 63, 72, 80-81, 93-97, 99, 108-109, 134-135, 143, 147-149, 151, 163-164, 175-178, 180.
virility, 39, 121, 148.
See also "Desire of the heart," Impotence, Love, Sterility.
Shropshire Lad, 11.
Snopes trilogy, 139, 153-173. *See also The Hamlet, The Mansion, The Town.*

Soldier's Pay, 4-7, 10-12, 16-25, 28, 32-33, 42, 52, 94, 160, 183-184
Aunt Callie, 183
Emmy, 4, 7, 10-11, 16, 20, 22-25, 32, 42
George Farr, 4, 7, 18-20, 23
Joe Gilligan, 4, 7, 17-18, 21-23, 25, 35
Janarius Jones, 4, 19-24
Julian Lowe, 4, 6-7
Donald Mahon, 4, 6-7, 10-12, 16, 18-23, 25, 32, 35
Margaret Powers, 4, 6-7, 11, 17-18, 21-25, 42, 94
Cecily Saunders, 4, 7, 10-11, 17-25, 29, 37, 42, 94, 176-177.
The Sound and the Fury, 45-72, 93, 111-112, 141, 166, 180-182
Dalton Ames, 62, 64-65
Gerald Bland, 61-62
Dilsey, 46-47, 52, 66-70, 181-184, 186
Benjy Compson, 47, 49-53, 64-66, 70
Caddy Compson, 46-57, 60-66, 93, 141, 180
Caddy's Quentin, 47, 65-67, 69
Caroline Compson, 46-47, 60-61, 68, 93
Jason Compson (father), 54-55
Jason Compson (son), 49, 51, 60, 65-67, 70
Quentin Compson, 46-48, 53-65, 71, 112, 140-141, 143, 177.
"The Spotted Horses," 153, 158-160.
Spring, See Seasons.
Sterility, 5, 8-9, 15, 23, 27-28, 31, 34-35, 38, 41, 99, 101-103, 132, 148-149, 163, 169-170, 178, 187.
Structure, 4-6, 11-12, 34, 36, 143-144, 153.
Survival, 36, 46, 107-109, 112-113, 119-120, 122, 129-130, 134, 142, 144, 146, 148, 151, 172-173, 179-182, 186-188.
Sustenance, 70-72, 89-90, 93, 140, 143, 147-148, 150, 154-156, 158, 163, 172, 175, 177, 180-186, 188.
Symbolism, 11, 14-15, 19-20, 23, 29, 31-33, 35, 38-39, 41-42, 45, 53-63, 72-73, 81, 84-87, 99-102, 104-108, 115, 121, 130, 135, 140, 143, 146, 154, 156, 158, 160-165, 168, 175, 181-182, 187-188. *See also* Imagery.

The Tangled Fire of William Faulkner, 40.

Tension, 4, 33, 42, 146, 153-168, 171-173, 175. *See also* Female principle; Force of death, of life; Male principle; Polarity.

"There Was a Queen," 38.

Time, 2, 40, 55, 59, 102, 126, 156
timelessness, 31, 33, 56.

The Town, 165-171, 176, 182
Margaret Mallison, 182-183. *See also Intruder in the Dust*
Ratliff, 165-166, 168
Eula Varner Snopes, 165-171, 181-184. *See also The Hamlet*
Flem Snopes, 165-171. *See also The Hamlet, The Mansion*
Linda Snopes, 168-171, 176. *See also The Mansion*
Manfred de Spain, 165, 167
Gavin Stevens, 165-171, 181. *See also The Mansion.*

Tragedy, 9, 34, 36, 40, 46, 49, 65, 67, 71, 88, 94, 99, 102, 104, 108-109, 113, 122, 124, 129, 131, 133, 143-144, 146, 150, 163-164, 170, 172, 178, 184.

Trees, See Imagery.

"Uncle Willy," 184.

Unity (oneness), 7, 25, 32-33, 41-42, 46, 53, 112, 115-116, 121, 127, 143, 172. *See also* Idealism.

The Unvanquished, 179-180, 183
Drusilla Hawks, 178-179
Louvinia, 183,
Rosa Millard, 179-180, 182, 184
Bayard Sartoris, 180.

"Verse Old and Nascent: A Pilgrimage," 31.

Violence, 35, 101, 147-149, 151, 155-156, 158, 162-163, 171, 178-180.

Virginity, 8, 20, 23, 29, 32-37, 45-49, 52-55, 62-73, 84-86, 89, 98, 103, 107, 126, 163, 166, 176-177
ideal of virginity, 30-32, 41, 140-141. *See also* Idealism, idealization of woman; "Ode on a Grecian Urn."

The Wild Palms, 94, 122-135
Old Man, 132-133
Charlotte Rittenmeyer, 94, 122-135, 143, 178
Harry Wilbourne, 122-129, 131-132.

Women
characterization of women, 5, 11-12, 15, 17, 25, 33, 41-42, 45-47, 90, 111, 118, 140, 143, 165-166, 171-172, 175-188. *See also* Appearance
character types
girls, 3, 15, 18, 21, 37, 48, 176-177
ghosts, 79, 104
spinsters, 99, 103. *See also* Adolescence, Motherhood, Virginity
nature of women, 5, 16-17, 21-22, 32-33, 35-36, 41-42, 45-46, 73, 90, 111-113, 140, 143, 147, 154-156, 166, 169, 177, 186. *See also* Female principle
personal qualities of women
attractiveness, 1-2, 4-5, 16, 19, 41, 52, 162, 171
allure, 2-4, 15-16, 19-21, 33, 42, 161-163, 169, 171, 176
creativity, 5, 11, 16, 28-29, 33, 42, 46, 57-58, 72, 93, 101, 115, 128-130, 134, 139, 157, 161-162, 164, 169, 171-173, 175, 178. *See also* Fertility; Force of life; Process of life; Sex, reproduction
dominance, 36, 49, 123, 182, 184
endurance, 10, 36, 38, 41, 68-70, 88, 108, 114, 131, 133, 143-144, 157, 163, 171, 179, 182, 184-186, 188
innocence, 17-18, 29, 141, 171, 177
maturity, 21-22, 36, 64, 72-75, 87-90
mystery, 2-3, 5, 16, 21, 28, 48, 100
power, 2-5, 17-18, 20, 29, 37, 42, 108, 130, 151, 161-162, 164-165, 169, 176
purity, 11, 16-18, 37, 46, 48-49, 53, 72-73, 141, 180
serenity, 16-17, 33, 39, 41-42, 45, 63, 65, 93, 97, 101, 139-142, 147, 159, 162, 169, 180
submissiveness, 46, 65, 72-73, 87-90, 93, 141, 155, 158, 160, 169, 172, 178, 184-185
tranquility, 11, 16, 37, 39, 42, 99, 134, 141-142, 159, 162
wisdom, 16, 21, 36, 89, 162, 180, 184
See also Beauty of woman; Destructiveness; Idealism, idealization of woman; Morality, moral decay, order; Responsibility; Sacrifice; Sex; Survival; Sustenance, and specific women characters.

Words, 10, 19, 22, 24, 28, 38, 55, 116-118.